IMAGES
of America

Wisconsin State Reformatory

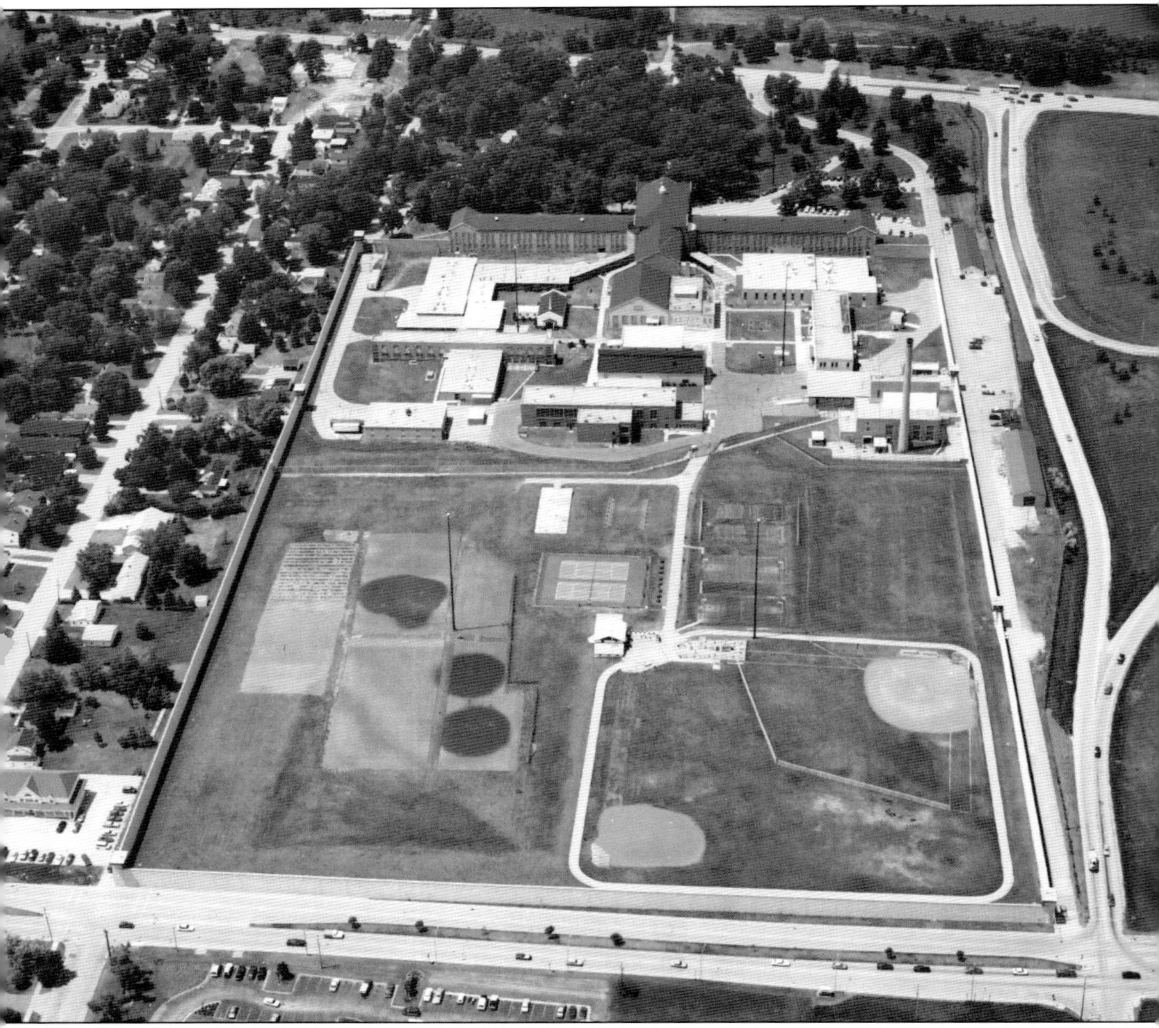

This aerial view of the institution, taken in the 1990s, illustrates the close proximity of the neighboring residential areas of the village of Allouez. Recreational facilities dominate the eastern half of the 29-acre facility, with the track and baseball diamonds visible at the lower right quadrant of the prison grounds. The road bordering the lower portion of the photograph is Webster Avenue. (Courtesy Green Bay Correctional Institution.)

ON THE COVER: Photographed in the 1990s, this view of the South Cell Hall illustrates the typical prison cell layout of the late 19th century. Additional lighting and stairs have been added to assist corrections officers in their duties, but the six-foot-by-nine-foot cells that were designed to minimize contact between prisoners remain the same. For more than 75 years, the Wisconsin State Reformatory housed thousands of youthful first-time offenders in the South Cell Hall.

IMAGES
of America

WISCONSIN STATE REFORMATORY

Michael E. Telzrow with the
Neville Public Museum of Brown County

ARCADIA
PUBLISHING

ISBN 978-0-7385-7715-9

Published by Arcadia Publishing
Charleston SC, Chicago IL, Portsmouth NH, San Francisco CA

Printed in the United States of America

Library of Congress Control Number: 2009933698

For all general information contact Arcadia Publishing at:
Telephone 843-853-2070
Fax 843-853-0044
E-mail sales@arcadiapublishing.com
For customer service and orders:
Toll-Free 1-888-313-2665

Visit us on the Internet at www.arcadiapublishing.com

This book is dedicated to the memory of J. Emory Temple, whose photographs have provided a window to the past.

CONTENTS

ACKNOWLEDGMENTS

This book would not have been possible without the contributions of the following individuals: staff members of the Neville Public Museum of Brown County, Green Bay, Wisconsin, including Louise Pfotenhauer for helping make available the Wisconsin State Reformatory photo collection; Larry LaMalfa for his efforts in scanning original prints and negatives; and Jeanine Mead for her patience and understanding during my visits to the museum's library and archives. Also deserving of special recognition are Allouez residents Rita Houston and former Wisconsin State Reformatory (WSR) employees Rosemary and Butch Mianecki, Jerry Tierney, and Dudley Smith for graciously providing photo identification; Mary Jane Herber; Carol Jones for her photographic contribution; and William J. Pollard, warden of the Green Bay Correctional Institution (GBCI), for his assistance in securing the use of some very early WSR photographs still held at the facility. I would be remiss if I did not mention Daniel Bertrand, former warden at the GBCI. Absent of his efforts in 1998 to secure the collection for the Neville Public Museum, it is likely that the WSR photographs would have remained hidden from public view and perhaps eventually lost to posterity. Finally, a special thank-you goes to my wife, Libby, and my sons, James and Thomas, for allowing me to work late nights in order to make deadline.

In 1998, while developing an exhibit on the Wisconsin State Reformatory, I was introduced to the comprehensive photographic archive that forms the basis of this book. From glass plate negatives of the earliest inmates to modern era silver gelatin prints, the WSR collection spans the history of the reformatory and provides a virtually unbroken visual link to its past. Most of that collection is now held at the Neville Public Museum of Brown County; a small portion remains at the Green Bay Correctional Institution.

Unless otherwise noted, all images appear courtesy of the Neville Public Museum of Brown County.

INTRODUCTION

The theory of the reformatory is not leniency, but discipline, correction, and reformation.
—James E. Heg, superintendent, Wisconsin State Reformatory, 1897–1901

The idea for the Wisconsin State Reformatory (WSR) was born during a period of profound change associated with the late 19th-century correctional reform movement. Liberal progressives, seeking to save youthful first-time offenders from the harsh realities of traditional prisons, began to question the strictly punitive approach employed by American penal institutions. Instead, they favored a new approach that sought to enhance the rehabilitative effort through training and education rather than punishment only. Major changes in sentencing followed, and traditional practices like the flat sentence gave way to the parole concept. Equally revolutionary was the implementation of vocational and educational programs within the framework of the traditional prison model.

In 1885, two Wisconsin proponents of the new system, Charles Lulling, chair of the state board of supervision, and H. H. Giles, his counterpart with charities and reform, visited the prototypical reformatory in Elmira, New York. Impressed with the new rehabilitative approach, Lulling and Giles immediately asked Gov. Jeremiah Rusk to establish a similar facility in Wisconsin. Rusk, however, felt that the idea was poorly developed, and in any case, Wisconsin's economy was in no shape to allow for the construction of a new prison facility. The idea went nowhere until 1897 when Green Bay assemblyman Thomas McGrath managed to successfully sponsor legislation that authorized the establishment of the WSR on a 200-acre site located on the Fox River between Green Bay and De Pere.

Situated on gently sloping wooded terrain, the WSR enjoyed close proximity to Green Bay, De Pere, and area farms—the latter would prove to be very beneficial to the development of the penal institution. Based upon the reformatory at Elmira, New York, WSR officials would establish a system that emphasized labor, education, and a just measure of discipline.

On April 15, 1898, the Wisconsin Board of Control named Beloit College alumnus James E. Heg the first superintendent of the WSR. Heg was the editor of the Republican *Lake Geneva Herald* and the son of Bvt. Brig. Gen. Hans C. Heg, formerly the colonel of the 15th Wisconsin Infantry Regiment. James Heg's appointment as the superintendent of the Wisconsin Board of Control, coupled with his father's Civil War record, all but assured his selection as the institution's first superintendent.

On August 31, 1898, the first inmates, all between the ages of 17 and 28, arrived from the state prison at Waupun, thus beginning the long history of the WSR. Although the Green Bay *Advocate* considered Heg's appointment a "political bargain," he was no mere political appointee. Within four months, he had successfully converted an abandoned bicycle factory foundation into a temporary cell house, filled key staff positions, and prepared the site for the eventual construction of a 600-cell facility.

Heg's successor, Charles W. Bowron, took over the reins in 1901 and continued the aggressive building programs of his predecessor. Under Bowron about half of the inmates at WSR engaged in building projects that included the construction of the largest portion of the original architectural plan. Between 1900 and 1924, the reformatory engaged in a series of contract labor initiatives. Vocational training and education combined with manual labor characterized much of the period between 1900 and 1924. During that time, WSR inmates produced overalls and jackets for Milton F. Goodman of Chicago, manufactured brooms, and leased a 40-acre granite quarry in Amberg. Pressure from trade unions and liberal-minded reformists, however, compelled the reformatory to voluntarily cease contract labor in 1924. Five years later, the Hawes-Cooper Act restricted transportation of contract labor goods from state to state, and by 1940, the Sumners-Ashurst Act drove the final nail in the coffin when it prohibited interstate transportation of convict-made goods.

Suddenly faced with a population of idle prisoners, reformatory officials looked to reverse the situation by increasing the amount of time devoted to vocational training and education. Under the direction of Supt. Earl H. Eklund, the reformatory added a number of new programs to its vocational offerings, most notably automobile body and engine repair. By the 1930s, inmates could take advantage of programs in plumbing, cabinet making, painting, and machine shop. Remedial educational instruction was offered, and older inmates lacking high school diplomas were permitted to take high school extension courses. In 1932, the University of Wisconsin ruled that academic credits earned in prison sufficiently met college admission requirements. The institution's commitment to education and vocation training continued under Eklund's successors, and in 1948, Supt. Benjamin P. Kramer added a school principal and vocational director to the reformatory's staff.

Sanger B. Powers continued the legacy of Wisconsin's progressive correctional tradition when he assumed control of the WSR in 1951. Powers, a product of Madison's well-oiled public welfare machine, instituted an array of reforms that fundamentally changed the reformatory's environment and established Wisconsin at the forefront of a new progressive correctional reform movement. In his attempt to enhance the rehabilitative effort, he moved quickly to abolish many of the traditional but seemingly archaic forms of discipline. During his five year tenure, he allowed inmates to send Christmas cards, increased food rations for those held in solitary confinement, allowed the publication of an inmate newspaper, and abolished the "silent rule" for inmates confined to "red band" tables in the dining room. Intramural sports and recreational activities were increased, including the reactivation of the reformatory swimming pool.

Powers's reform efforts also included substantial augmentation of the institution's academic and vocational training opportunities. He employed eight state-certified academic teachers and made available correspondence courses through the University of Wisconsin Extension Division. Powers also placed a premium upon staff development, increasing the level of professionalism among reformatory employees. This emphasis on rehabilitation and treatment programs continued well beyond his tenure even while other so-called "progressive" correctional jurisdictions around the country were eliminating programs.

Much has changed at the reformatory since 1898. The flimsy wooden fence that once kept prisoners from escaping was replaced with a 22-foot concrete wall in 1921, and the adjacent wooded areas and farms of 1898 have given way to middle class suburban property owners. In the mid-1970s, the last juvenile was released or transferred and WSR became an adult maximum security prison. On July 1, 1979, the name was changed to Green Bay Correctional Institution to better reflect its new status. The days of the silent rule, inmates in stripes, and prison guards wielding brass-tipped canes are over. The youthful first-time offenders of James Heg's era have been replaced by adult criminals convicted of serious crimes, and the close interaction between inmates and the local population that once characterized the early years of the institution has ceased.

However, despite these and many other profound changes, the basic reform philosophy endures at the Green Bay Correctional Institution. Indeed, its ability to adapt and change when necessary remains the defining characteristic of the institution. Even today educational reentry programs still constitute the basis of the reform effort, and concepts like the indeterminate sentence that once seemed revolutionary in the last quarter of the 1800s are standard practice.

Nestled in the heart of the village of Allouez, the former WSR remains one of Wisconsin's most historic institutions while boasting an unbroken operational history dating to 1898.

One

A New Kind of Prison

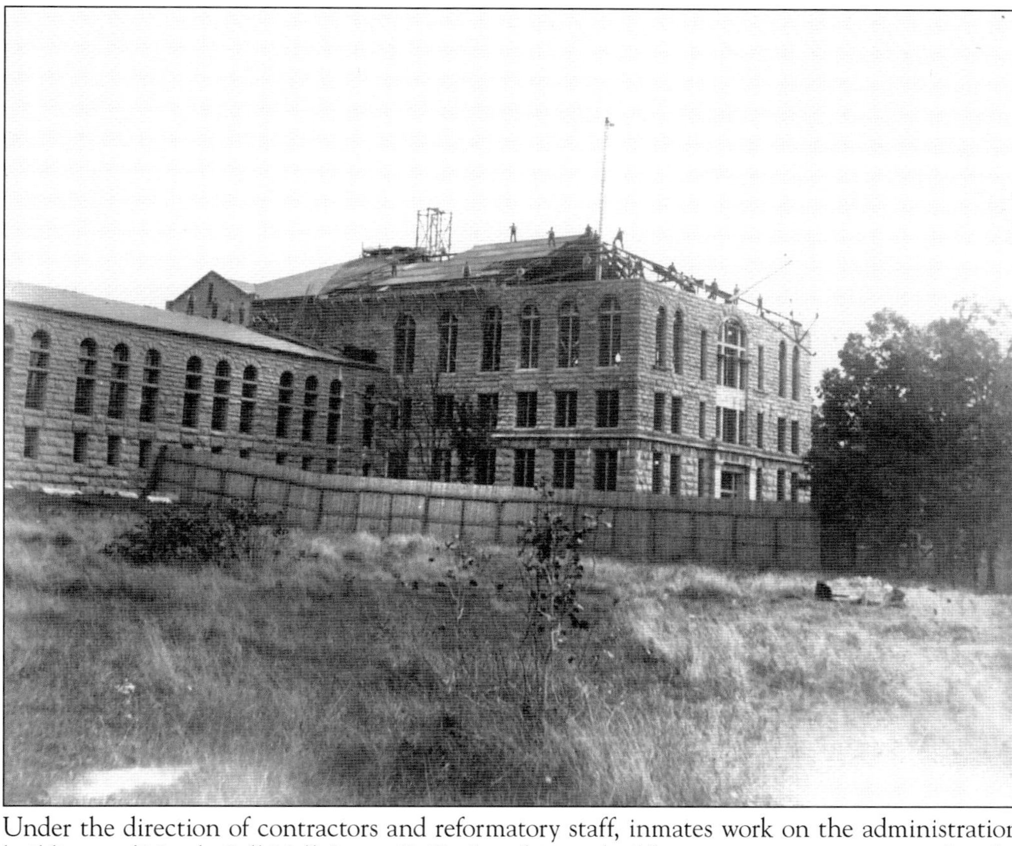

Under the direction of contractors and reformatory staff, inmates work on the administration building and North Cell Hall. James E. Heg's ambitious building projects were continued under Charles W. Bowron (1901–1917). During this period, about half of the inmates incarcerated at Wisconsin State Reformatory (WSR) worked in building construction. In 1910, Bowron told Wisconsin Board of Control officials "All of the construction has been done by our inmates." (Courtesy Green Bay Correctional Institution.)

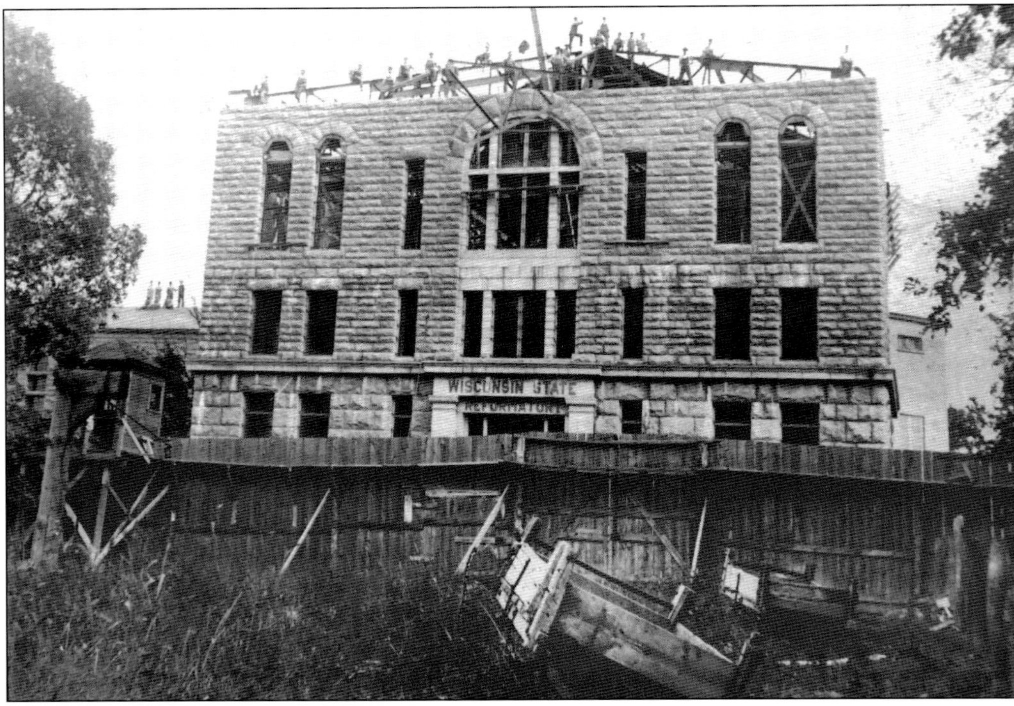

High atop the administration building, inmates and reformatory staff erect the roof support system. A stone and concrete stairway led up to an impressive entrance pavilion. The arched bar windows, massive granite blocks and Romanesque aesthetic was meant to convey the seriousness of the institution and its role as a place of reform. A pair of granite eagles guarded each side of the door. (Courtesy Green Bay Correctional Institution.)

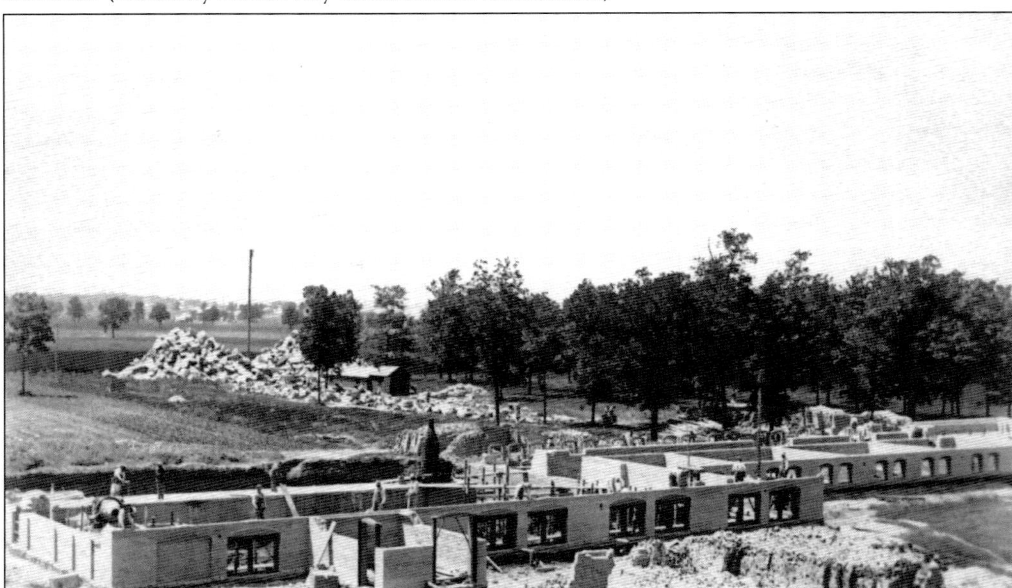

A mountain of Amberg granite lies behind newly constructed foundations and walls in this c. 1905 photograph. The wooden reformatory fence can be seen in the background of this early building project scene. (Courtesy Green Bay Correctional Institution.)

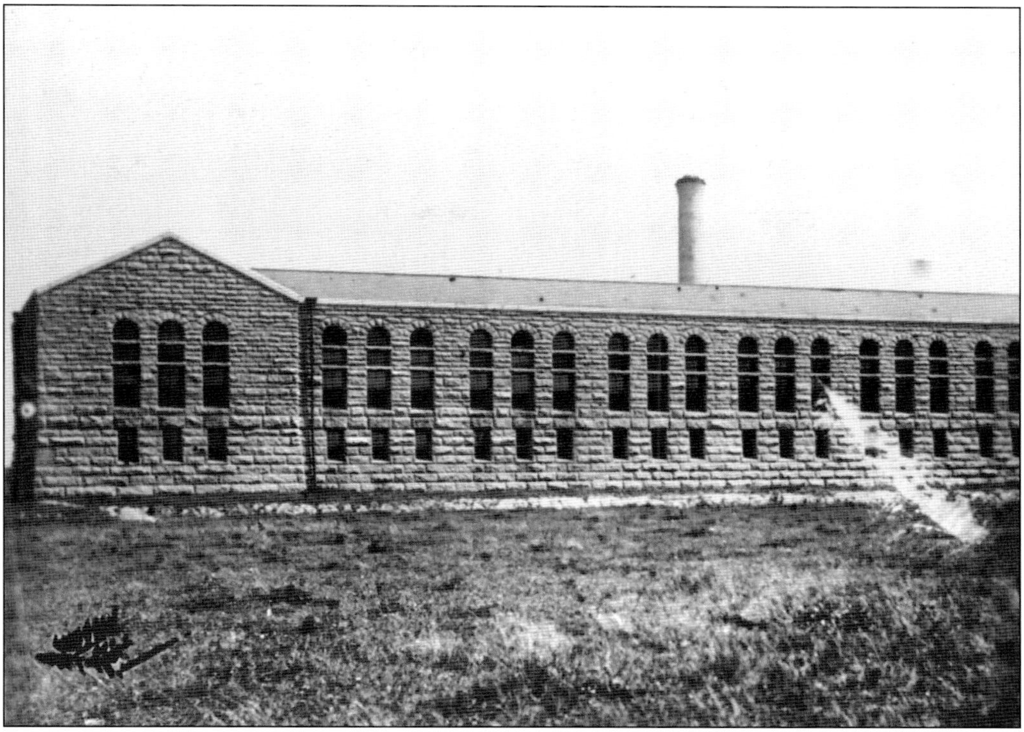

Construction began on the North Cell House in 1898 and was completed in 1903, about the time this photograph was taken. It is the earliest building in the complex. It was constructed of cream brick and sheathed in rusticated dark gray Amberg granite, creating a look common to the period that exemplified the grave nature of penal institutions.

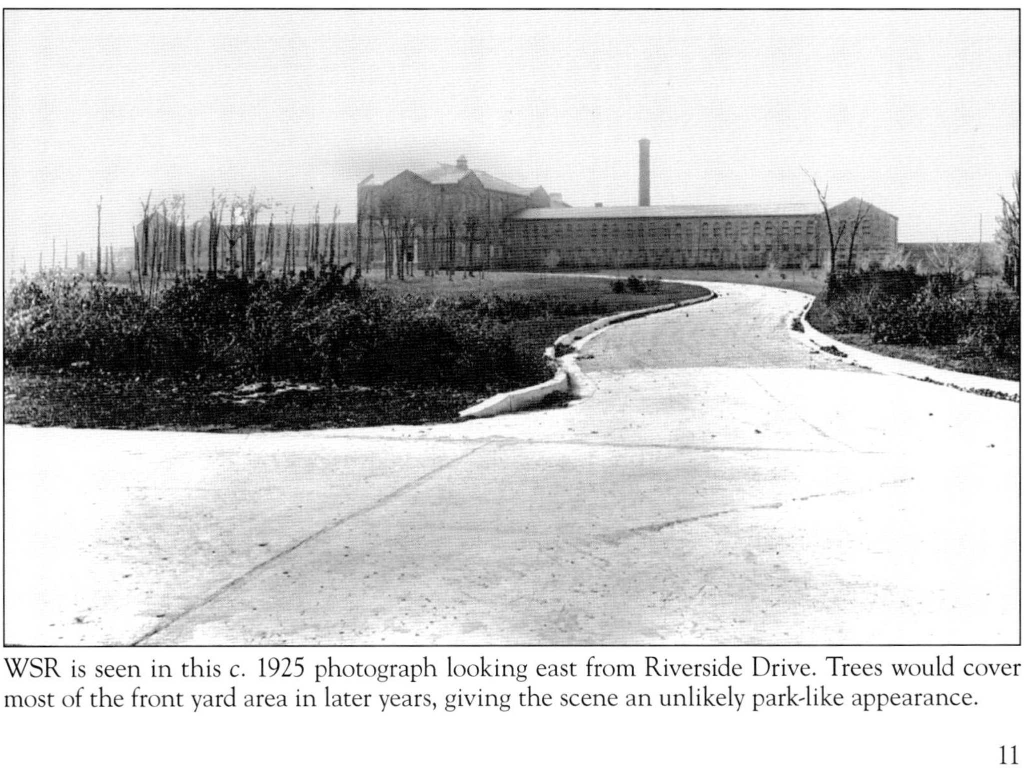

WSR is seen in this *c.* 1925 photograph looking east from Riverside Drive. Trees would cover most of the front yard area in later years, giving the scene an unlikely park-like appearance.

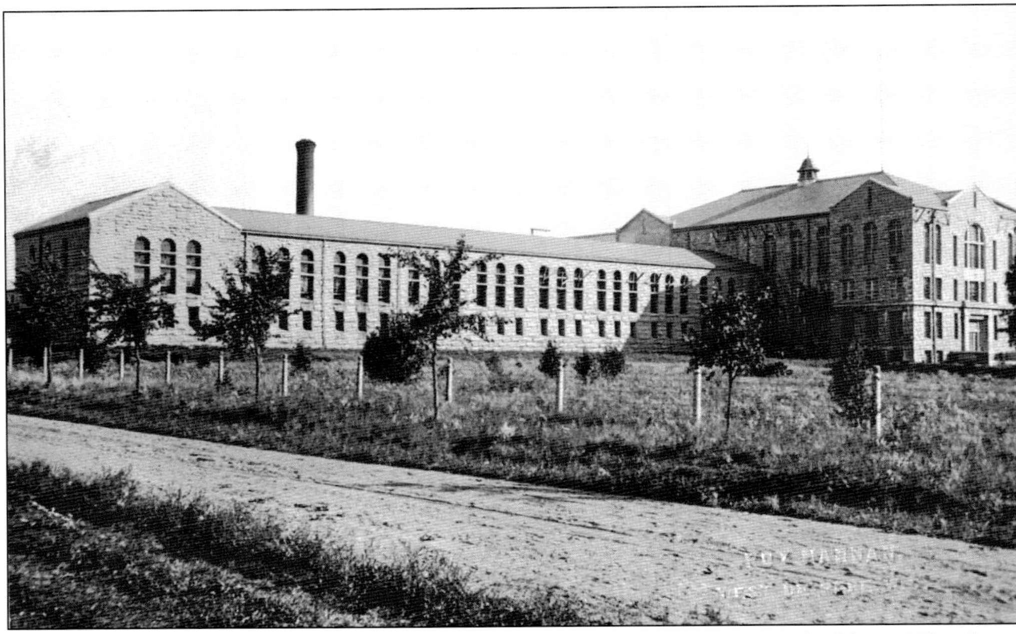

Visible here are the North Cell Hall and completed administration building. The latter functioned as the nerve center for the facility and included the hospital building. A long road ran the length of the north wall to Riverside Drive. The photographer is Roy Hannan of nearby West De Pere.

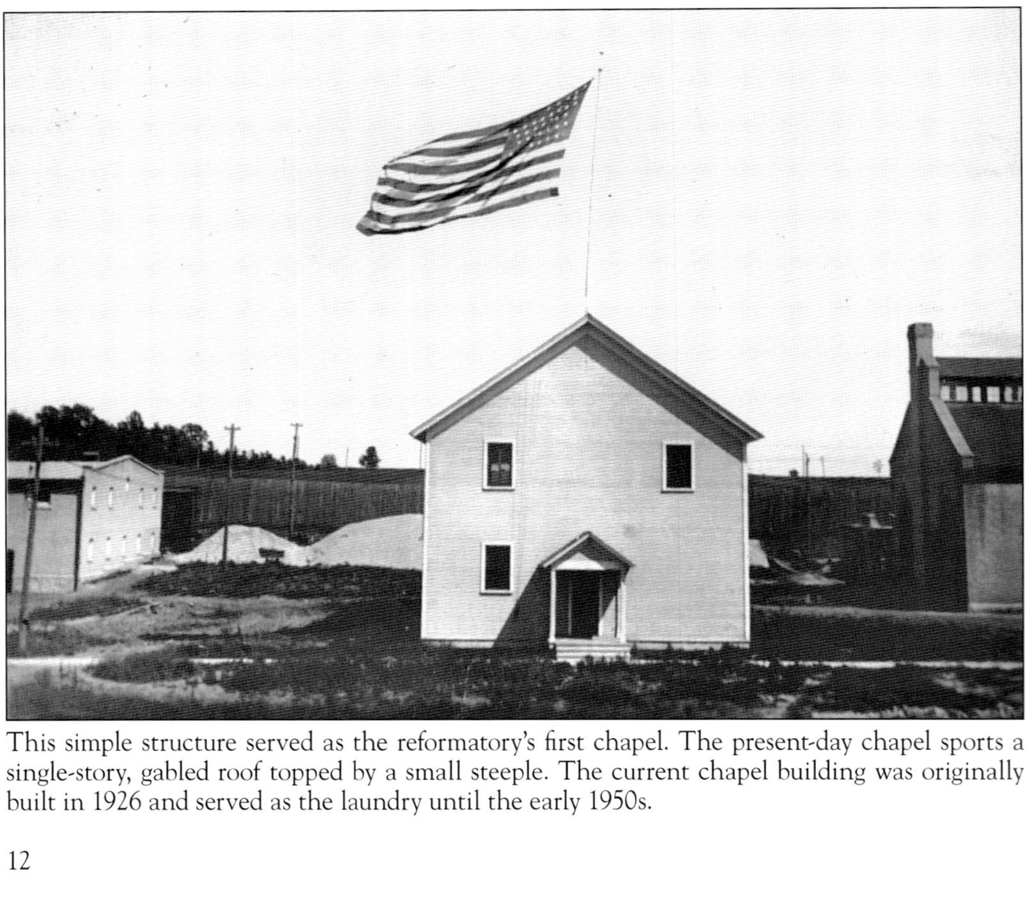

This simple structure served as the reformatory's first chapel. The present-day chapel sports a single-story, gabled roof topped by a small steeple. The current chapel building was originally built in 1926 and served as the laundry until the early 1950s.

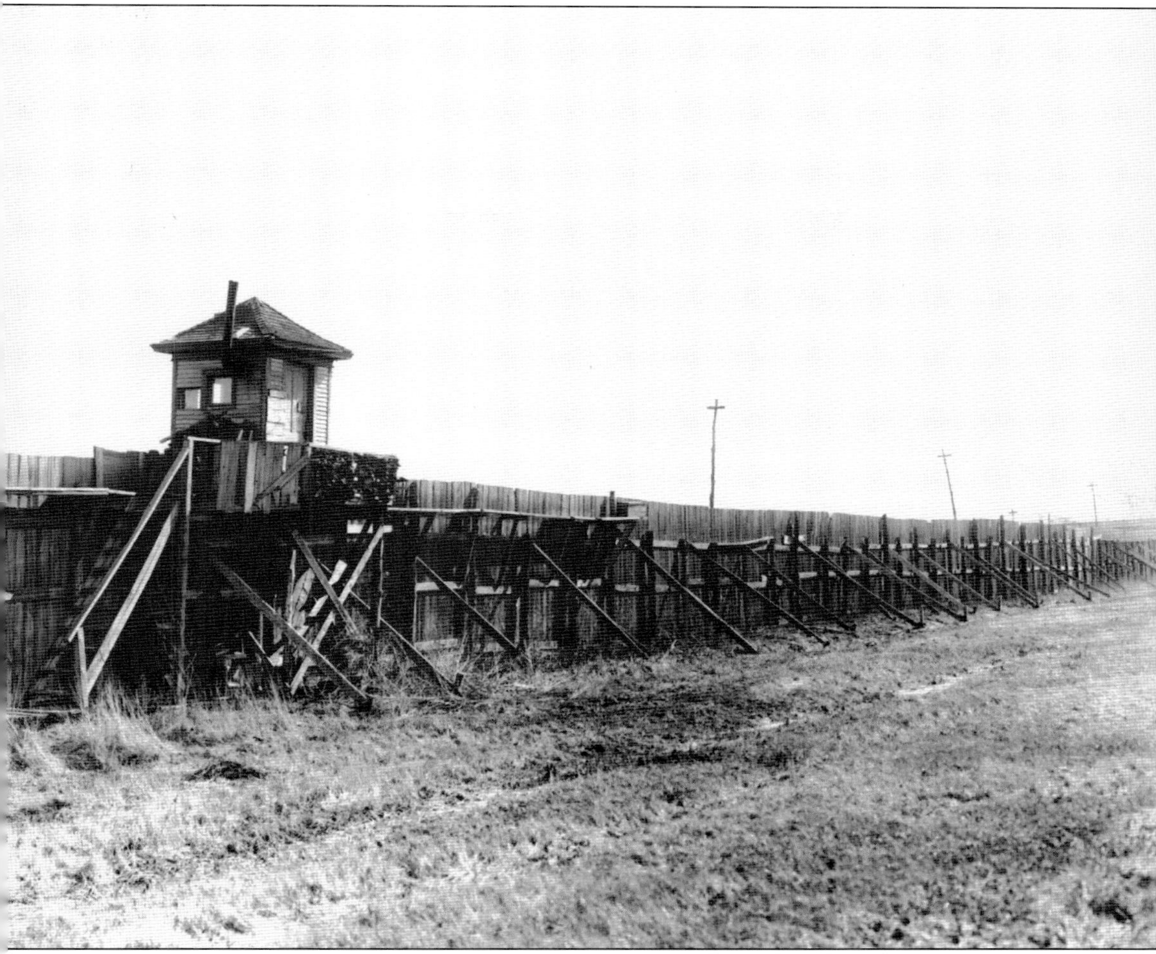

With a wood stove chimney jutting from its side, a guard tower sits atop the 12-foot high wooden stockade. It was all that separated the inmates from the outside world. The guard towers were heated by wood stoves and contained no lavatory facilities. Strong winds often flattened sections of the stockade, and it was known for its lack of stability over time. Keeping prisoners secure behind an imperfect wooden stockade proved problematic. This photograph was taken around 1910, about 21 years before the erection of an inmate-constructed, 22-foot-high concrete wall. The 1921 version still stands. (Courtesy Green Bay Correctional Institution.)

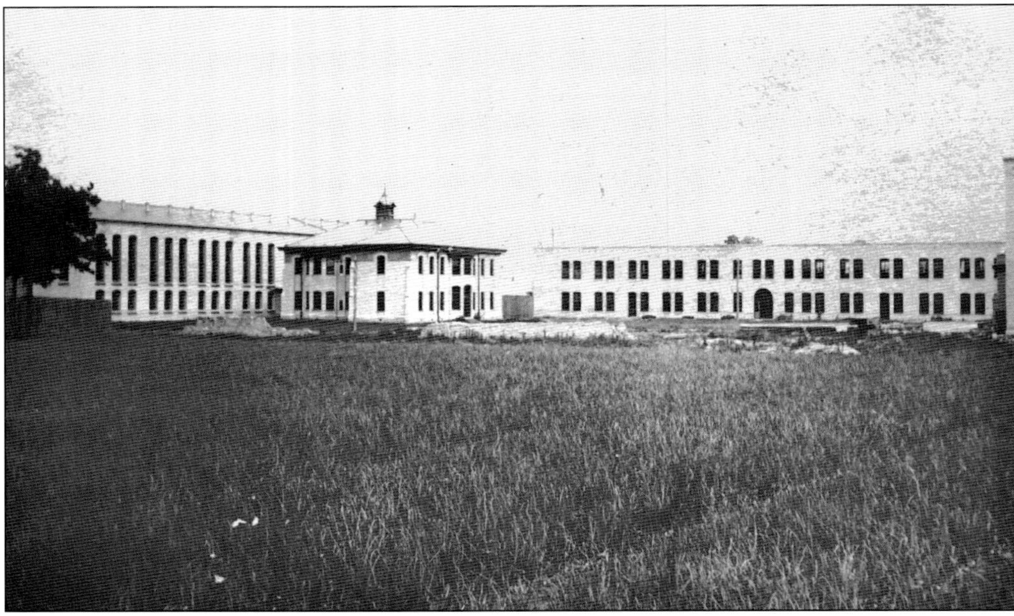

Photographed around 1901, this view looking northwest toward the North Cell Hall, administration building, and old dormitory gives a good indication of how the site developed architecturally. The stockade, shown at the far left near the lone tree, only encompasses a portion of the facility. The old dormitory still remains today, but the hospital building at the center, which also served as a temporary cell house, is long gone. (Courtesy Green Bay Correctional Institution.)

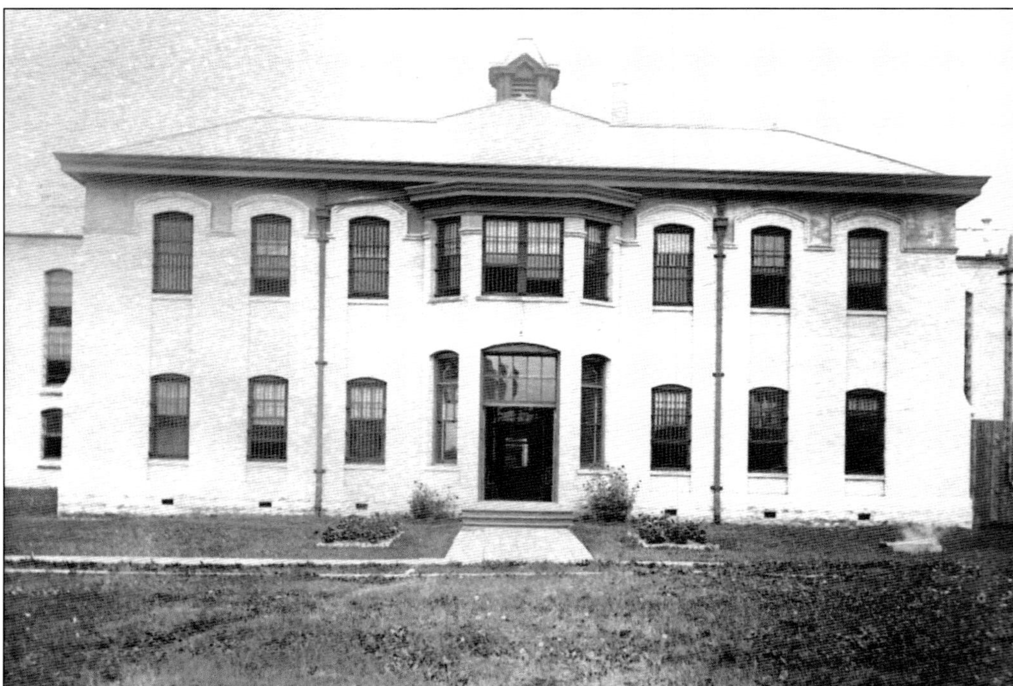

The hospital was the first permanent structure built at WSR and was completed in 1901. It also served as a 104 unit cell house for a time. This view is looking west toward the Fox River.

This photograph, taken during the early construction phase around 1901, is one of the earliest photographs of the ambitious building projects started by Supt. James E. Heg and carried on by his successor Charles W. Bowron. Scaffolding can be seen erected on the side of the reformatory administration building.

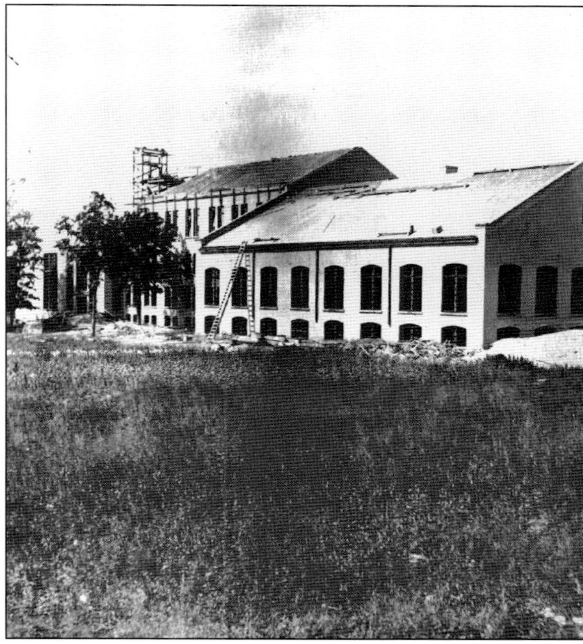

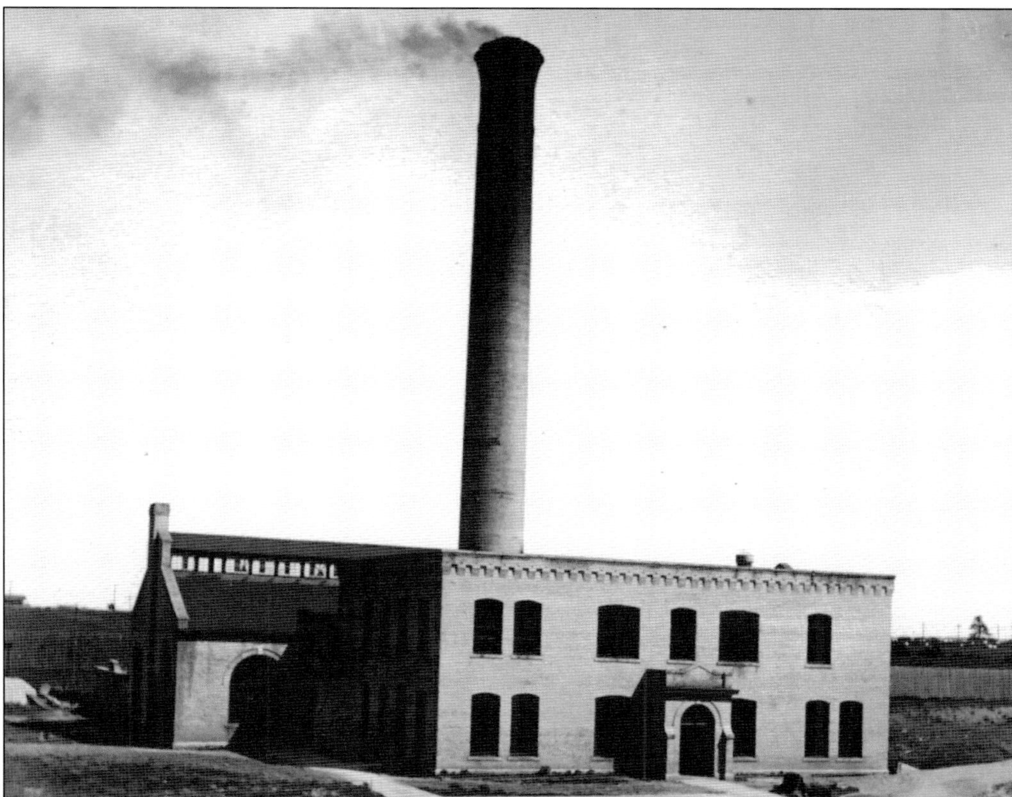

Black Smoke belches from the coal-fired reformatory plant in this *c.* 1905 photograph. The plant remained in service until it was demolished in 1957. (Courtesy Green Bay Correctional Institution.)

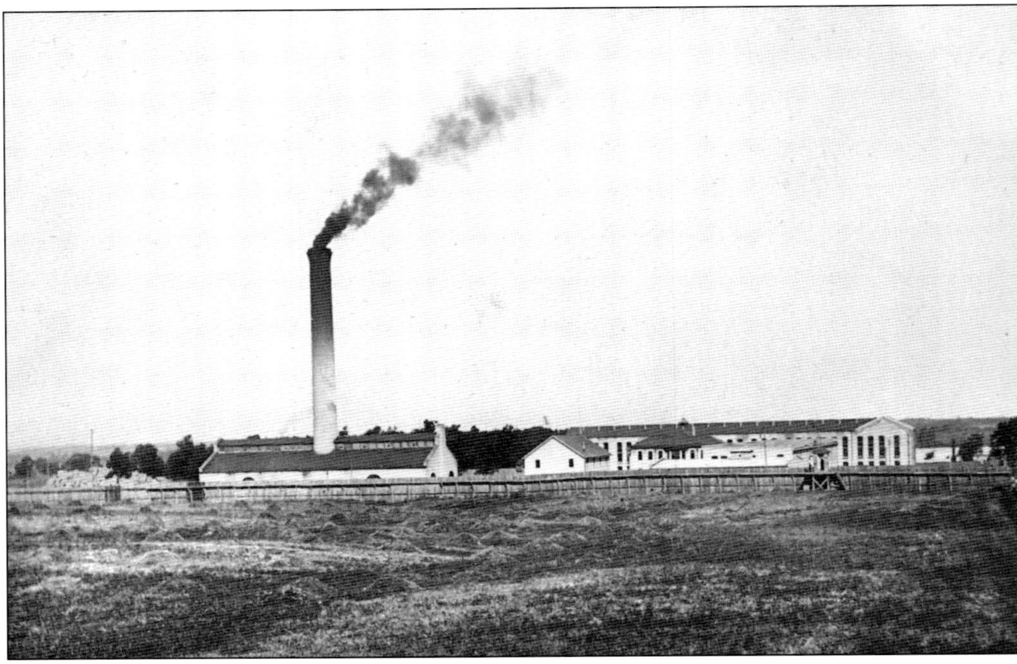

The prison power plant smoke stack is visible from the east in this photograph from about 1910. The land surrounding the prison was largely uninhabited with the exception of a few farms. Today this view is now intersected by Highway 172, and the prison sits comfortably within the boundaries of the village of Allouez. The reformatory's first power plant was demolished in 1957. This scene is from Webster Avenue looking west toward the main complex and North Cell Hall.

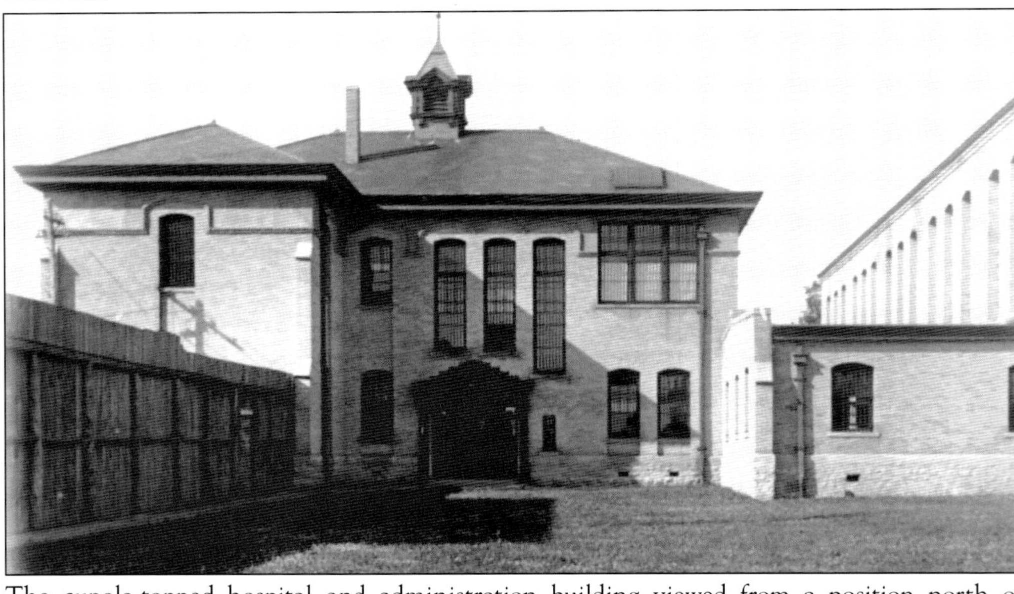

The cupola-topped hospital and administration building viewed from a position north of the institution, around 1910, gives a good indication of the minimal security level outside the cell halls visible at the far right of the building. The wooden stockade fence seen at the far left of the photograph did not encompass the cell hall structure. (Courtesy Green Bay Correctional Institution.)

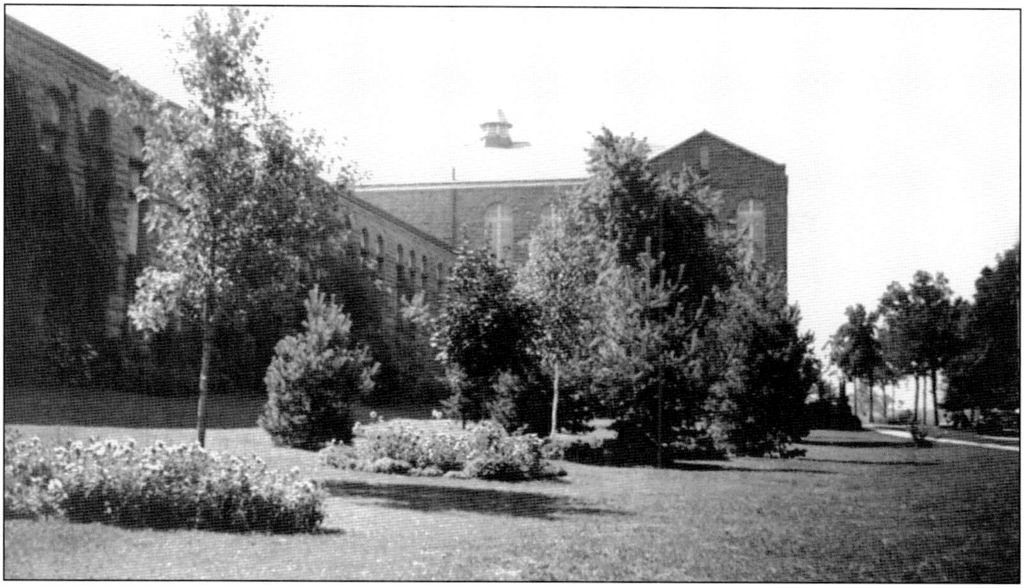

Between 1910 and 1915, inmate labor enabled the reformatory administration to complete the largest portion of the architectural plan. Looking south past the North Cell Hall and administration building, this photograph was taken sometime around 1925.

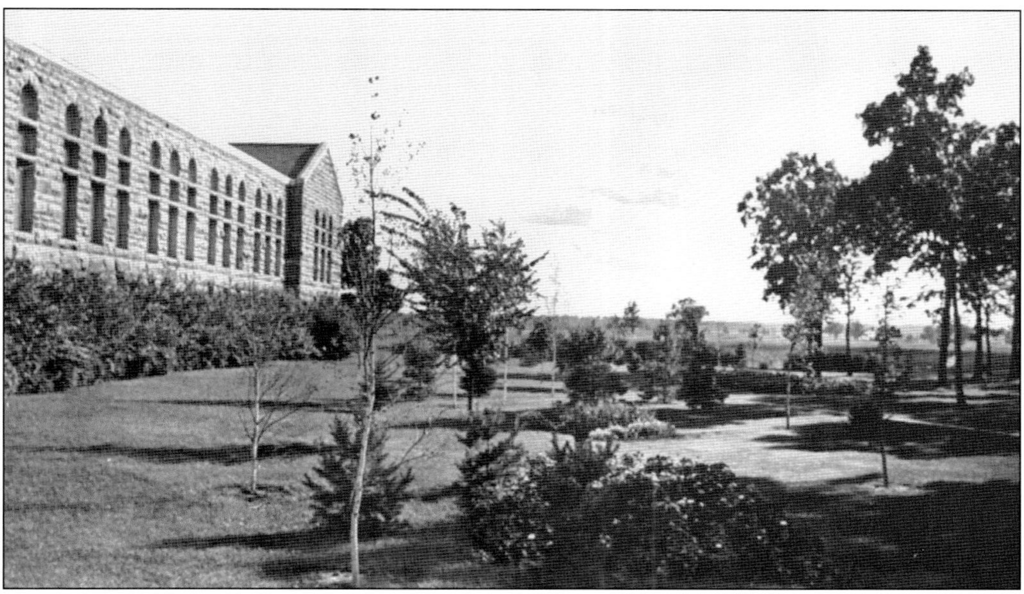

The rural nature of the environment surrounding the WSR is evident in this photograph taken in the 1920s. The view is looking south past the South Cell Hall. The area had yet to experience the rapid residential growth that would start during the post World War II era and continue through the 1970s.

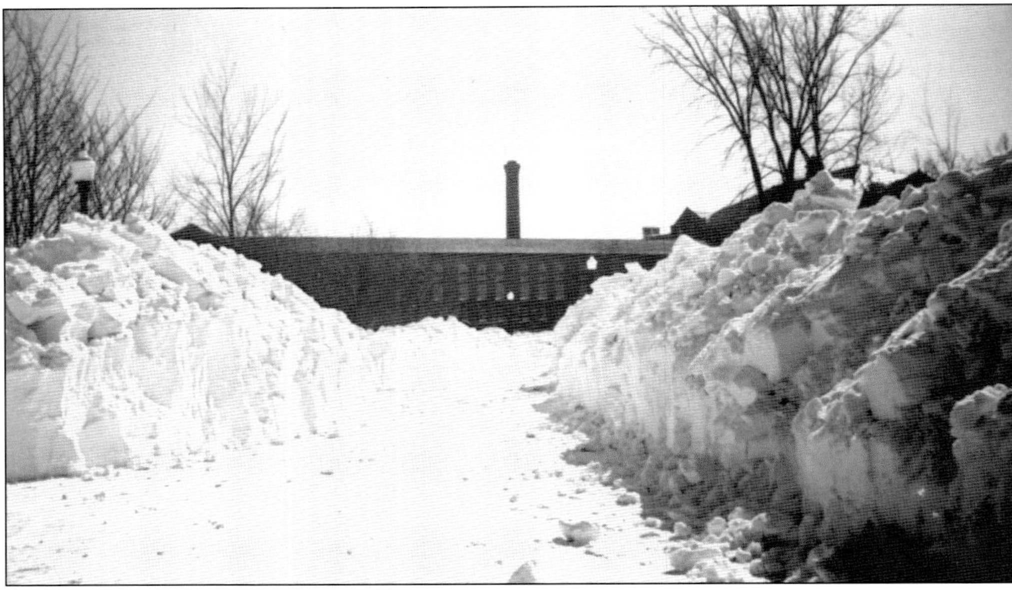

Snowbanks obscure the view of the North Cell Hall. The old power plant smoke stack is visible in the background of this photograph taken by reformatory employee J. Emory Temple during the 1930s.

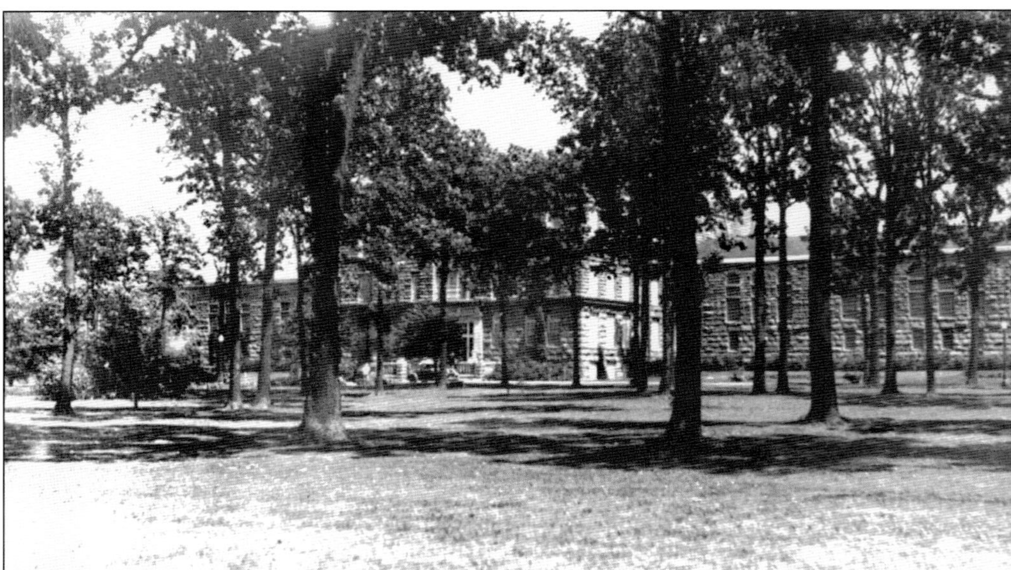

The front of the reformatory retains a park-like environment that belies the nature of the institution. Its imposing facade has changed little since the early 1900s.

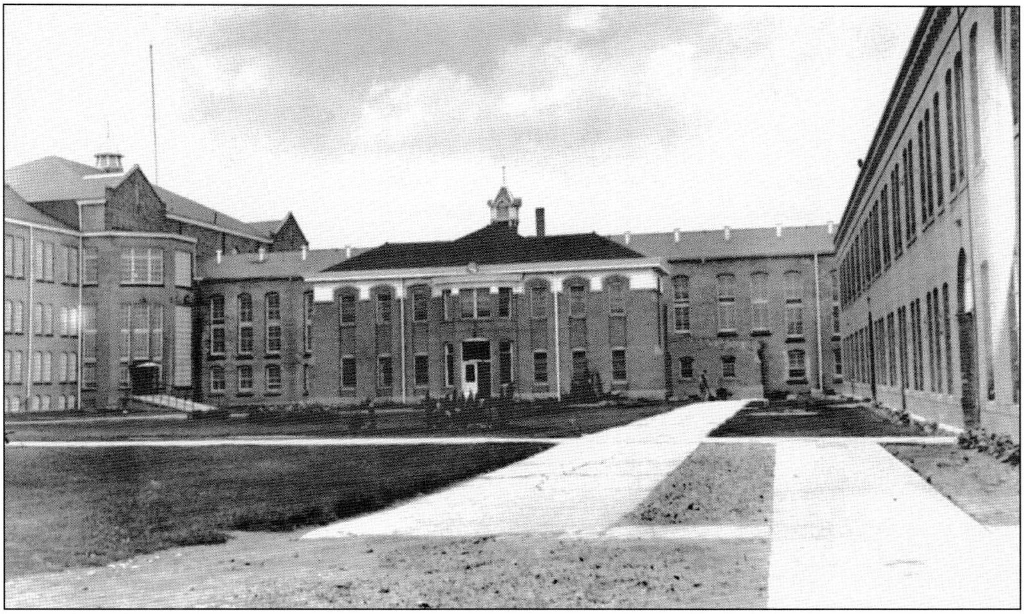

The old hospital and surrounding buildings are visible in this photograph taken early in the 1930s. It is no longer extant, having been replaced with a new treatment center in the 1960s.

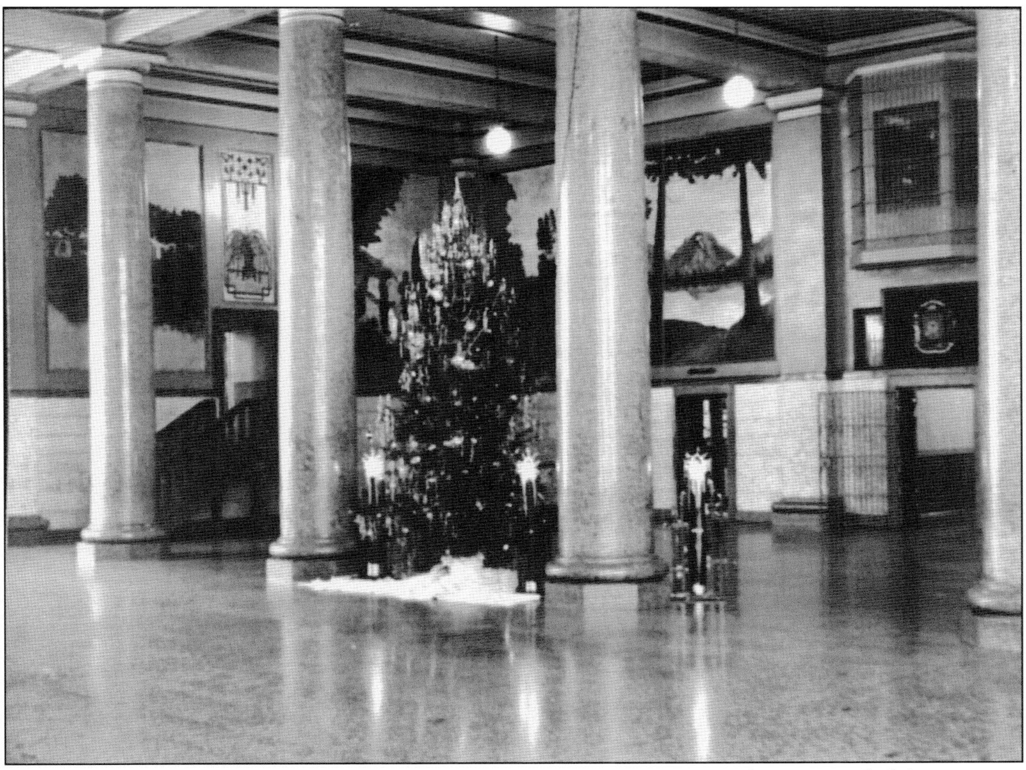

A reminder of the world outside, a decorated Christmas tree stands surrounded by massive columns inside the reformatory's rotunda during the 1937 holiday season. Christmas gave the inmates an opportunity to interact with the citizenry through holiday concerts featuring the reformatory band.

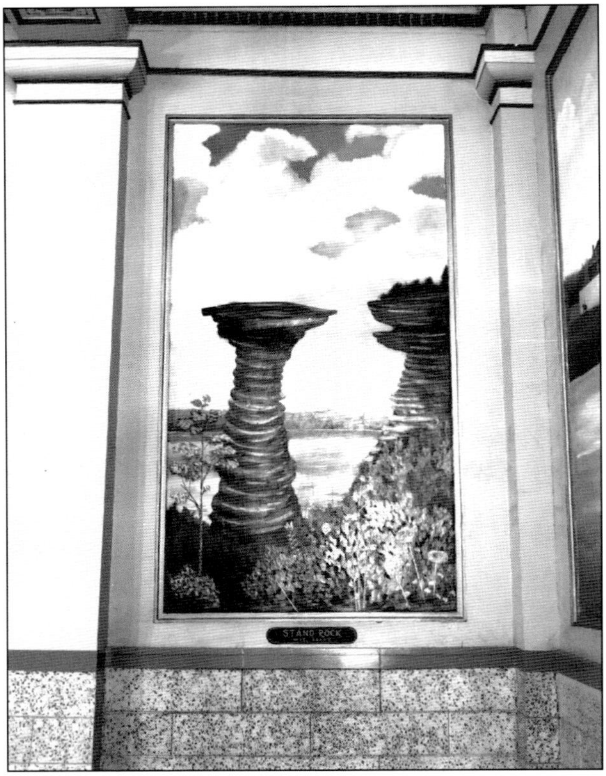

Throughout the prison's history, inmate talent h.as played a major role in the building and beautification of the physical environment. The upper portion of the rotunda walls are graced with large paintings depicting various historic and natural scenes painted by inmates. *Stand Rock, Wisconsin Dells* is located on the west wall of the rotunda and was painted in 1924 by an inmate named E. Hubbard.

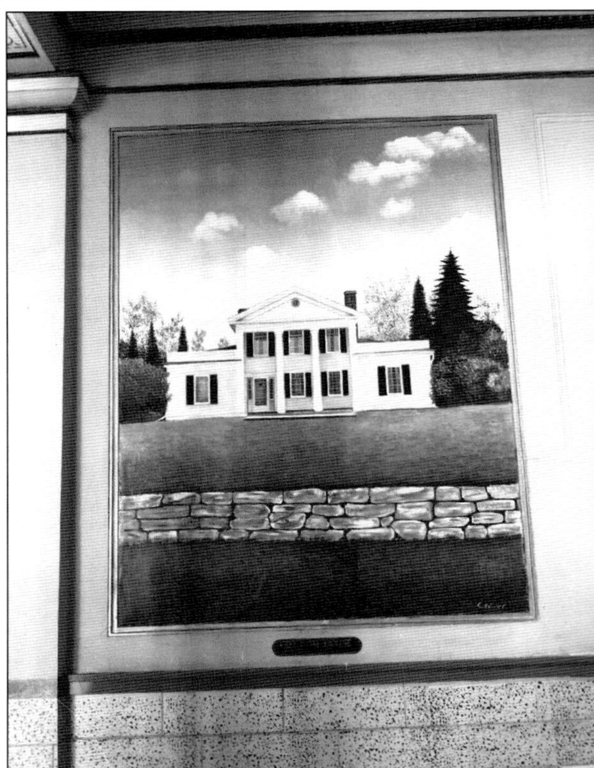

A painting of the Cotton House adorns the south wall, another example of inmate art painted by Charles Waite sometime around 1964. Built in 1826, the home was originally owned by Louis Beaupre. In 1938, it was moved to its present location at Heritage Hill State Historical Park.

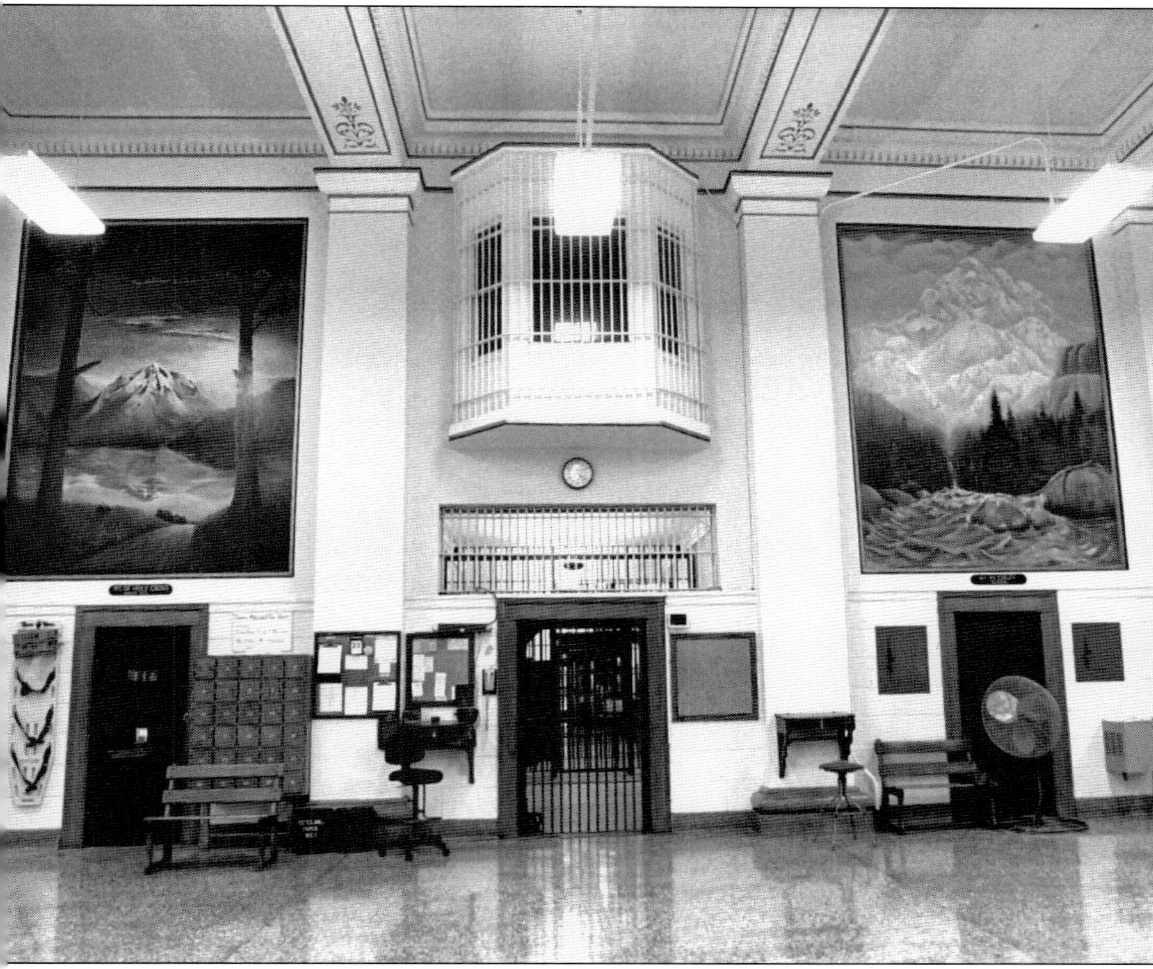

Gate 4 at the west rotunda entrance gives a good indication of the size and placement of the inmate art that depicts natural and historic scenes of the United States and Wisconsin; from left to right are *Mt. of Holy Cross* (artist unknown) and *Mount McKinley*, painted by E. Hubbard in 1924. The use of inmate labor was common among the reformatory setting during the late 19th and early 20th centuries.

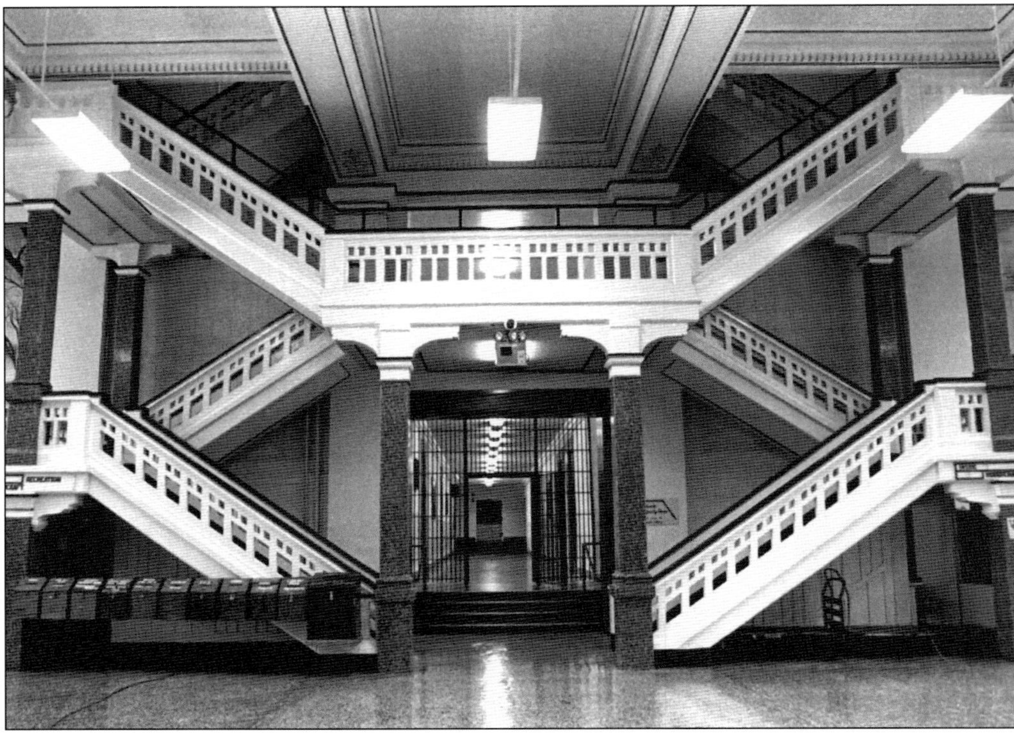

The rotunda is an open rectangle with polygonal bays on the north and south sides. Its two-story construction measures approximately 70 feet by 70 feet. Its floors, columns, baseboards, and wainscoting are clad in rose-colored terrazzo. The east end of the rotunda features a spectacular poured concrete staircase featuring Craftsman-inspired bracketing and balustrade spindles. The staircase provides access to the dining area and classrooms.

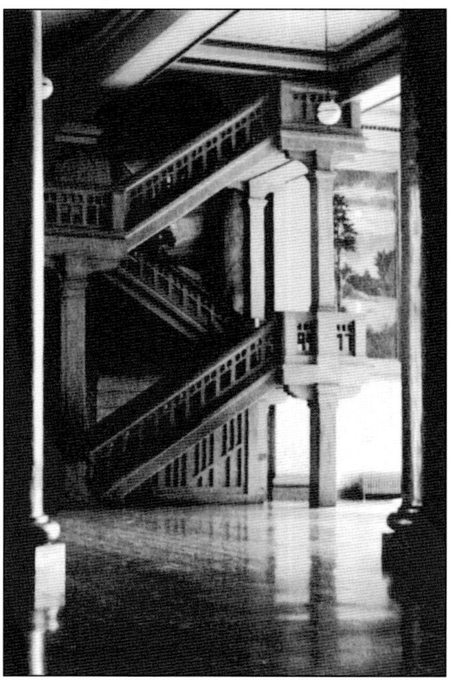

The rotunda is seen here looking toward the staircase, photographed early in the morning by reformatory employee J. Emory Temple. (Courtesy Green Bay Correctional Institution.)

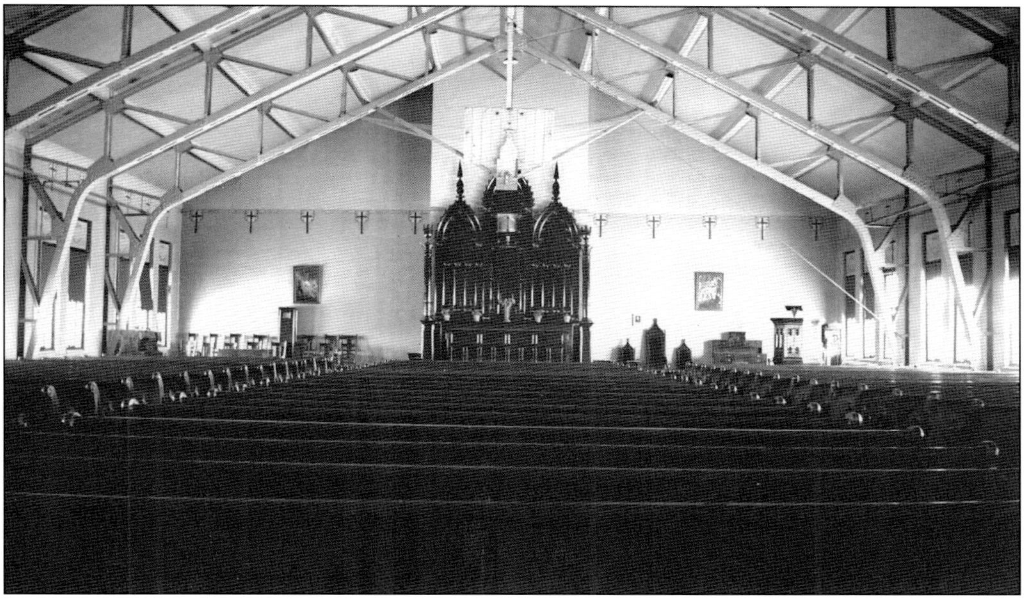

This interior shot of the reformatory chapel was taken sometime during the 1930s. The vast majority of the inmates during that period regularly attended Catholic and Protestant services.

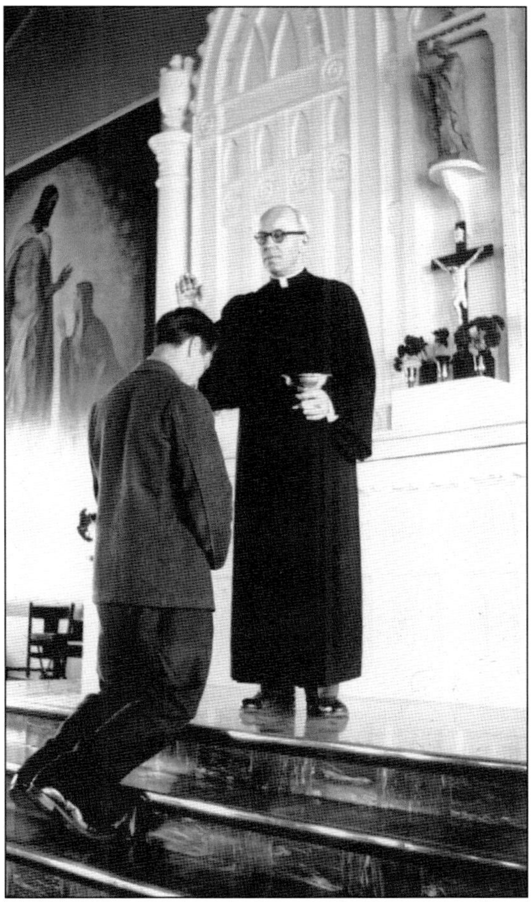

Fr. Roland Hoffman gives his blessing to a Catholic inmate on the steps of the high altar. Religious instruction and observance were considered prime elements of the rehabilitative process. American prisons traditionally relied heavily upon religion to induce a change of heart among prisoners. Solitary prayer encouraged penitential reflection and gave birth to the term "penitentiary."

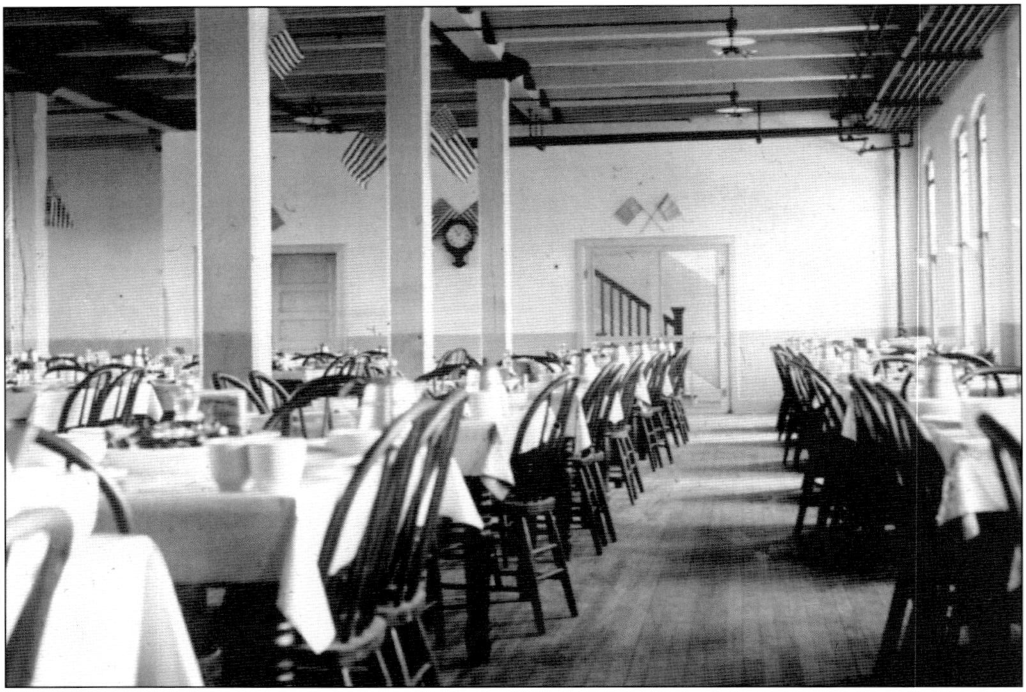

The Wisconsin reformatory may have been considered a progressive institution in 1900, but it still held fast to many of the traditional disciplines that regulated the life of an inmate. Until Supt. Earl H. Eklund (1924–1941) abolished the silent rule, inmates were prohibited from speaking to one another. Conversation was permitted only during a 10-minute period at the evening meal. A ringing bell at the end of the meal signified a return to the silence. Photographed during the 1930s, the old dining hall reflected the typical dining arrangements before the advent of the cafeteria system.

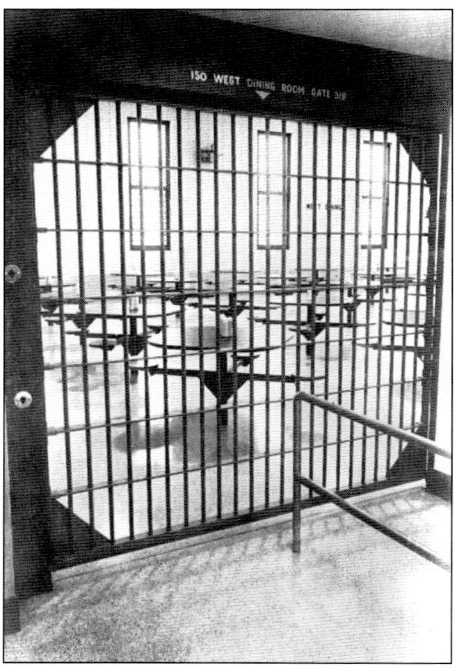

Much has changed at the prison, including the construction of a new dining hall in 1982. Gone are the wooden tables, long ago replaced with a cafeteria-like setting.

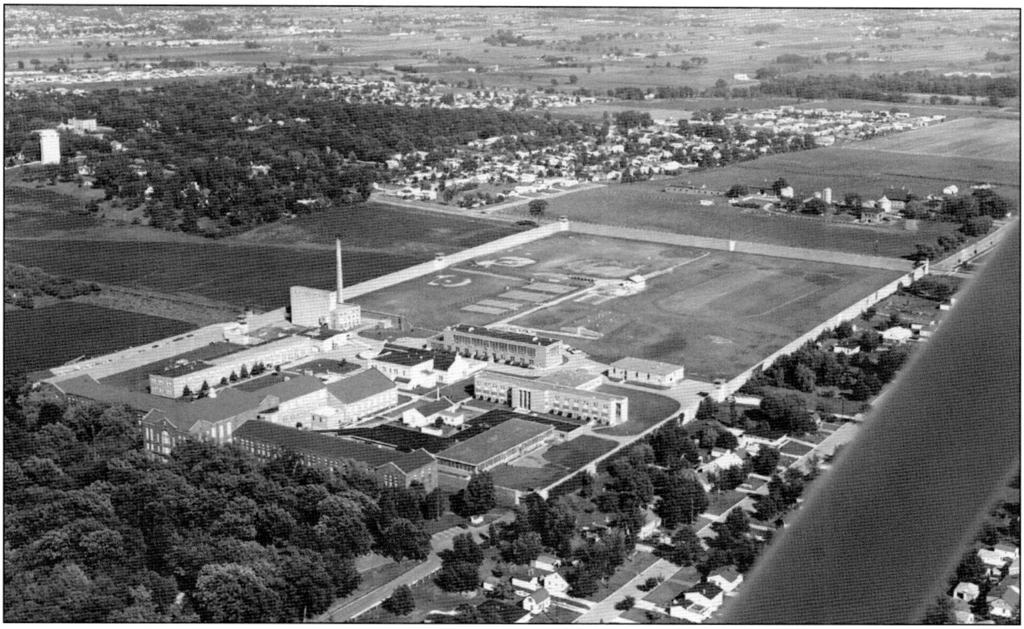

A birds-eye view of the institution, looking slightly northeast, provides a good indication of the institution's geographical footprint. This photograph was taken prior to the construction of Highway 172, which now runs parallel to the eastern wall visible alongside the power plant smoke stack. The Webster Avenue farm complex can be seen just beyond the north wall. The residential area to the north of the farm complex has spread south to encompass the last remaining parcels of farmland.

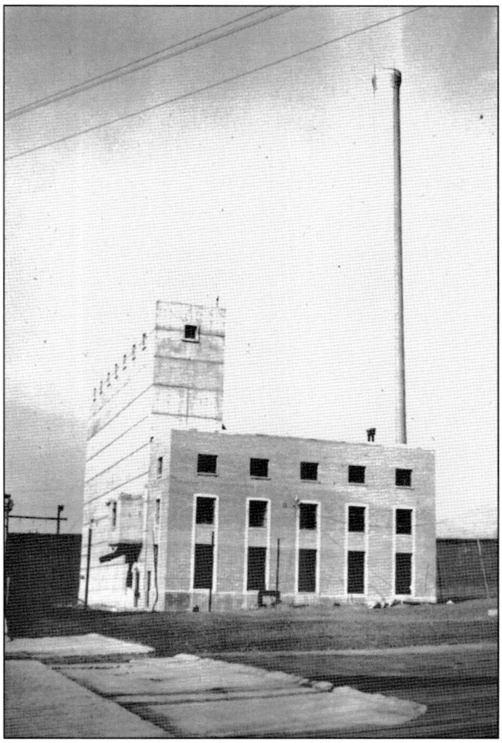

The new power plant was constructed in 1957. It is situated along the north wall of the facility and is one of the most visible reformatory structures.

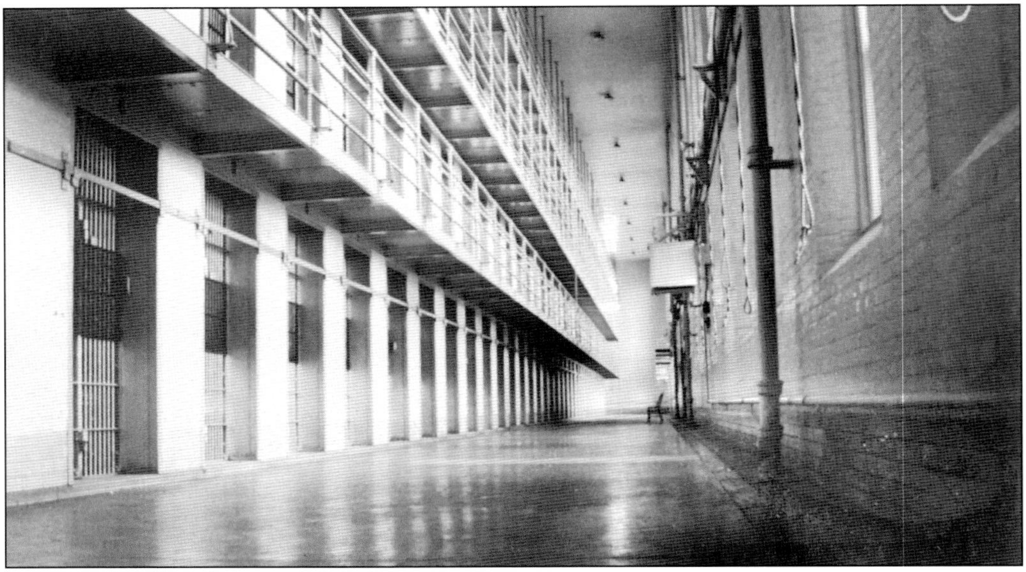

North Cell Hall construction was started almost immediately and is one of the oldest buildings in the complex. Construction was completed in 1903. The rectilinear Romanesque Revival–style structure is attached to the main building. The basement windows have been bricked in for security reasons.

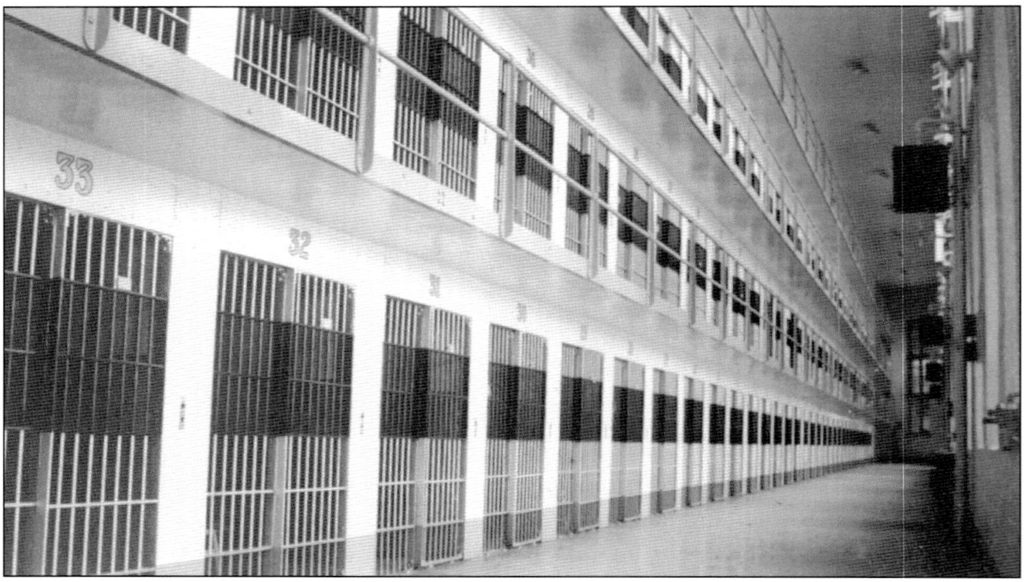

Reformatory architecture typically followed a formula that included high walls, stone buildings, and guard towers. Interior layouts sought to minimize contact between inmates. The South Cell Hall is typical of American prisons built during the late 19th century based upon the Auburn design, which favored tiered cell wings. The cell house consists of four tiers of cell blocks. Gang walks separate each tier, and there are about 70 cells of 50 square feet on each level. The two-story South Cell Hall, completed in 1922, is a mirror image of the North Cell Hall.

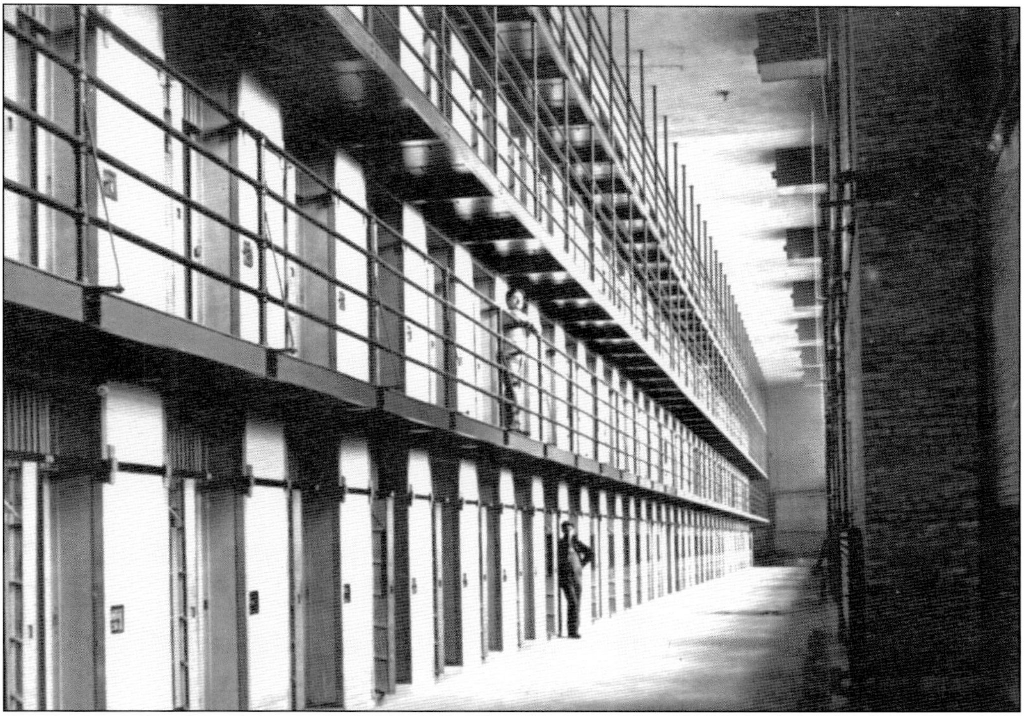

Two inmates stand outside their cells in the South Cell Hall. The hall was designed to minimize contact between inmates and allow guards to easily control movement from cell to workplace. (Courtesy Green Bay Correctional Institution.)

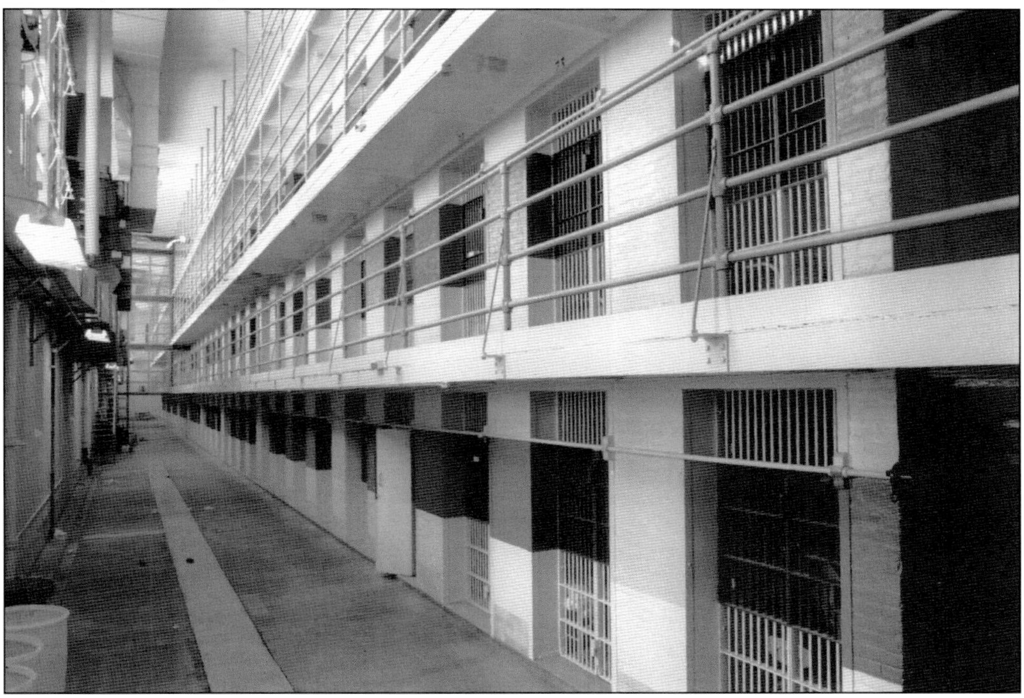

Sometime in the 1970s, each cell section received a color coded paint scheme to better assist the guards in identifying particular areas. (Courtesy Green Bay Correctional Institution.)

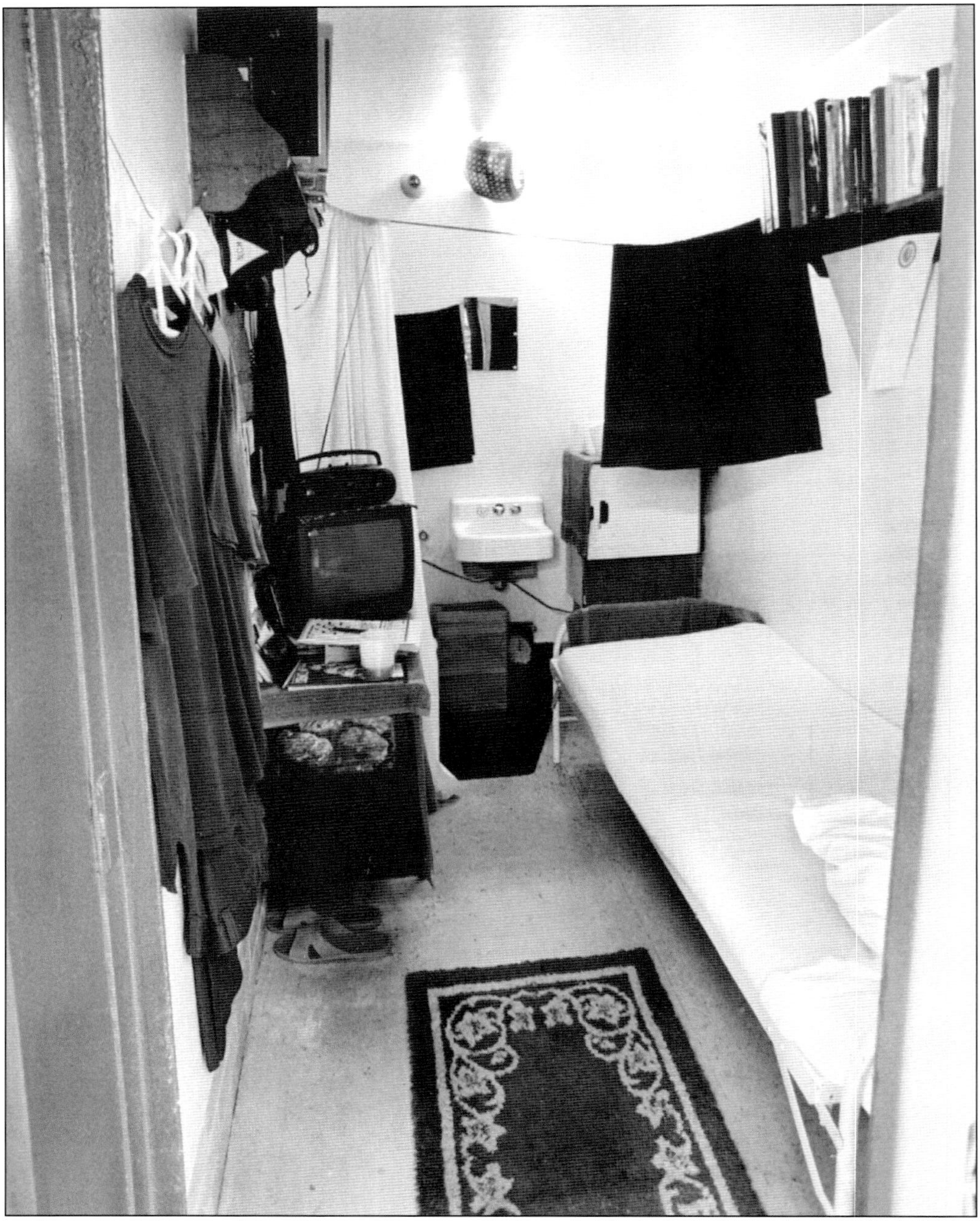

Single cells are typically cramped, but when they were originally constructed, prisoners were prohibited from having personal belongings in their cells. Cells in the north and south halls measure 5 feet 8 inches by 9 feet and contain a sink, toilet, and bed. Approximately 1,090 inmates now call the Green Bay Correctional Institution their home. The old North and South Cell Halls were built to house approximately 588 prisoners. Additional dormitories handle the overflow. (Courtesy Green Bay Correctional Institution.)

Two

GUARDS

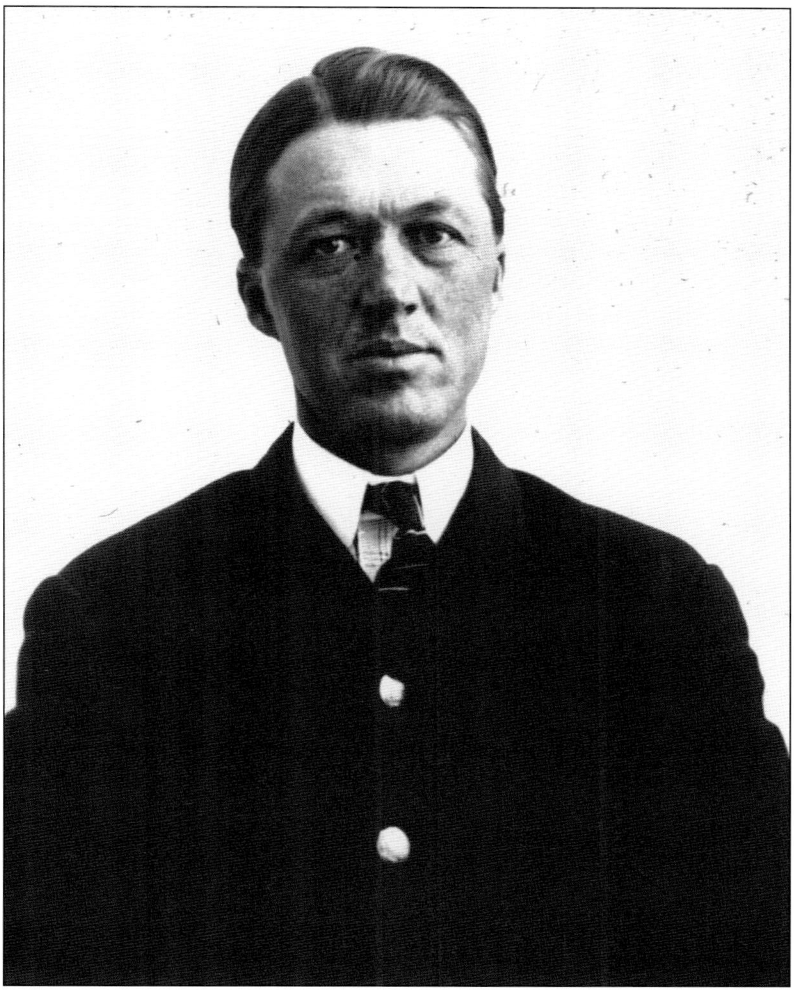

Reformatory guard Bruce Dodge opened and closed the gate on the first inmates transferred from Waupun on the morning of August 31, 1898. All were first-time offenders between the ages of 17 and 28. James E. Heg personally met the prisoners as they stepped off the train between De Pere and Green Bay.

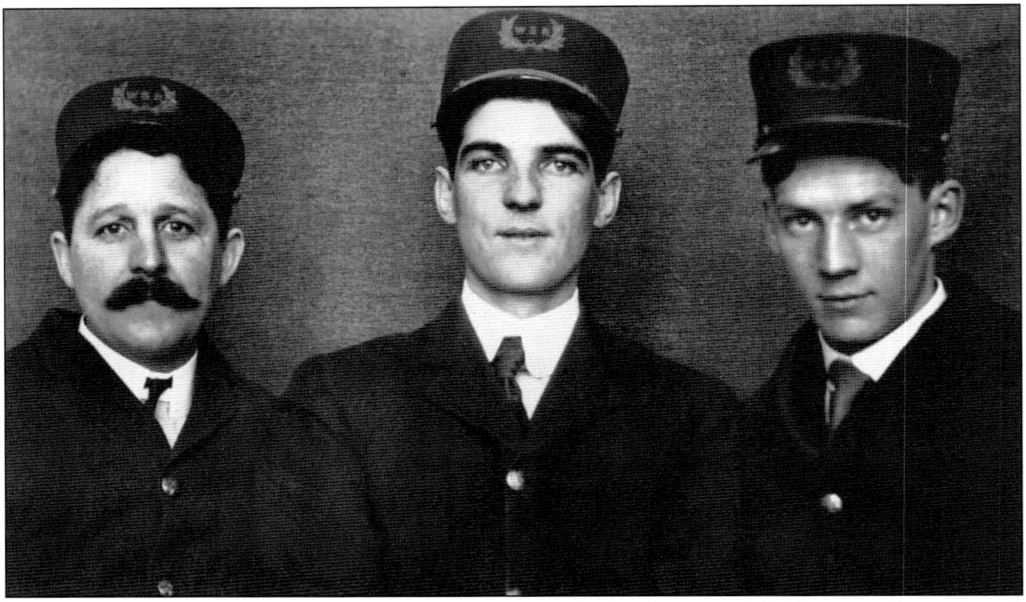

Deliverers of discipline, guards like these three, identified only as Boyd (left), Gross (center), and Clifford, doled out harsh punishments for such minor infractions as "gazing about while working" and the catch-all charge of "general crookedness." Blue-uniformed guards often employed corporal punishment and felt no compunction in striking unruly prisoners with brass-tipped canes in order to modify behavior. Punishments ranged from the imposition of small fines, to the reduction of rations, to bread and water coupled with solitary confinement.

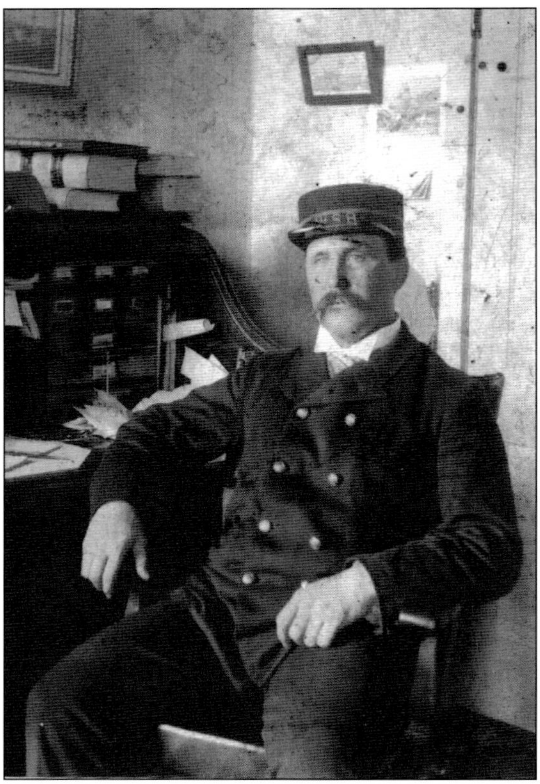

Joseph Rafael Junion was born in Red River, Kewaunee County, in 1867. He moved to Green Bay in 1899 and took a guard and teaching job at the reformatory. During his tenure, the reformatory tailor shop cut cloth for the Reliance Company in Mattoon, Illinois. In 1913, Junion was named assistant superintendent of production at the Reliance Company, where he oversaw the construction of Big Yank overalls made from cloth cut at WSR. (Courtesy of Carol Jones.)

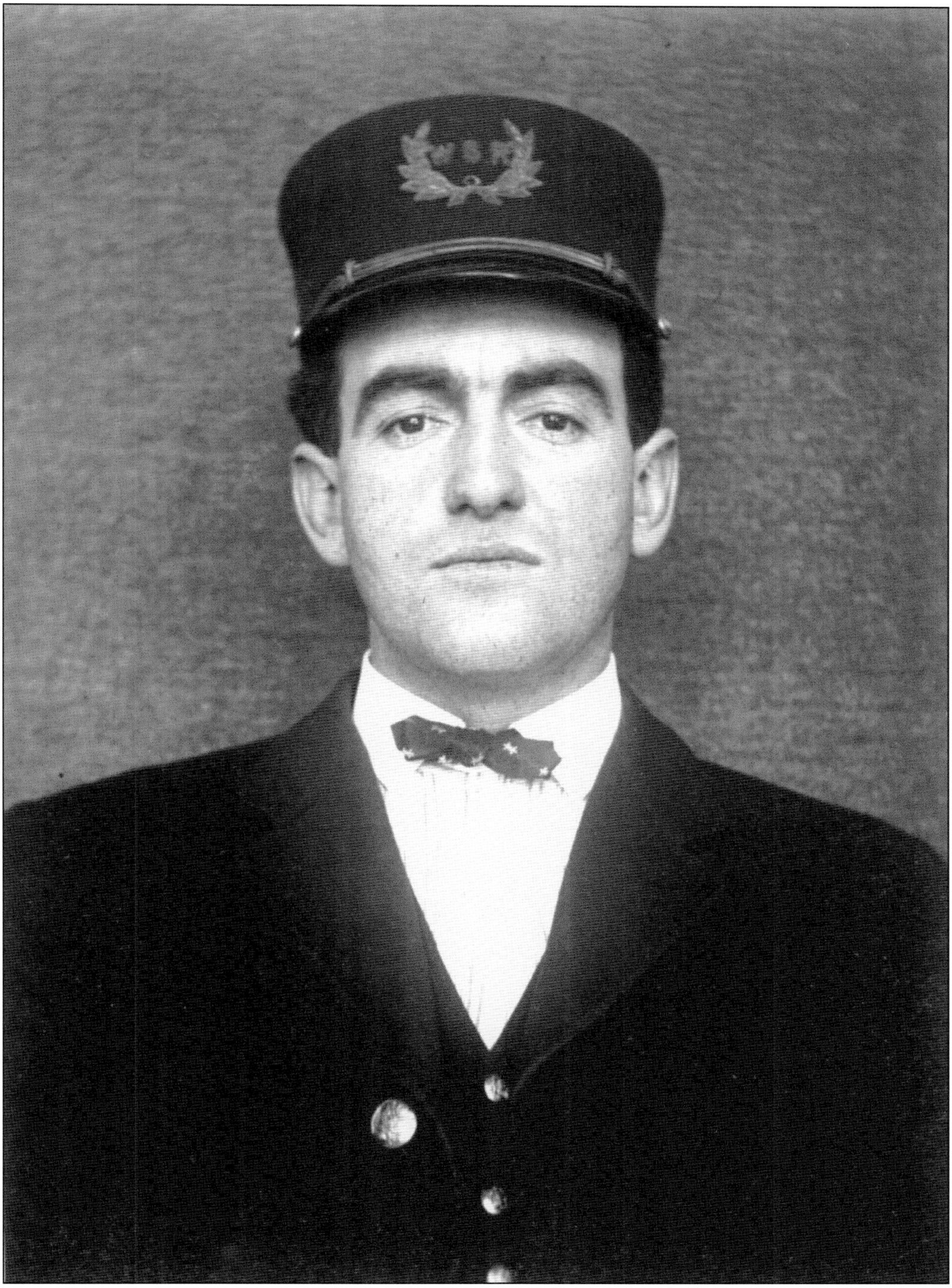

Tough men like C. R. Watson made good guards during the early days of the reformatory. Considered untrained by today's standards, guards like Watson relied upon the cane and a just measure of pain to compel inmate compliance. Their blue uniforms were meant to copy police uniforms—a daily reminder of who was in charge at the institution. Discipline at the reformatory remained severe, particularly prior to the 1950s, but in practice it generally differed from the arbitrary brutality common at penitentiaries of the period.

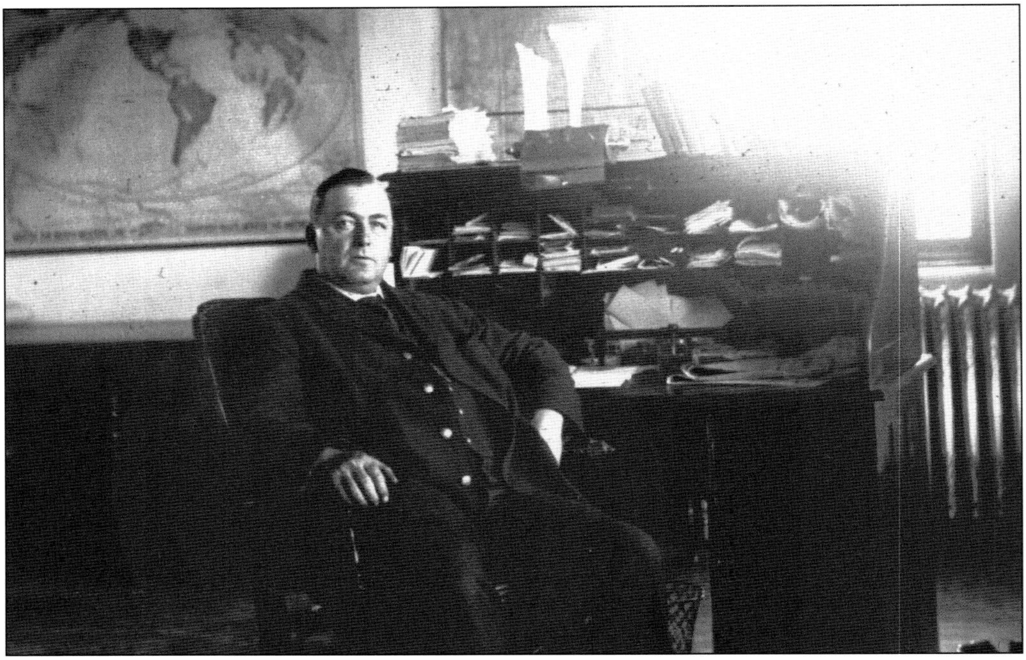

O. E. Bickford, assistant superintendent, began his corrections career in 1887 at the state prison in Waupun. In July 1902, he transferred to WSR and served 17 years before retiring in 1937.

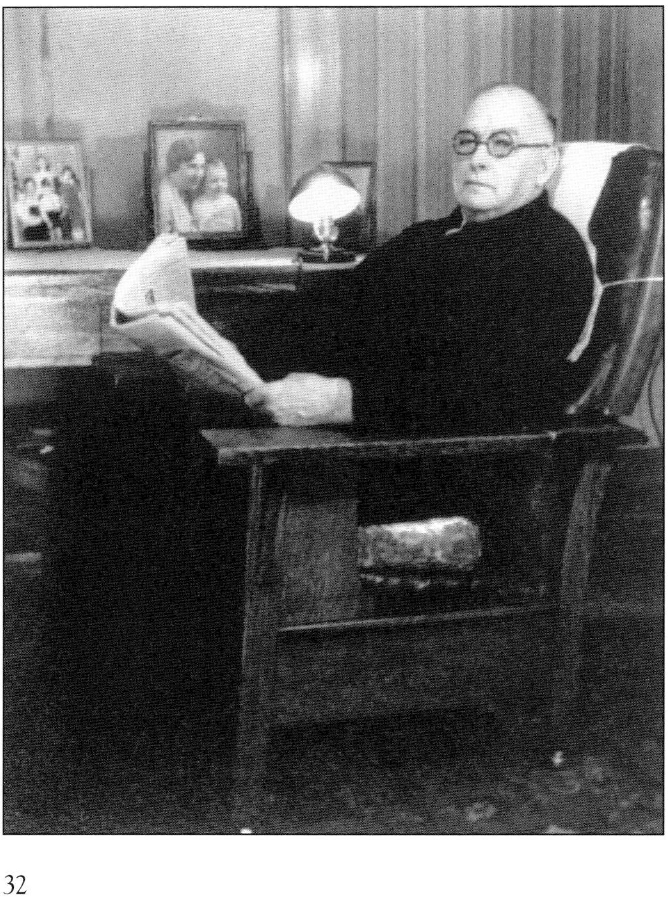

When Bickford arrived at WSR in 1902, inmates observed the silent rule, wore striped uniforms, and marched in lockstep. By the time he retired 50 years later, much had changed.

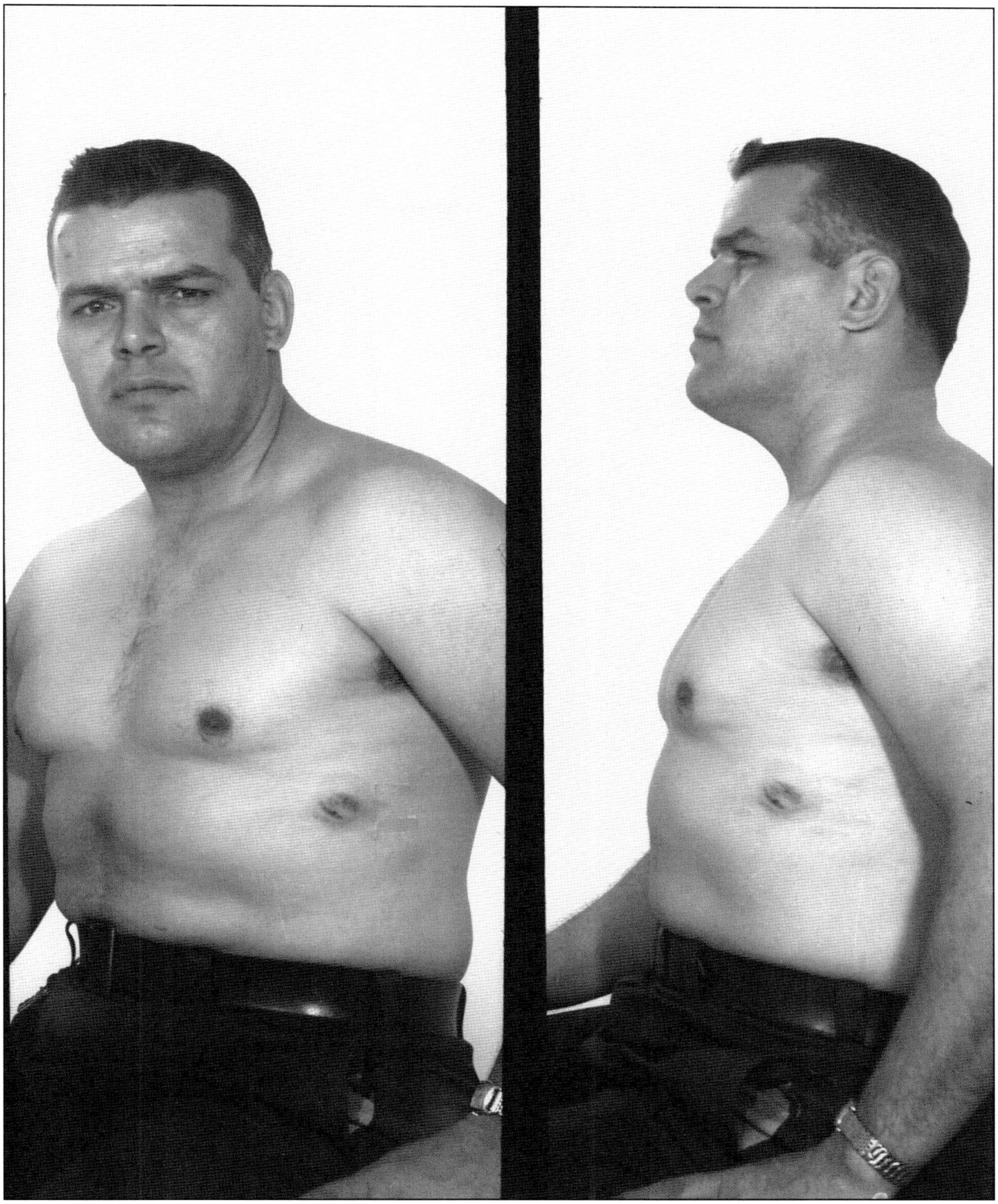

Like any prison, WSR housed its share of violent criminals despite its status as a facility for youthful offenders. Guard Dick Benzschawel shows the effects of a scuffle with a hostile inmate around 1960.

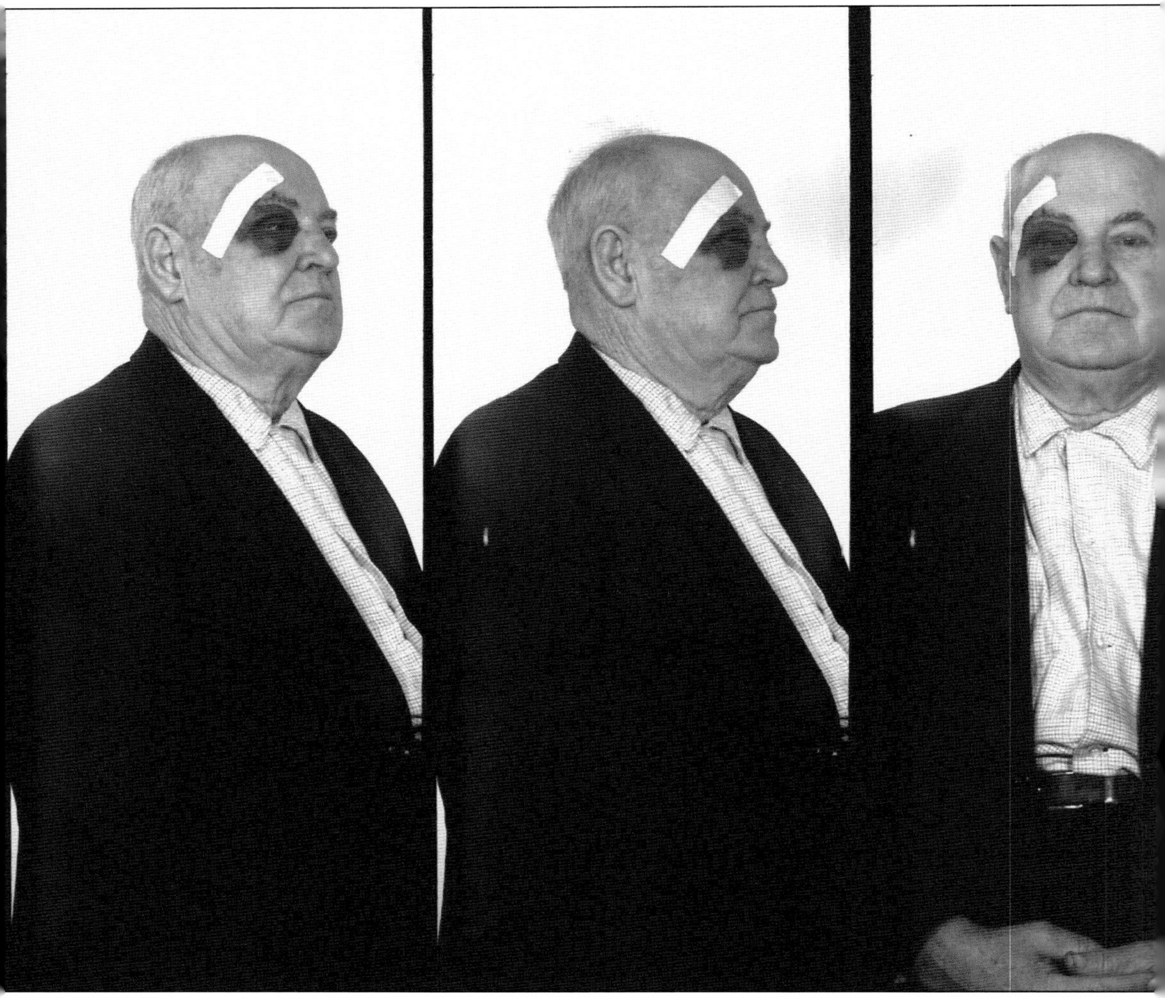

Although they held the upper hand, guards and prison officials were not immune to inmate violence. Reformatory employee Otto Muenster sports a nasty black eye and laceration, possibly administered by an unruly inmate.

Three

PEOPLE AND PLACES

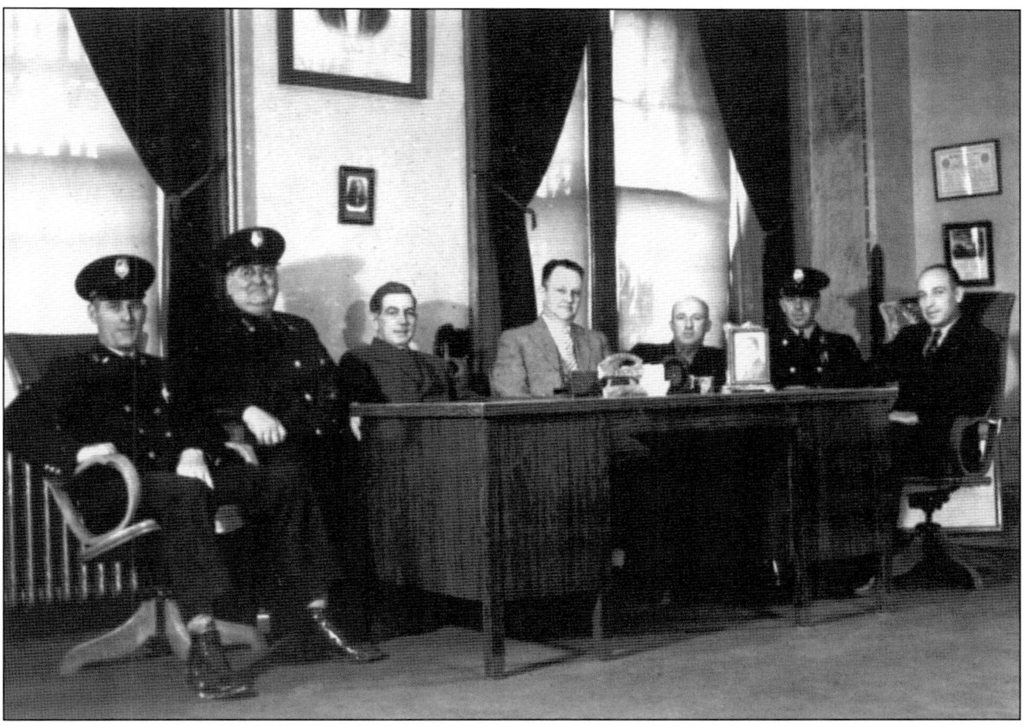

In a scene evocative of the era, members of Supt. Earl H. Eklund's staff sit for a photograph at his desk around 1935. From left to right are assistant deputy Joe Marchant, deputy assistant C. W. McCready, superintendent Eklund; business manager Benjamin P. Kramer, welfare officer Jim Daley, assistant superintendant N. J. Nuss, and director of education Stephen C. Govin.

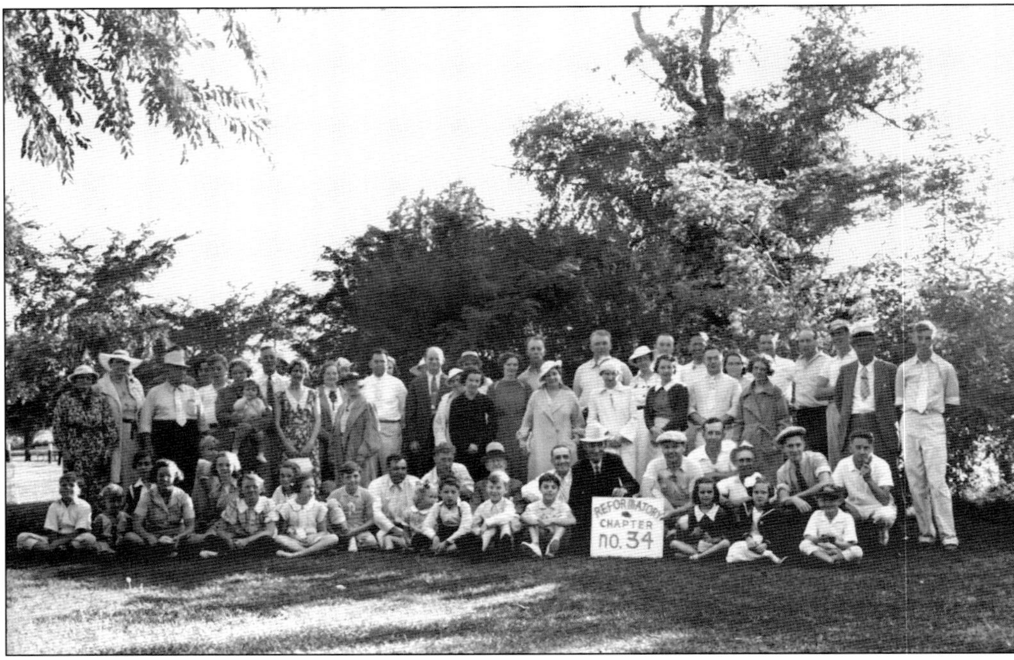

Members of the Wisconsin State Reformatory Employees Union, Chapter No. 34, gather at Bay Beach on July 31, 1937.

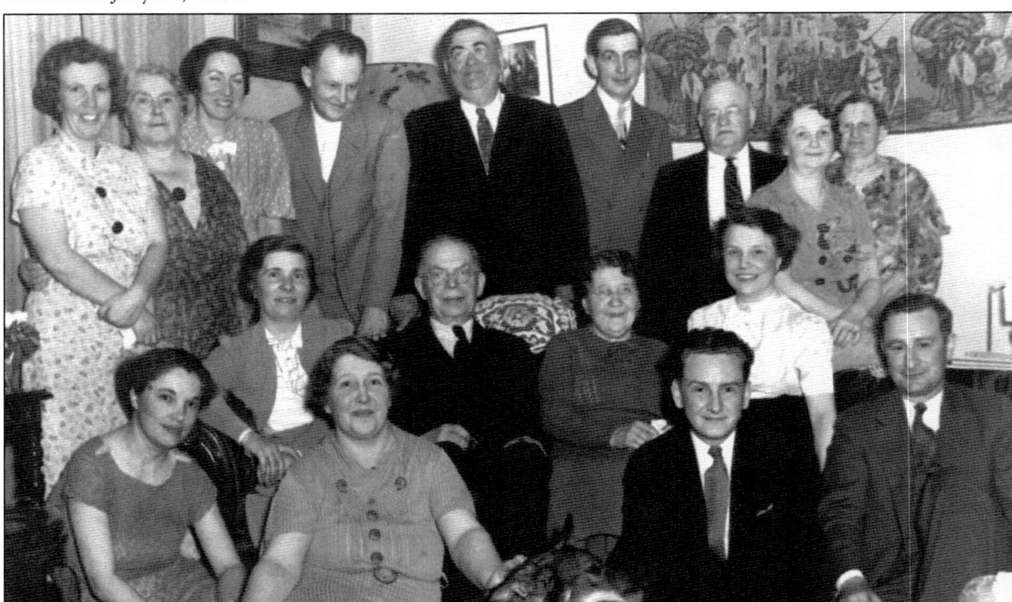

Reformatory employees enjoyed close working relationships. Many of them lived nearby the facility, with some of the higher ranking officials occupying reformatory housing. This scene is from A. "Teddy" Aalbers's retirement party. Assistant steward B. P. Kramer, reformatory deputy C. W. McCready, and Supt. Earl H. Eklund stand in the third row fourth, fifth, and sixth from the left respectively. Aalbers is shown seated in the center of the sofa with his wife to his left. The photograph was taken by J. Emory Temple, whose wife, Jean, is pictured standing in the third row, far left.

When this photograph was taken in 1921, J. Emory Temple had just started working as a records clerk at WSR. Starting in the 1920s, he tirelessly photographed reformatory personnel and inmates, special events, building construction, the Amberg granite quarry, and the satellite farms at Oneida and on Webster Avenue. Before he retired 37 years later, he compiled a body of work that provides a photographic history of the institution during his tenure. Temple also preserved a number of early photographs that predate his employment at WSR.

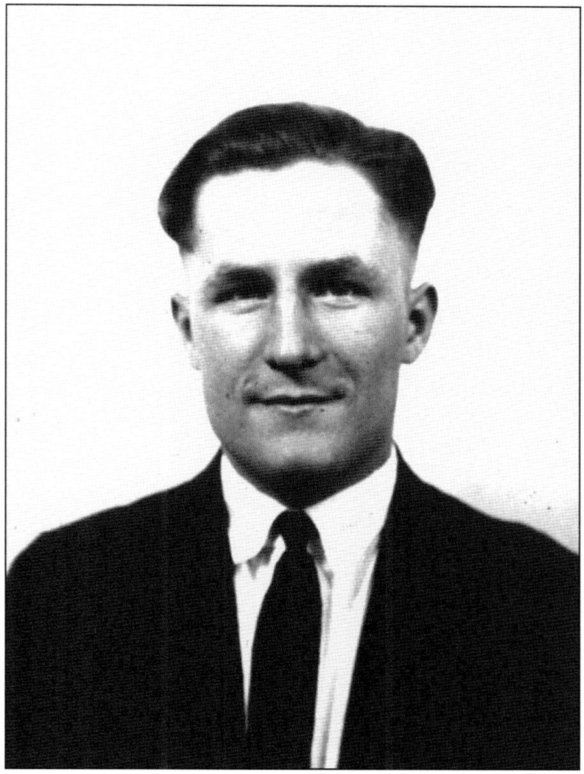

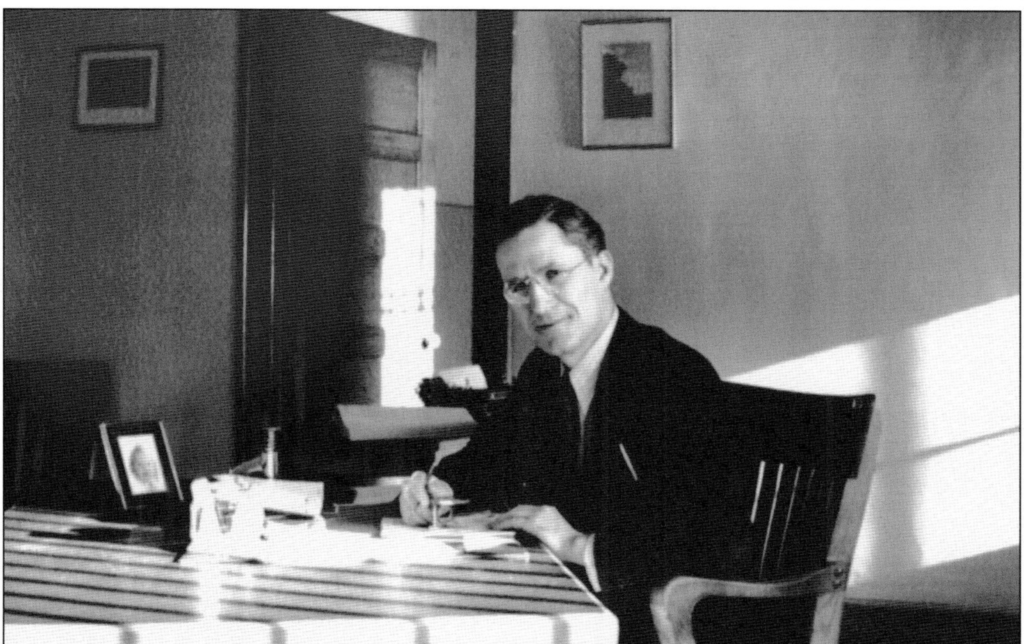

J. Emory Temple is seen here at his desk in 1939. Temple, the unofficial reformatory photographer, once presented a photo album as a gift to Earl H. Eklund, marking the superintendent's 15th anniversary at the reformatory. A portion of that album remains at the Green Bay Correctional Institution. (Courtesy Green Bay Correctional Institution.)

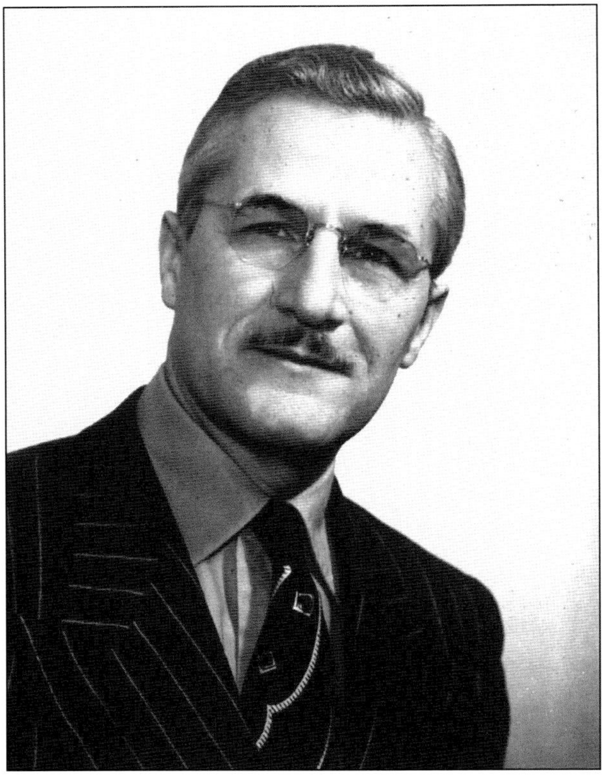

Temple, pictured here in 1952, six years before his retirement, became an expert fingerprint technician during is career at WSR.

Professor Alex V. Enna led the Wisconsin State Reformatory Band during the 1920s. During the summer, his band would often give public concerts from the steps of the administration building. Inmate-community interaction was not unusual and extended to many areas, including sports, community events, and business relations. The reformatory band provided a creative outlet for talented inmates and entertainment for their fellow prisoners. Such activity was designed to rehabilitate inmates and develop skills that might lead to success and a diversion from a life of crime.

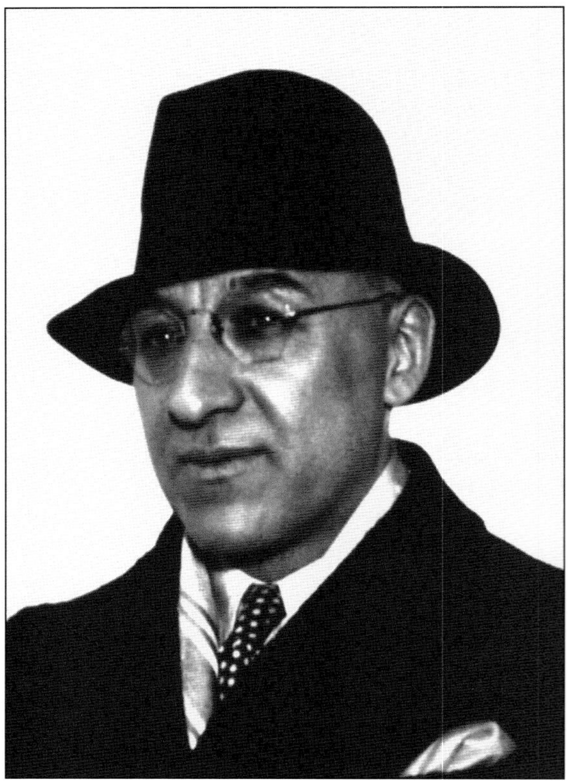

Howard Atkinson ran the reformatory's auto repair shop. Boys from all backgrounds were naturally drawn to the auto shop after its establishment in 1926, and its popularity soared in the 1950s as Americans turned increasingly to cars for their transportation needs. Atkinson posed for this photograph in 1950.

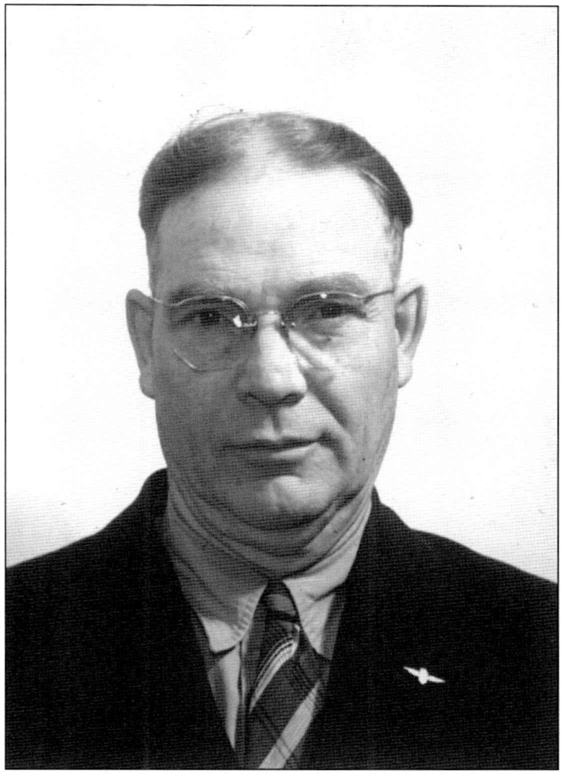

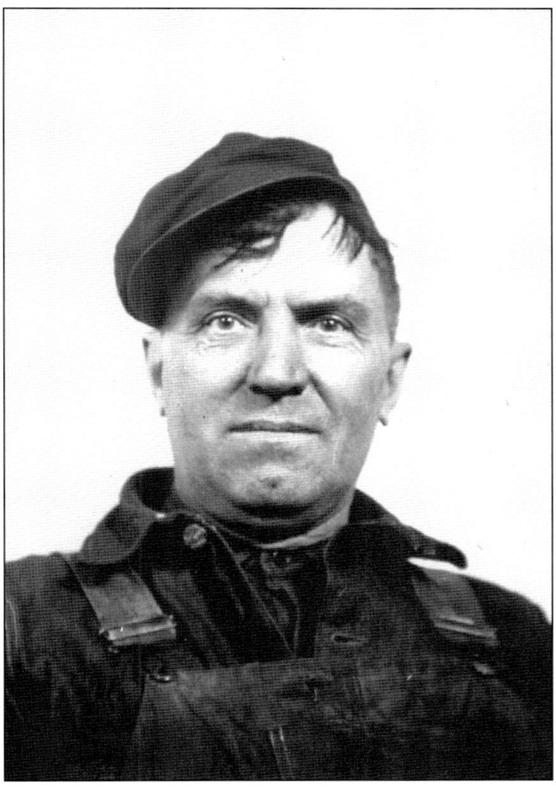

C. J. Daley was the reformatory's chief engineer for much of the early period. This photograph was taken in 1950 by reformatory records clerk J. Emory Temple.

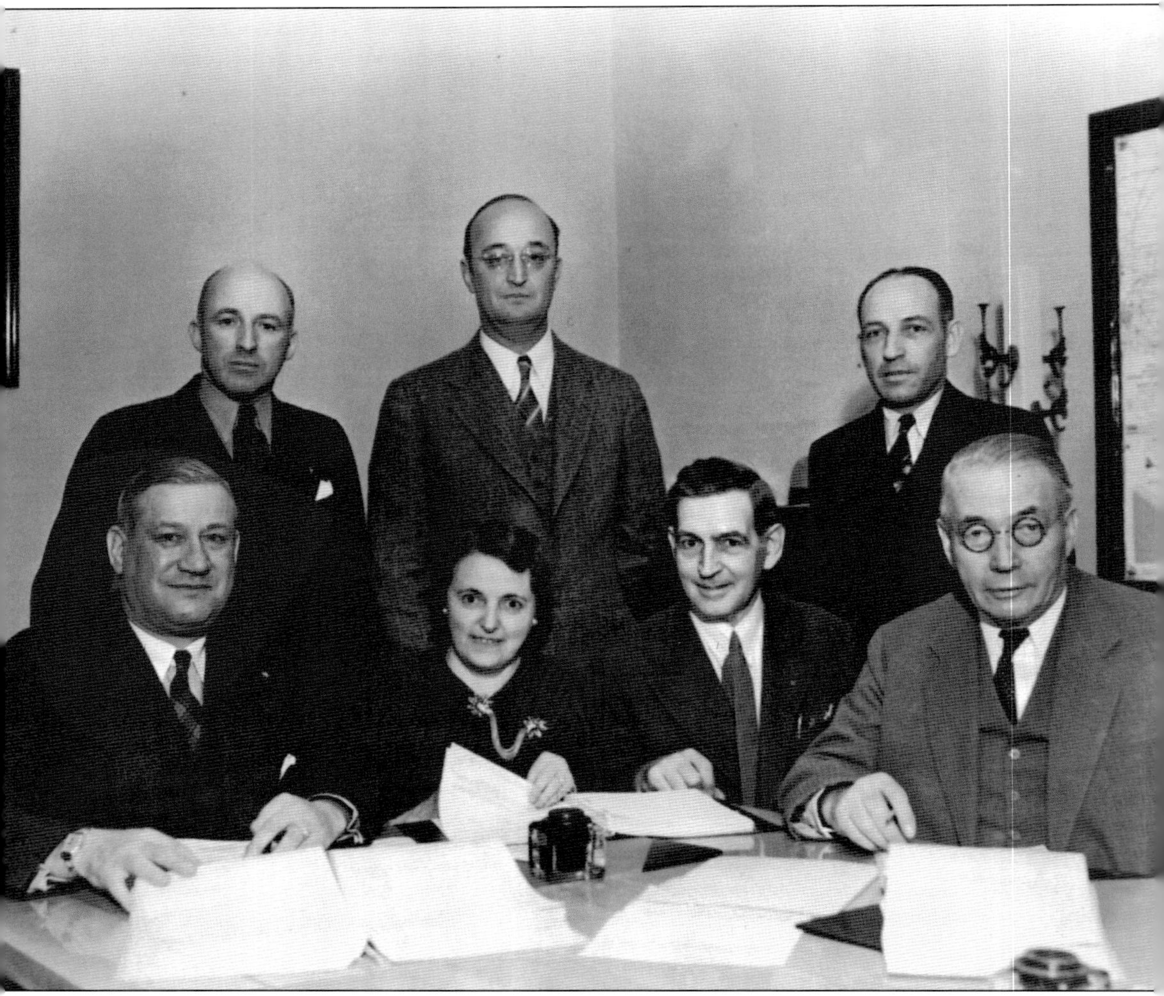

Earl Eklund was undoubtedly one of the most admired of all reformatory superintendents. His staff surrounds him at his desk in this photograph from the 1930s. Eklund's work in developing the reformatory's dairy herd and his devotion to public service were unsurpassed. Under Eklund's direction, it won a first place ranking among all of the nation's reformatories included in a survey of the American Prison Association. He expanded educational programs, completed building projects, abolished the silent rule, and helped the institution shift from contract labor programs to state-use industries. Upon his death in 1941, the *Holstein-Friesian* publication opined, "Fortunate was the young man who had the good fortune to share Supt. Eklund's fine philosophy of life." (Courtesy Green Bay Correctional Institution.)

Eklund was fond of dogs. Beans, a Boston terrier, was one of his favorites. (Courtesy Green Bay Correctional Institution.)

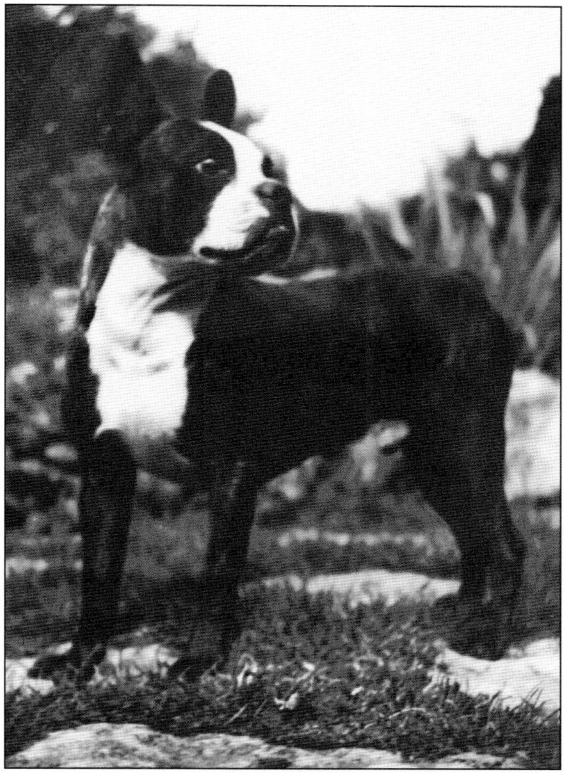

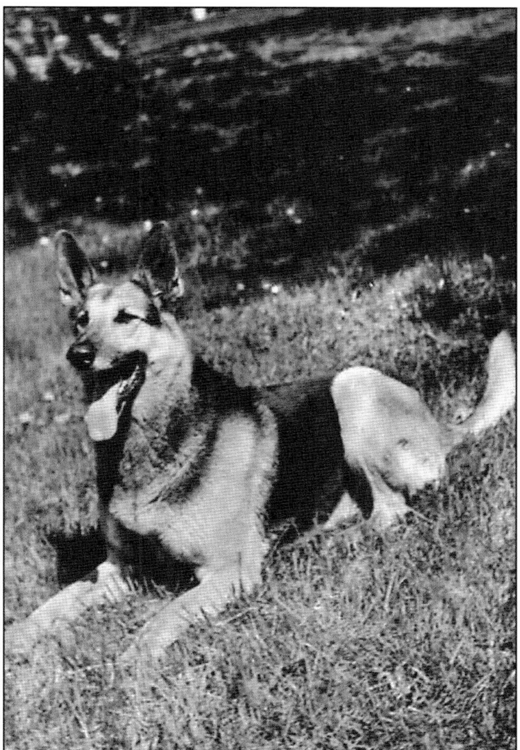

Eklund, the fifth WSR superintendent, also owned a German Shepherd named Jet.

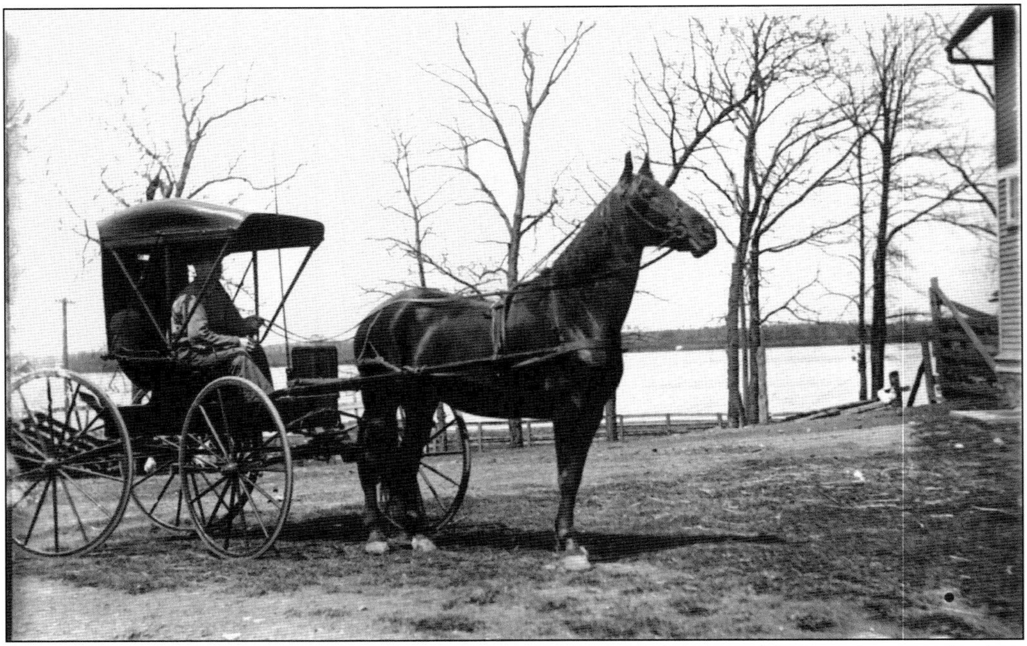

In 1900, the superintendent's mode of transportation was this horse and buggy photographed on the Fox River farm site just east of the reformatory.

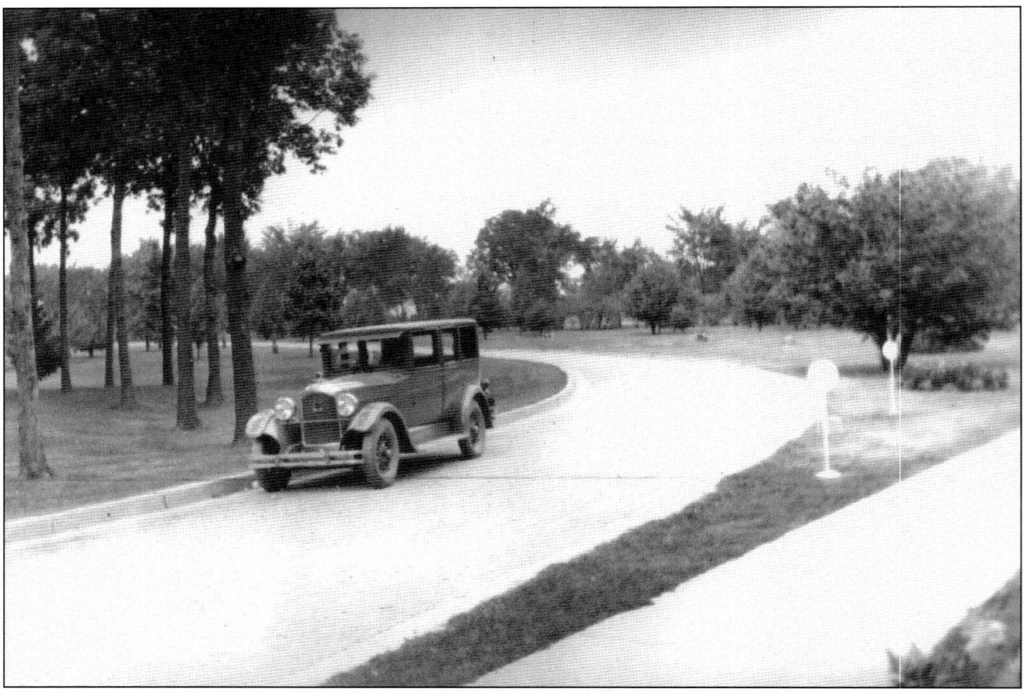

The horse and buggy soon gave way to automobiles as the preferred mode of transportation for WSR officials. Supt. Earl H. Eklund makes his way to the reformatory along the entrance road from Riverside Drive in 1938. The approach remains the same today, but the grounds are now heavily wooded.

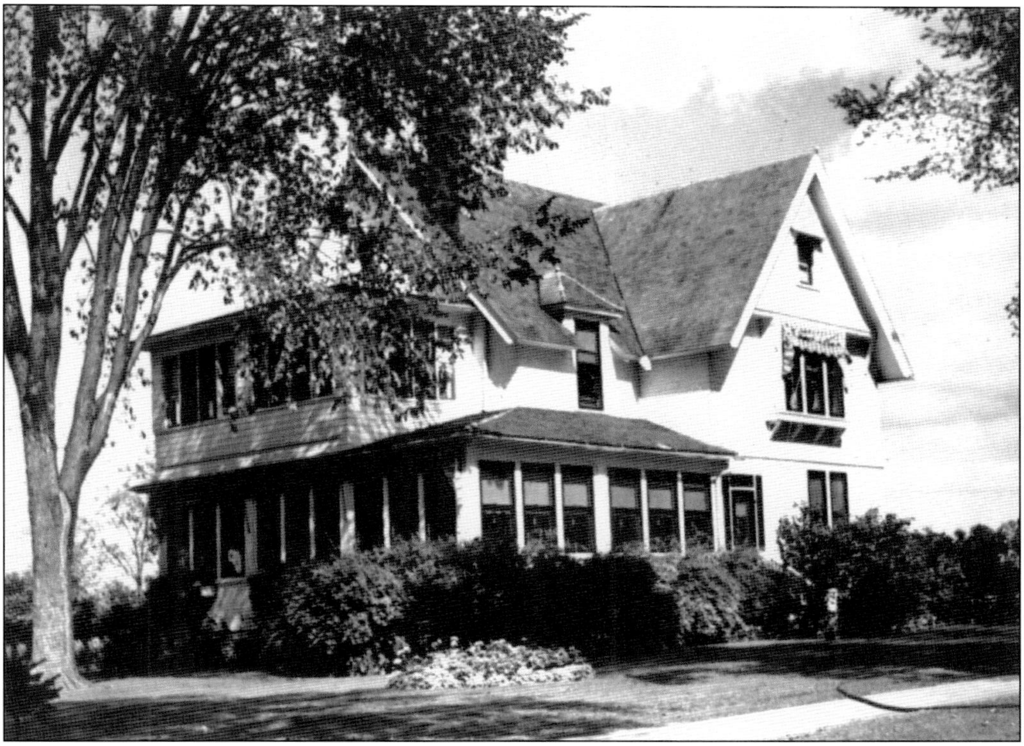

WSR superintendents lived in housing provided by the state located on Riverside Drive, or Highway 57, just west of the reformatory. This photograph was taken by J. Emory Temple in 1939 during Eklund's tenure as superintendent.

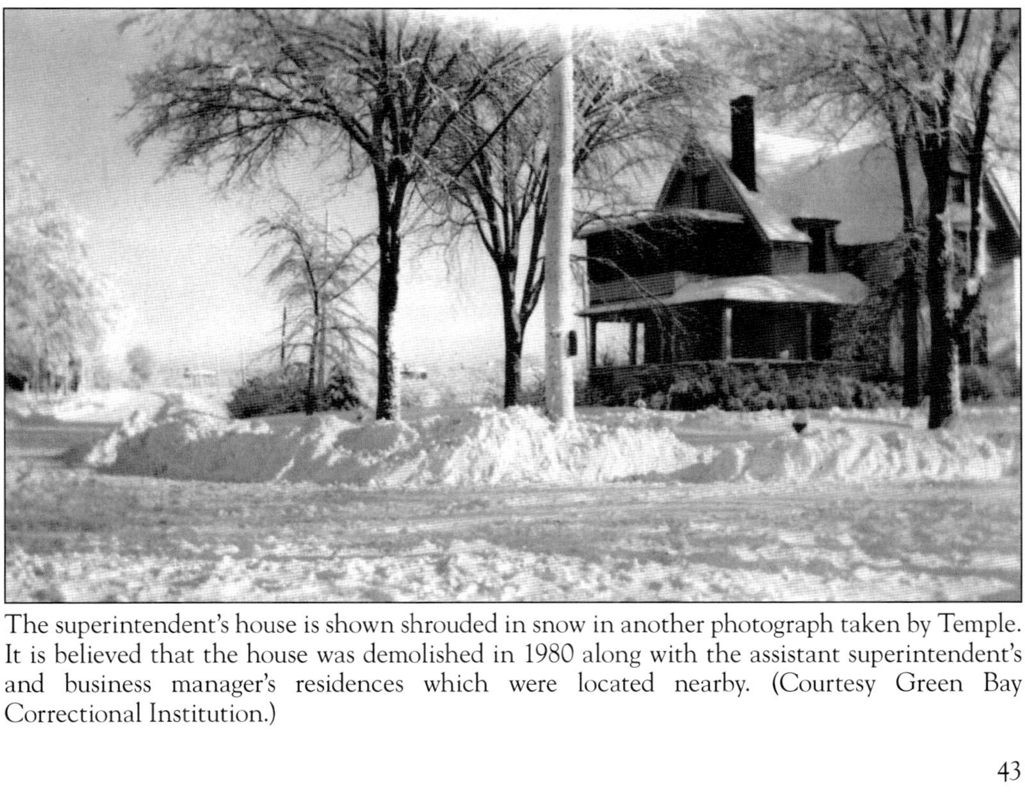

The superintendent's house is shown shrouded in snow in another photograph taken by Temple. It is believed that the house was demolished in 1980 along with the assistant superintendent's and business manager's residences which were located nearby. (Courtesy Green Bay Correctional Institution.)

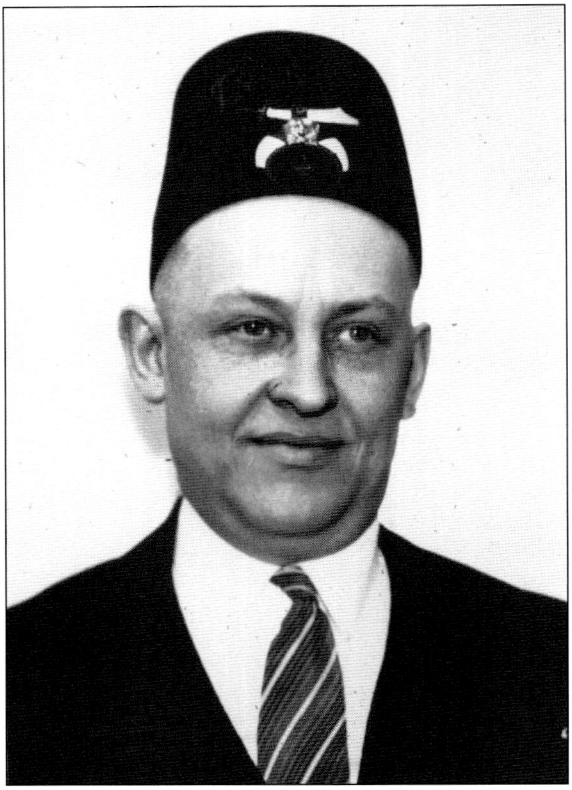

Benjamin P. Kramer assumed the duties of superintendent after Earl Eklund's death in 1941. Kramer would serve as superintendent for 10 years before retiring at the age of 61. By the time he finished his career, he had served over 30 years at WSR.

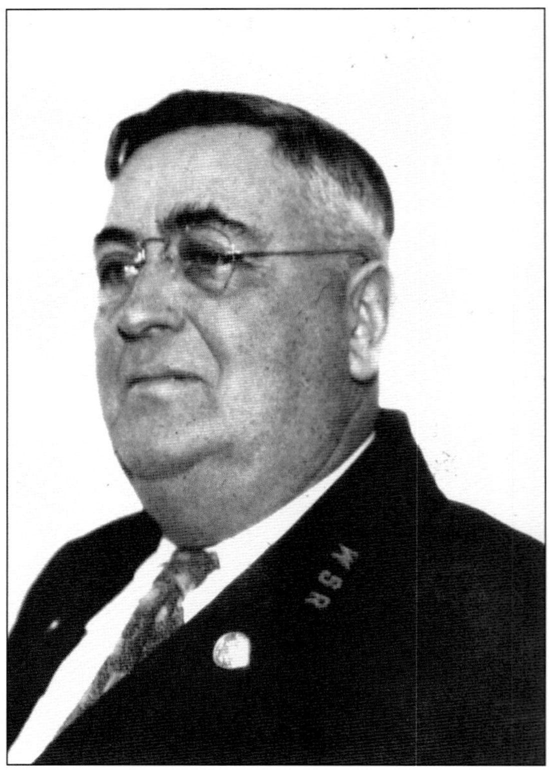

C. W. McCready served as deputy under Earl H. Eklund.

De Pere native Andy Janssen started working for the WSR as a clerk stenographer in October 1922. His compensation package included $65 per month and room and board. When he arrived at WSR, it held only 125 inmates. By the time he retired in 1969, the inmate population numbered 860.

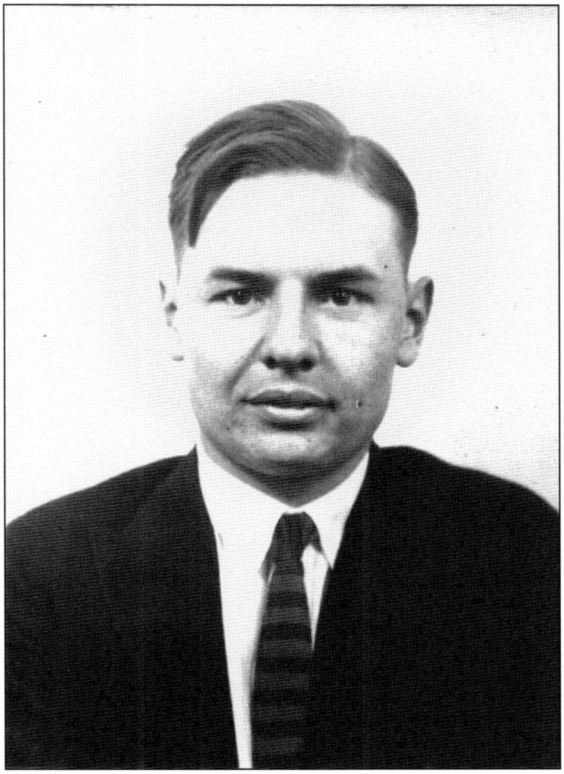

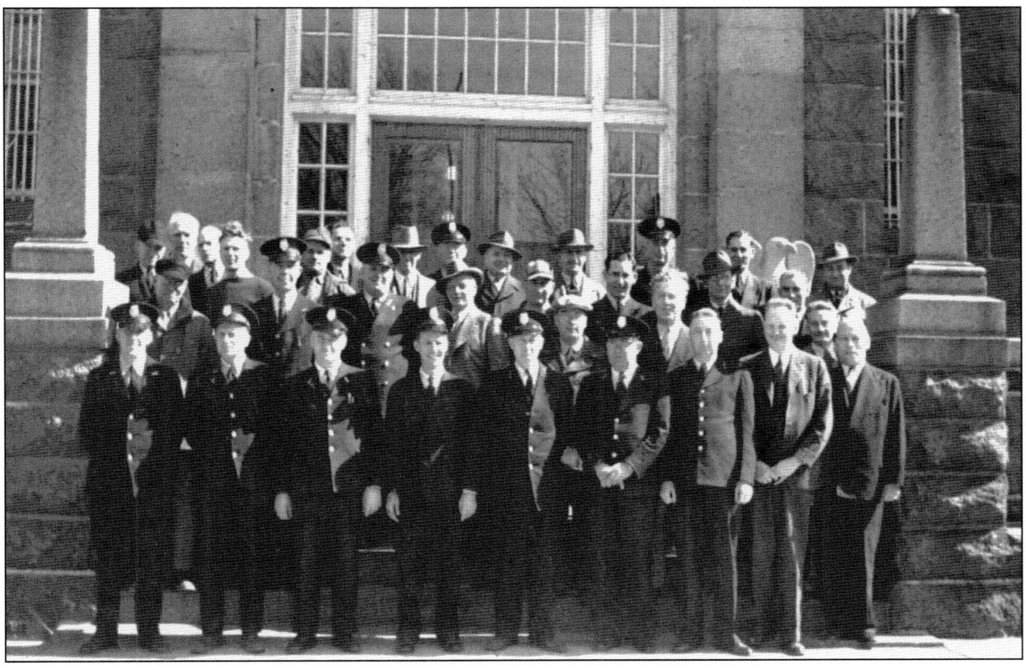

Supt. Sanger Powers (1951–1956) instituted a continuous system of in-service training. Professor Carl Johnson of the University of Wisconsin Extension taught many of the classes. In this photograph taken during Powers's tenure, in-service attendees pose on the steps of the reformatory.

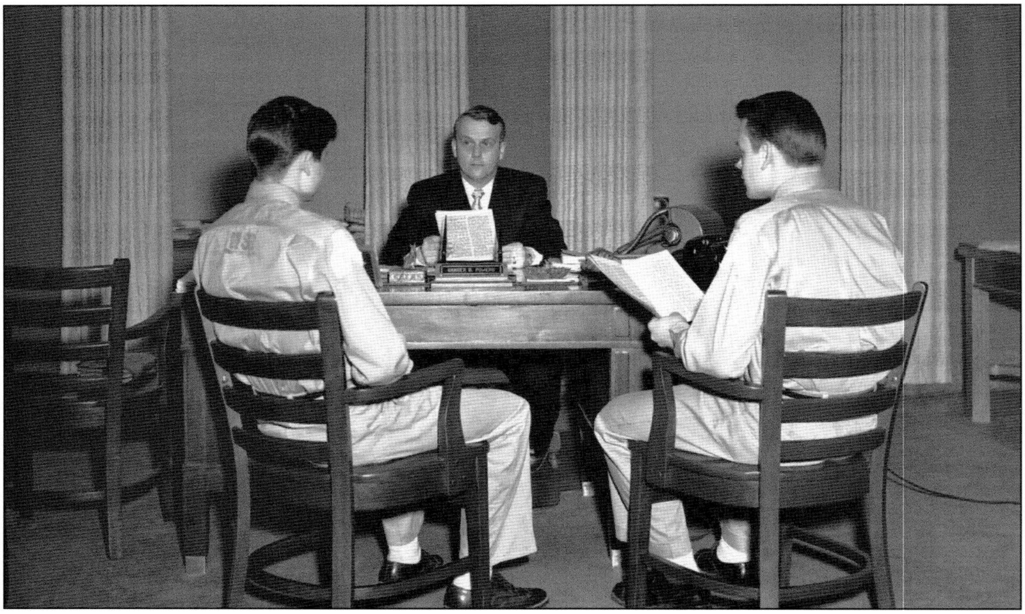

Sanger B. Powers, shown counseling two inmates, carried on Wisconsin's progressive correctional tradition by abolishing some traditional reformatory methods of discipline and by experimenting liberally with programs intended to humanize the rehabilitation effort. His influence on rehabilitation and treatment programs continued well into the 1970s and defined the mission of the institution in subsequent years.

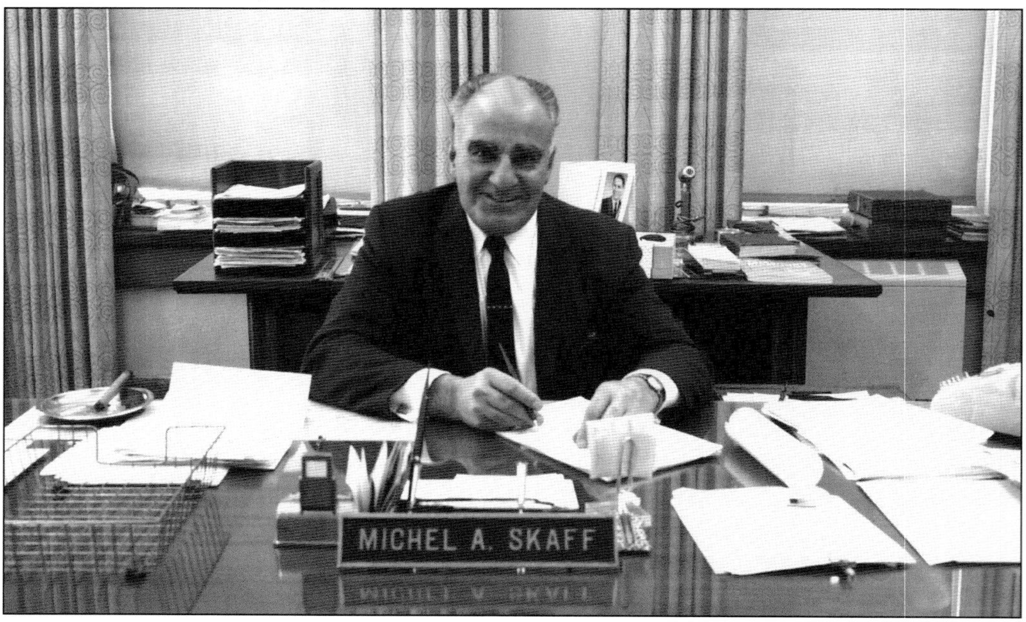

Michel A. Skaff started his career at WSR as temporary assistant superintendent under Sanger B. Powers. A former military intelligence officer, Skaff headed the Wisconsin Department of Jail Inspectors and served as superintendent at a number of state correctional facilities. A proponent of Powers's reform philosophy, Skaff did much to improve the prison environment. In 1957, he transformed the land adjacent to the South Cell Hall into an outside picnic area complete with 16 picnic tables and two swing sets to meet the needs of visiting families.

Four

A Good Neighbor

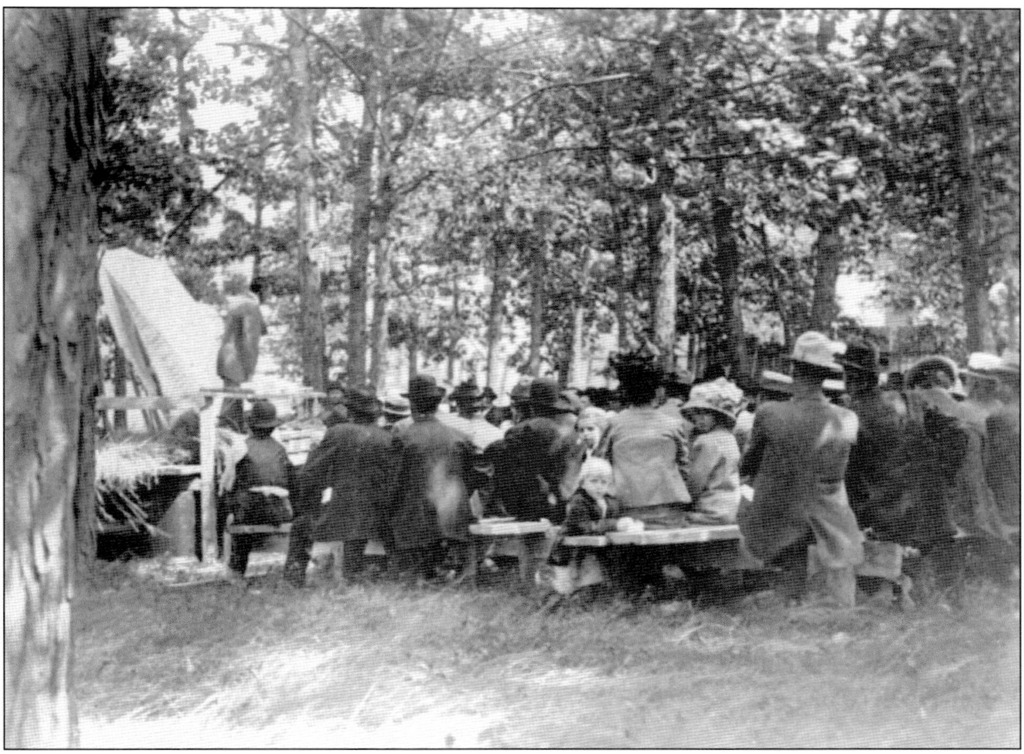

Local residents gather near the Riverside Drive farm facility around 1900. The local population looked upon the reformatory as a good neighbor. Frequent public concerts and interaction with inmate farm workers, who cultivated much of the vacant land around the reformatory, removed any sense of concern about the location of a penal institution near neighboring farms and homes.

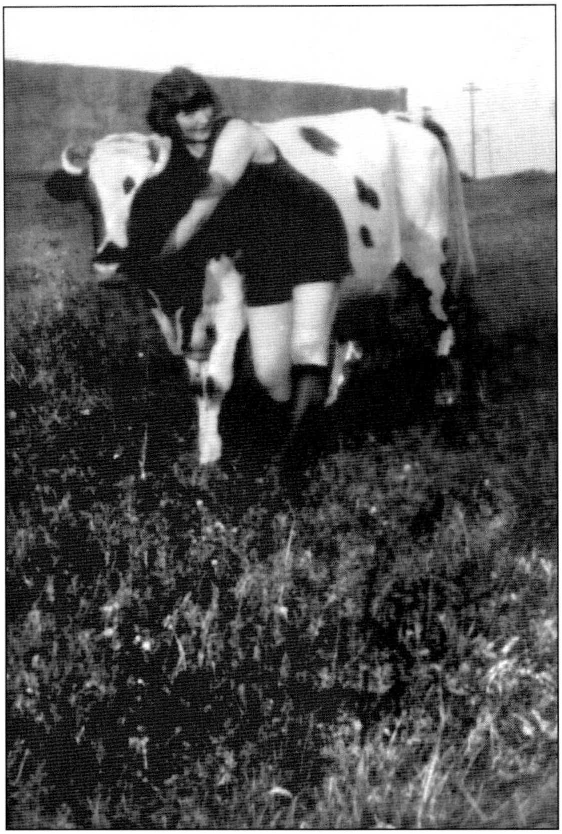

Netty Mainecki, photographed here with a favorite bovine friend, lived near the reformatory with her family. The reformatory wall, built in 1922, is visible in the background. (Courtesy Rita Houston.)

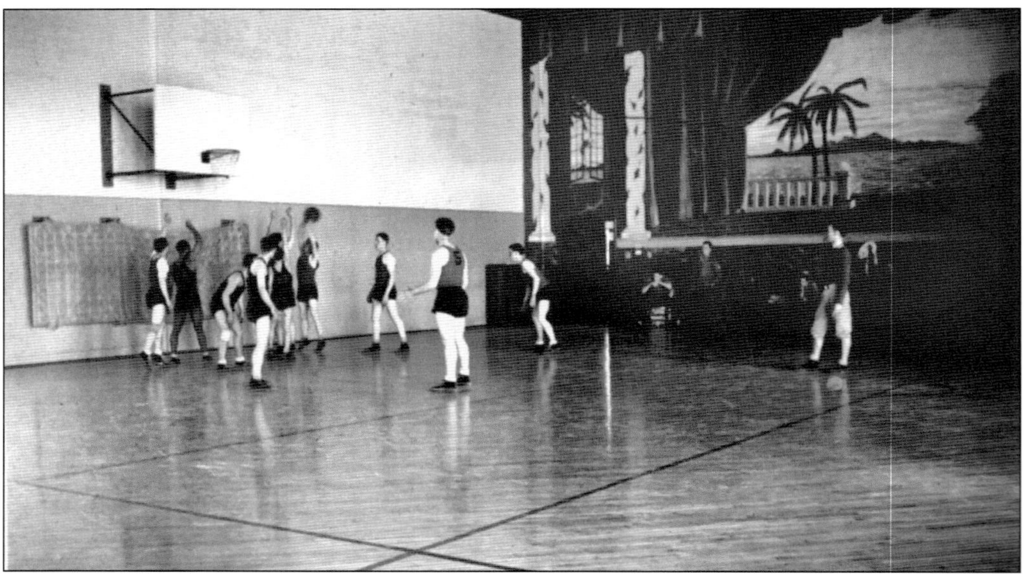

Inmates enjoy a game of basketball in the mid-1930s. Whether they were working or playing, physical activity played a major role in the daily lives of the inmates. Local residents enjoyed watching the reformatory basketball team play opponents every Thursday night during the winter months. For many area residents, the reformatory was a source of recreation, despite its mission of incarceration and criminal reform.

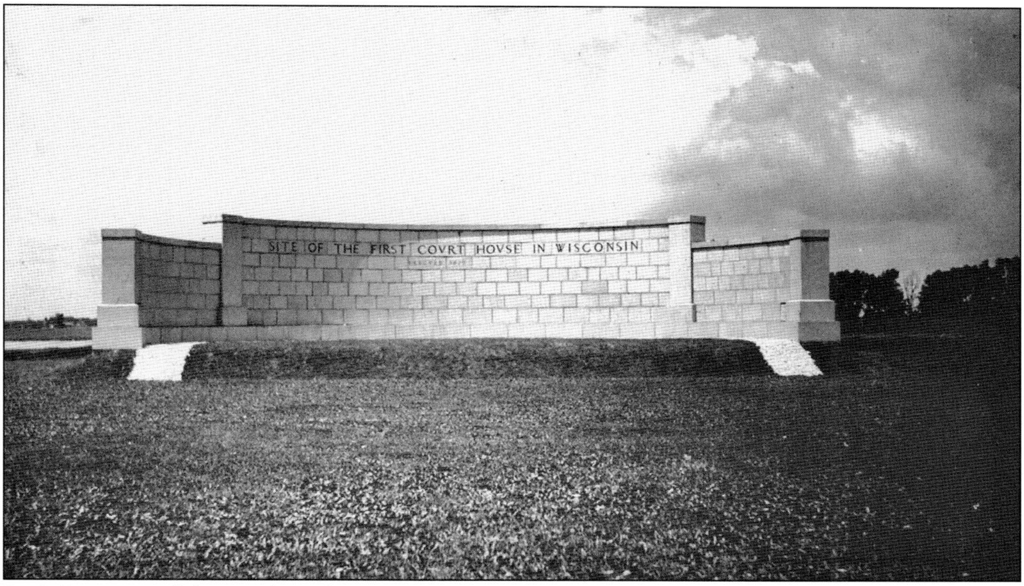

Built by inmate labor and cut from granite at the reformatory quarry in Amberg, this monument marking the site of the first courthouse in Wisconsin sits on property now owned by Heritage Hill State Historical Park near the east bank of the Fox River. J. Emory Temple once described it as "a fitting monument to those dauntless lawmakers of our early history." (Courtesy Green Bay Correctional Institution.)

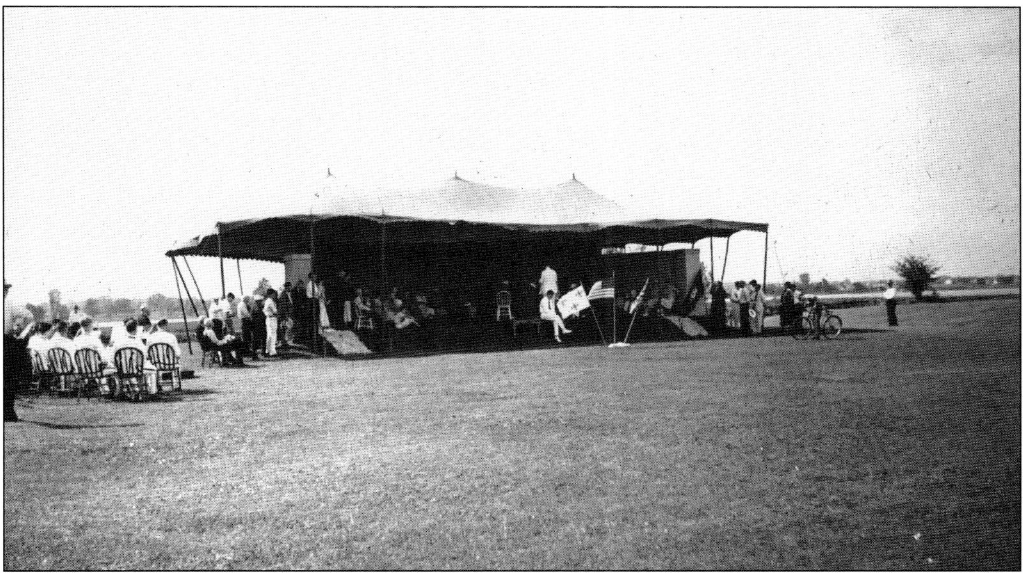

Col. John J. Hannan, president of the Wisconsin State Board of Control, dedicates the courthouse monument in 1934. British, American, and French flags signifying the region's multinational history fly in front of the canopy.

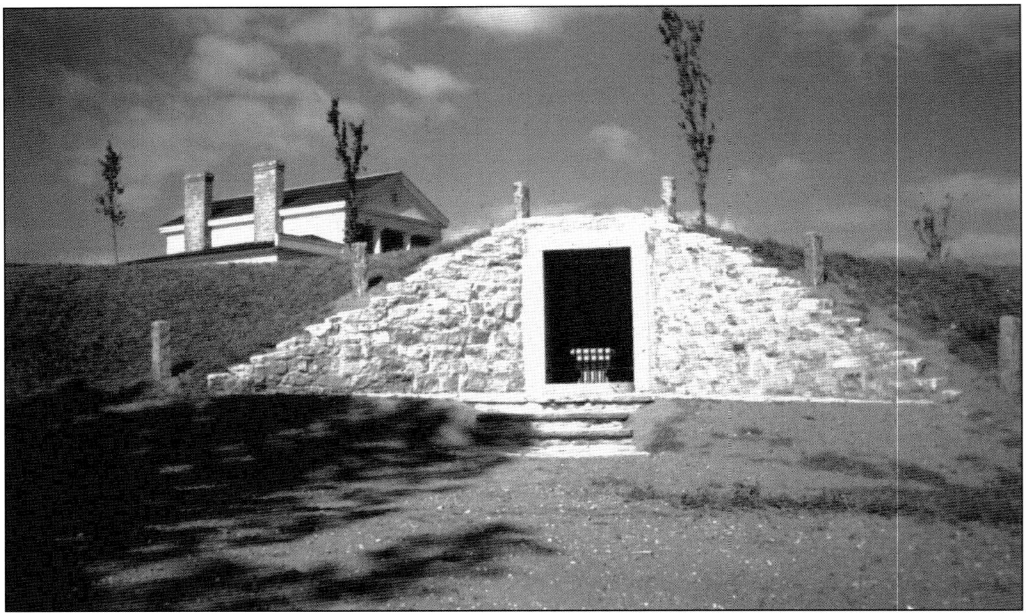

Historic land use near the reformatory included the brief presence of a military outpost between 1817 and 1821. Camp Smith was situated on the high ground overlooking the Fox River in present day Allouez. Named after Col. Joseph Lee Smith, the site was abandoned when Smith was relieved from duty at Fort Howard in 1821. During the occupation period, several soldiers died, probably from disease. The remains of one of the unknown soldiers are housed in this tomb, now part of Heritage Hills State Historical Park.

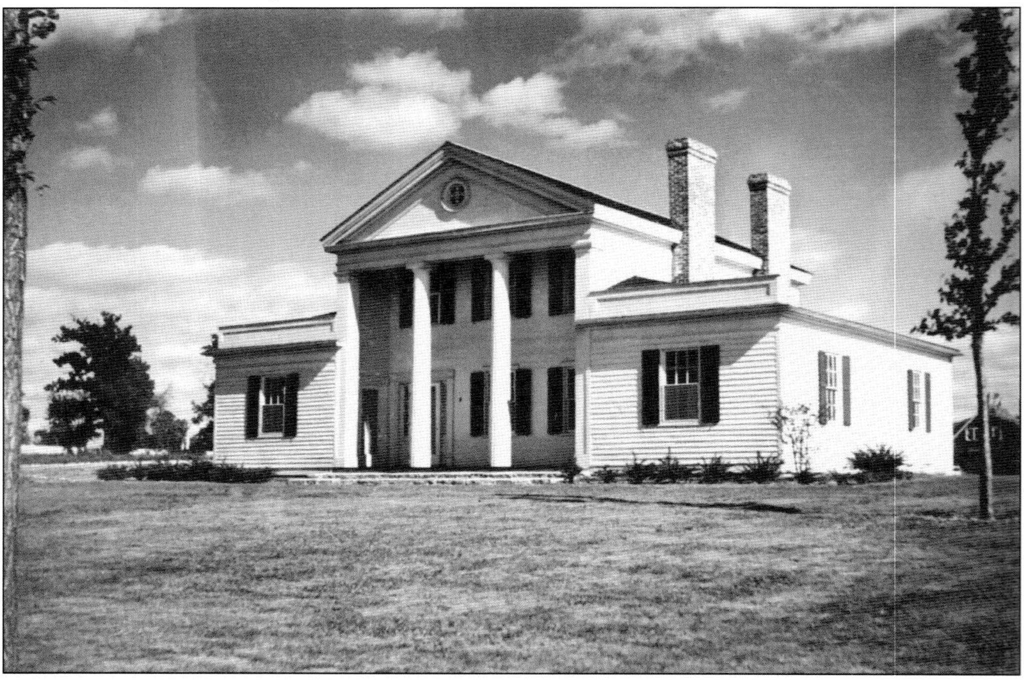

Cotton House is situated near land that was sometimes farmed by reformatory inmates and personnel. The historic structure is part of the Heritage Hill State Historical Park complex of historic buildings and overlooks the Fox River from the east.

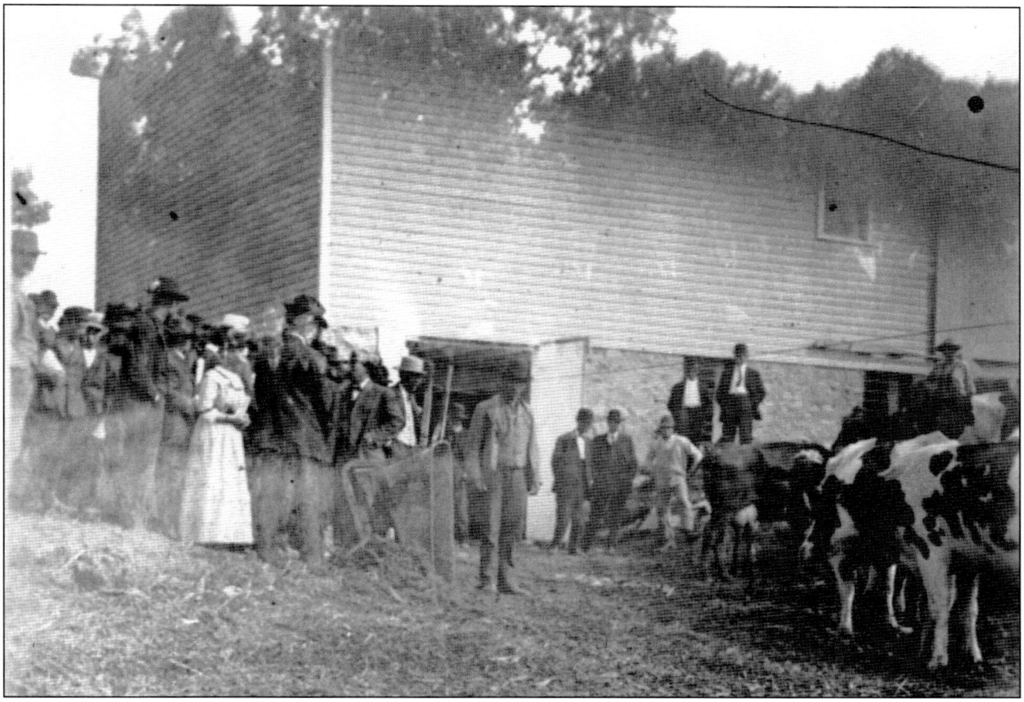

Interaction between local farmers and residents characterized the first 60 years of the institution. Here a number of area residents gather at the Fox River farm site in 1900 to view the latest livestock acquisitions.

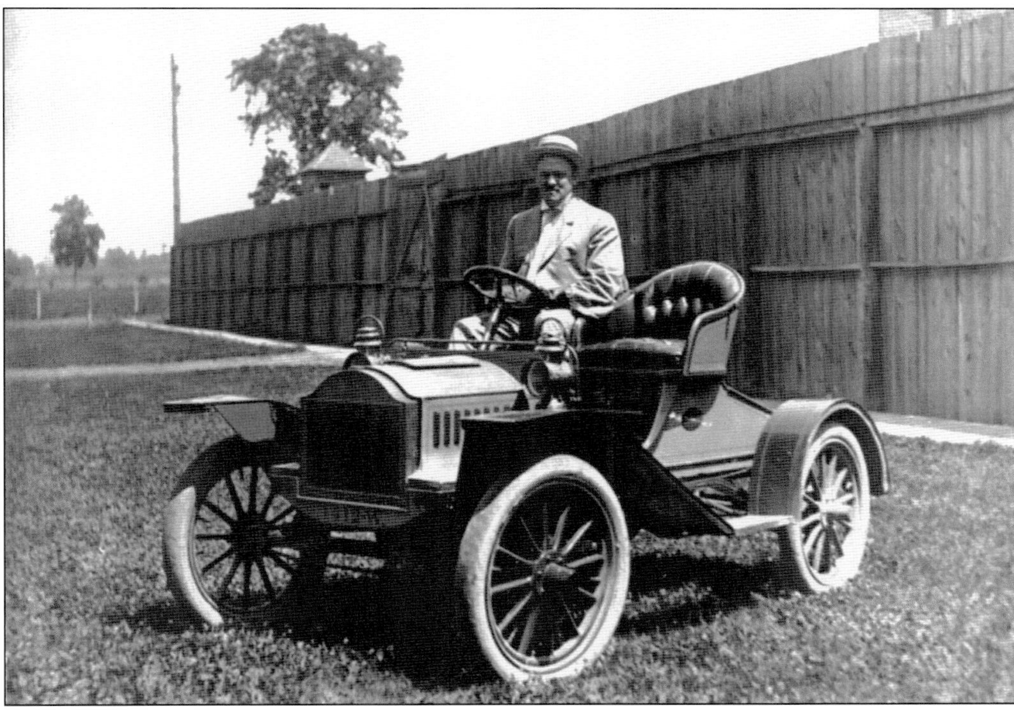

Dr. J. R. Lenfestey poses with his Oldsmobile just outside of the reformatory's wooden walls. Dr. Lenfestey tended to the medical needs of the prisoners and staff from 1906 to 1938.

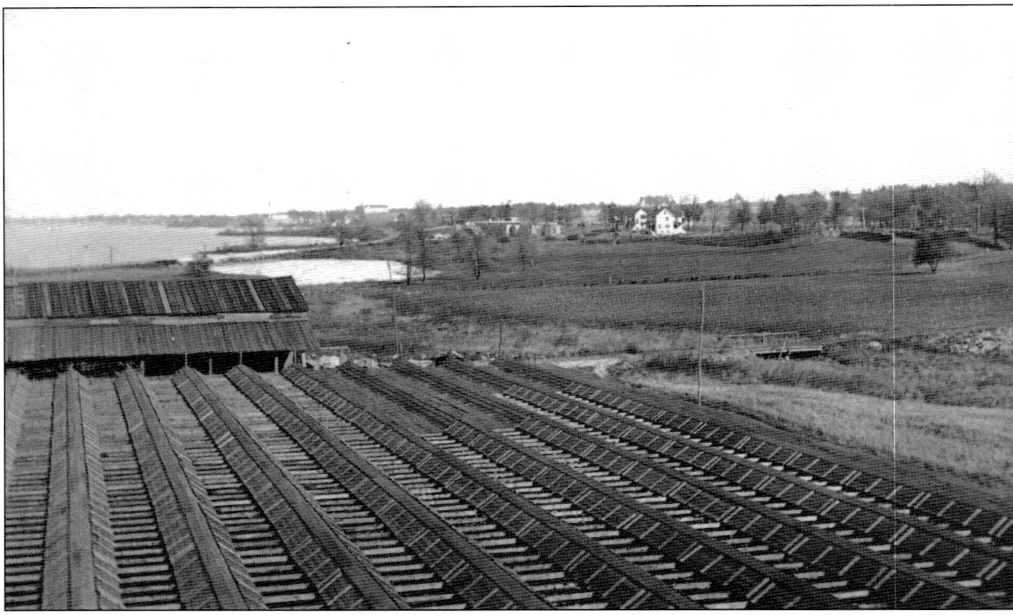

The land surrounding the reformatory was largely characterized by gently sloping terrain that supported farms, a brewery, and Hocker's brickyard facility shown in the foreground of this c. 1900 photograph. Inmates farmed much of the land surrounding this area, particularly during World War II when there was a reduction of local manpower due to the draft. (Courtesy Green Bay Correctional Institution.)

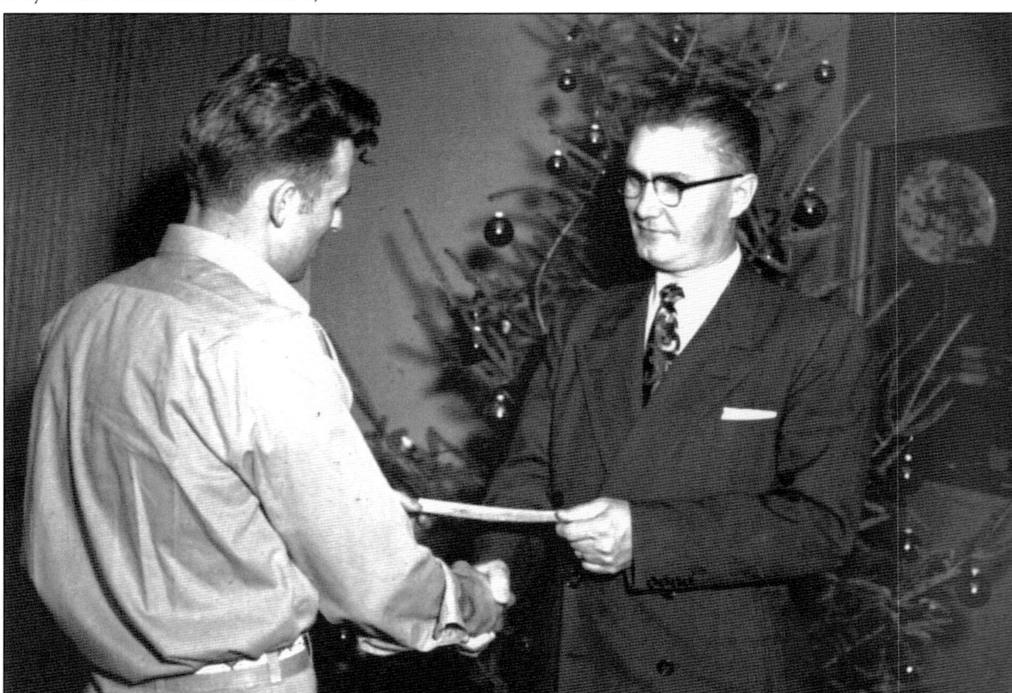

Community service was a major part of life at WSR. Here an inmate presents a check to an official representing the Lutheran Orphanage. Interaction with local citizens gave the community an opportunity to better appreciate the nature of WSR and its rehabilitative programs.

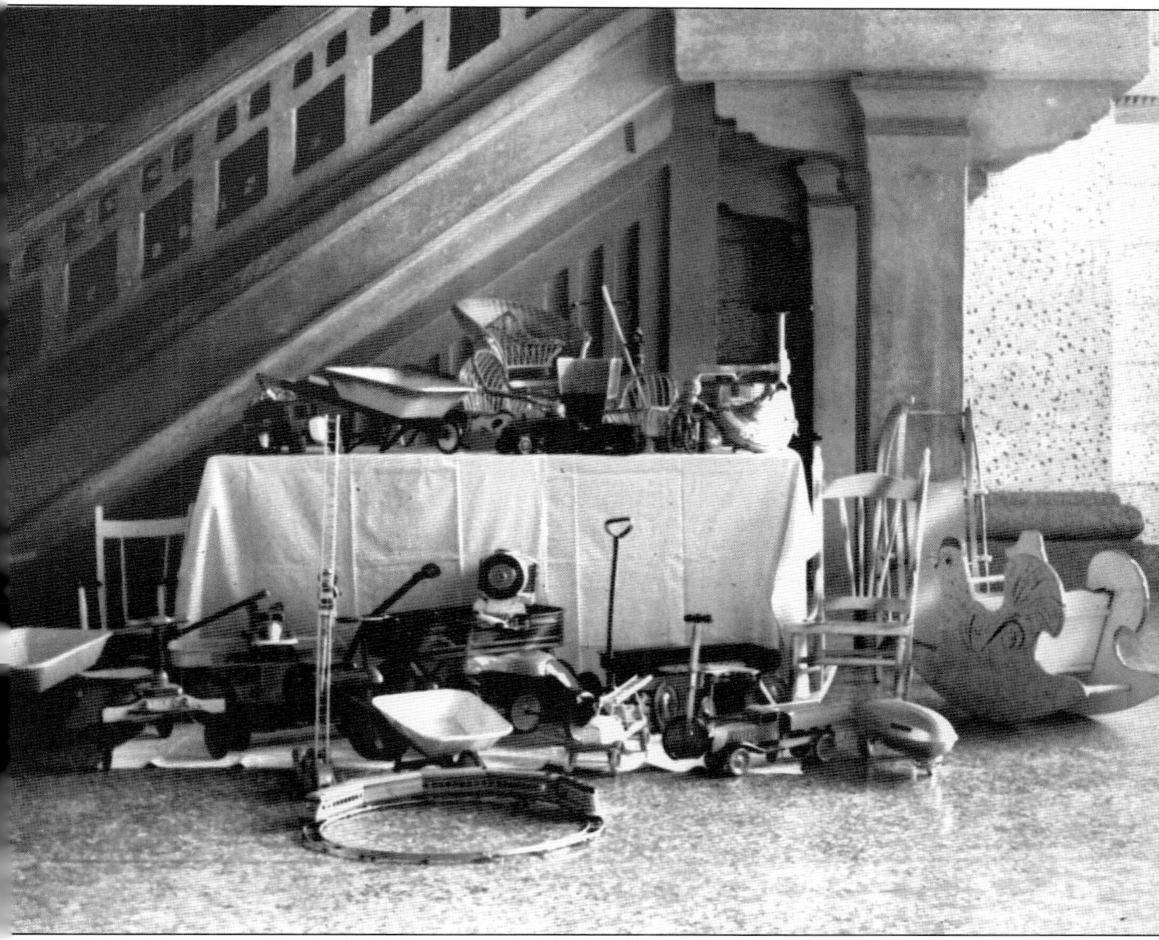

Toys built or refinished at WSR shops enabled prisoners to maintain a connection to the outside world and fostered good relations with the surrounding community. These toys photographed in the main hall at the prison were destined for local distribution. Most of the prisoners held at WSR were youthful offenders and not too far removed from a time when playing with toys, rather than marching in lockstep, marked their days.

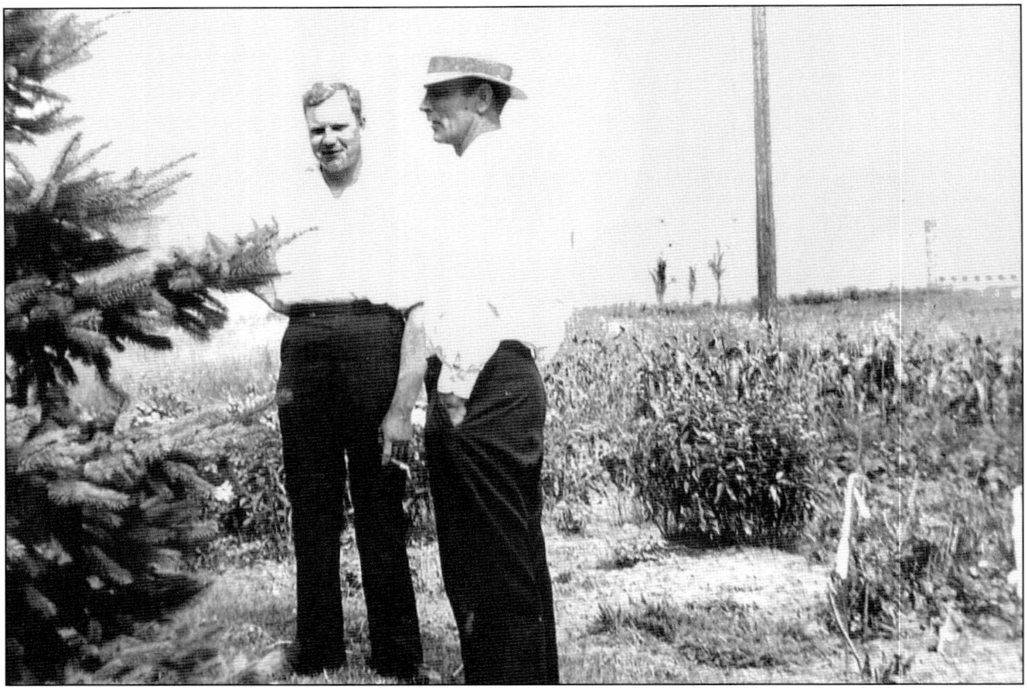

John Mainecki ran a nursery business near the prison's Webster Avenue farm. The 22-foot reformatory wall can be seen in the background of this photograph. Over the years, the area surrounding the reformatory has been the home to farms, businesses, and a vibrant residential neighborhood. Even today area residents generally consider the prison to be a good neighbor and are little concerned with the presence of a maximum security prison in their midst.

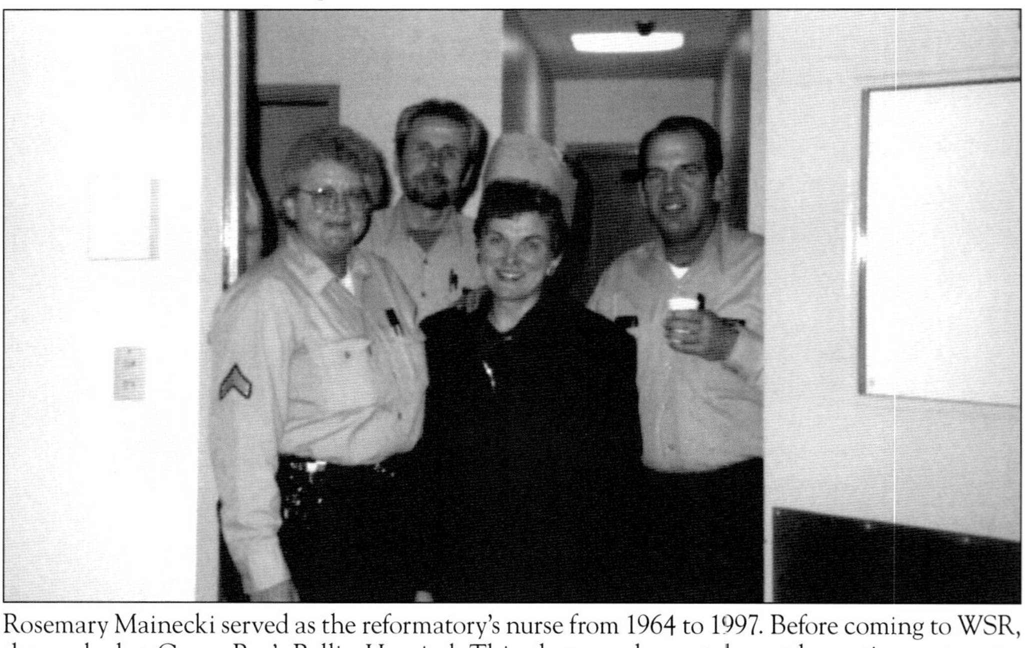

Rosemary Mainecki served as the reformatory's nurse from 1964 to 1997. Before coming to WSR, she worked at Green Bay's Bellin Hospital. This photograph was taken at her retirement party. She is flanked on the left by reformatory guards Kitty Thompson and Dick White and on the right by Craig Storm. (Courtesy Rosemary Mainecki.)

Five

FEEDING THE FELONS

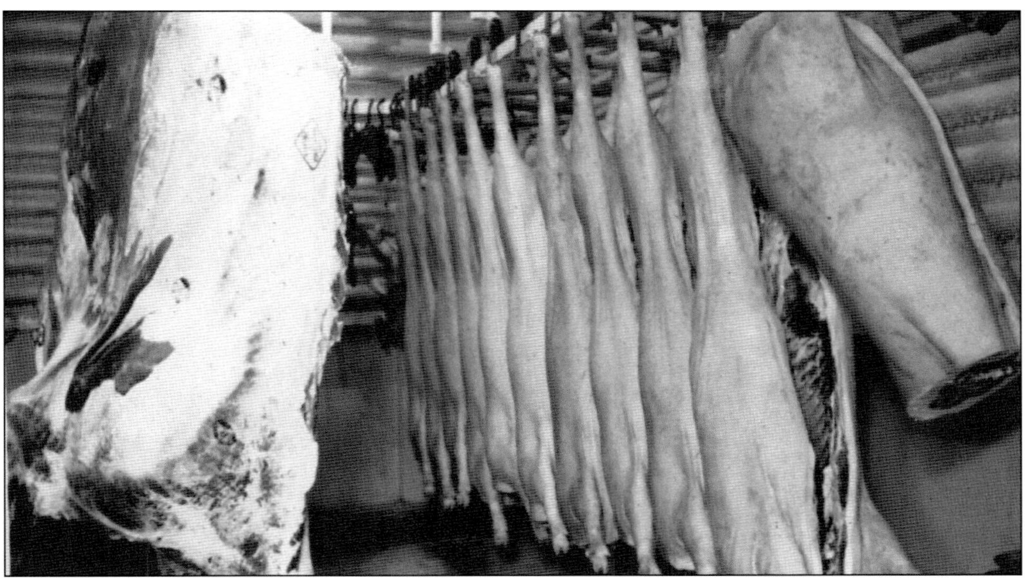

Hogs hanging in the reformatory cold storage are a visible testament to the productivity of the pork operation and the institution's level of self sufficiency. Business manager Andy Janssen once remarked, "I would say probably over 50 percent of what we fed the inmates was raised right there on the farm."

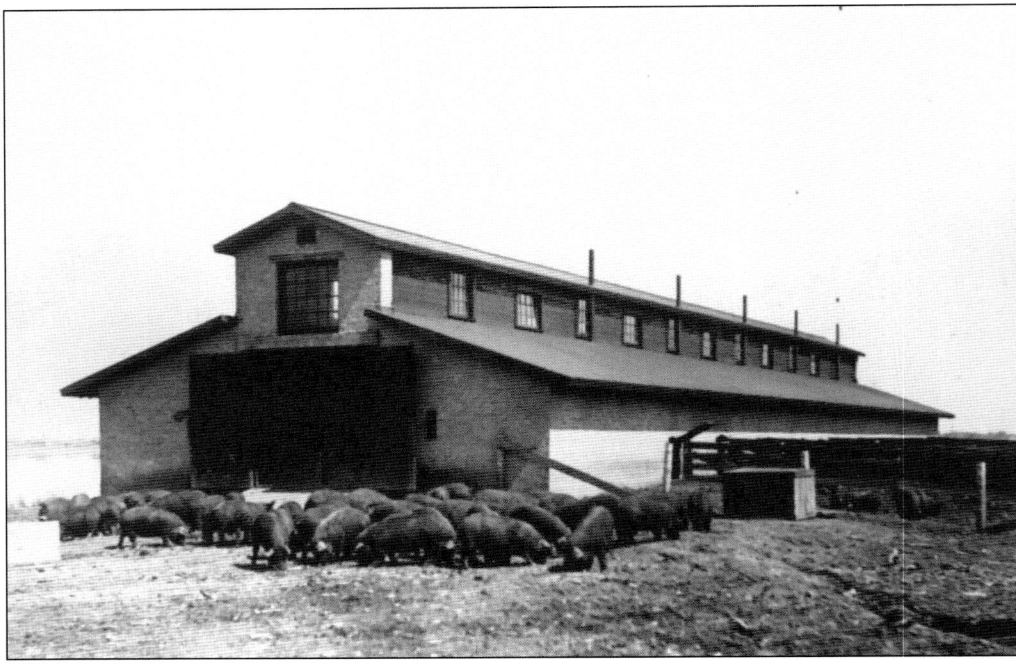

Hogs root outside the reformatory barn. Starting in 1900, prisoners tended a farm operation on the bank of the Fox River, west of the reformatory. The farming operation later moved to a location east of the reformatory along Webster Avenue.

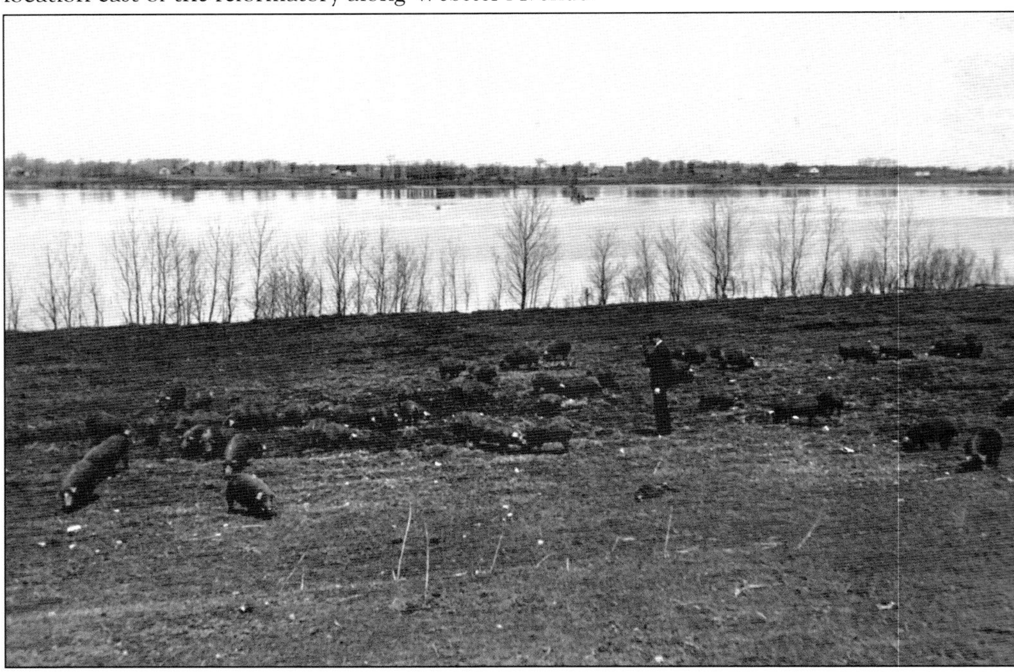

A reformatory farm worker watches over the pig herd along the Fox River in the first decade of the 20th century. The farm operation not only provided sustenance to the prisoners, it also provided a positive institutional image. Local residents, many of whom labored in their own fields, viewed with favor the work done at the farm, as it showed the salutary effects of the reformatory system. (Courtesy Green Bay Correctional Institution.)

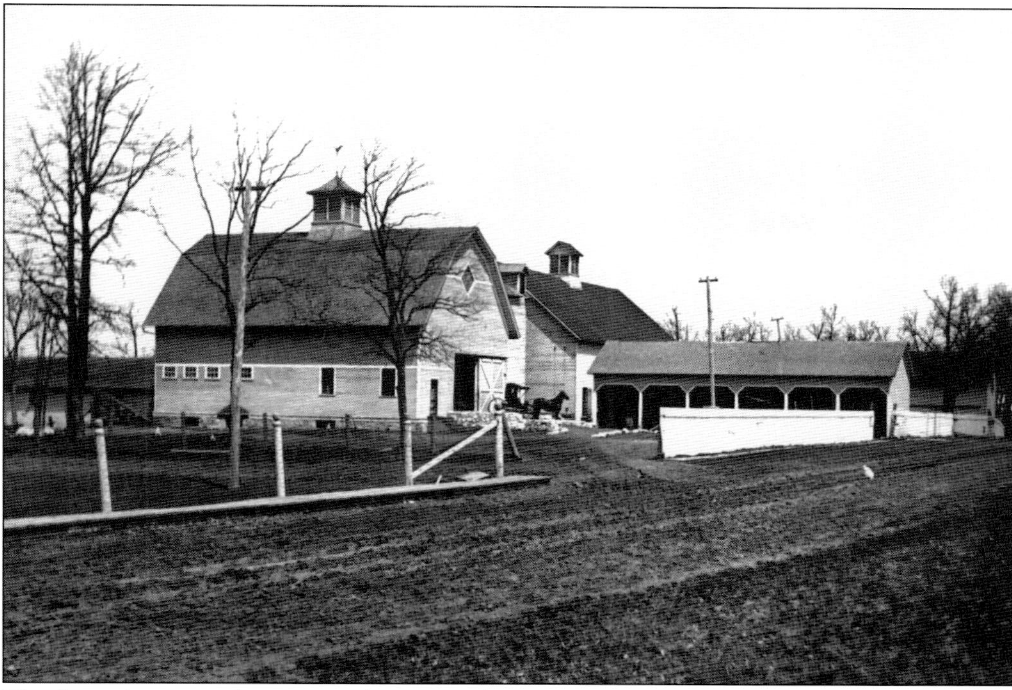

The first reformatory farm is seen here viewed from the south along present-day Riverside Drive. The piggery was eventually transferred to the Oneida Farm where the soil was less contaminated. Oneida raised 500 pigs annually, enough to completely satisfy the pork needs of the institution. (Courtesy Green Bay Correctional Institution.)

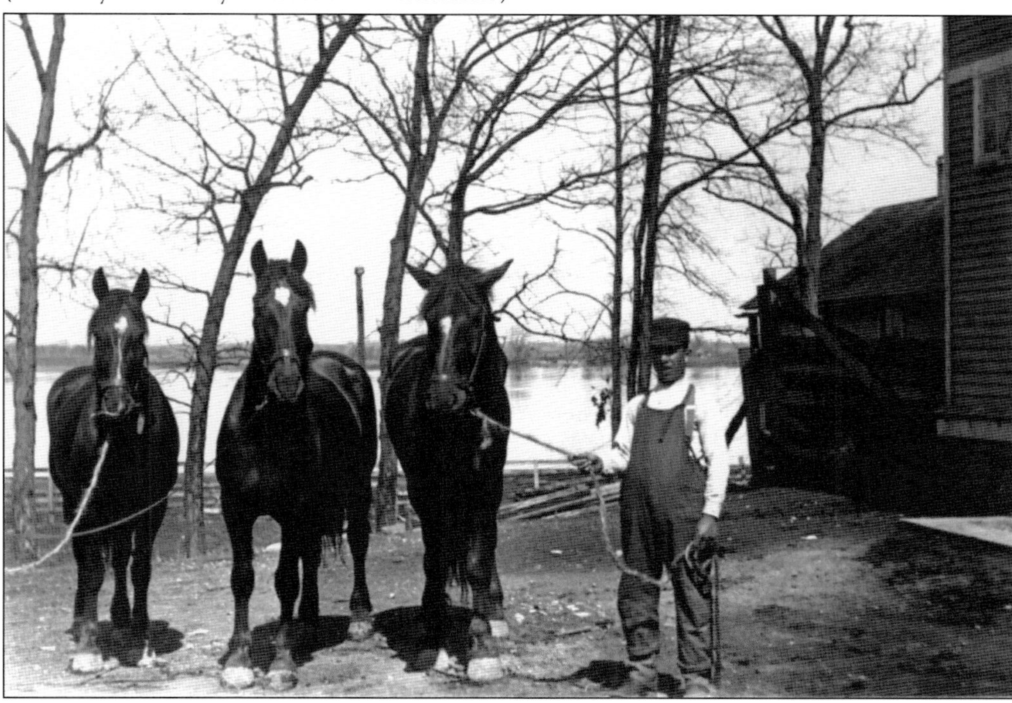

Workhorses Dan, Molly, and Riley stand with their handler near the reformatory's earliest farm on the east bank of the Fox River.

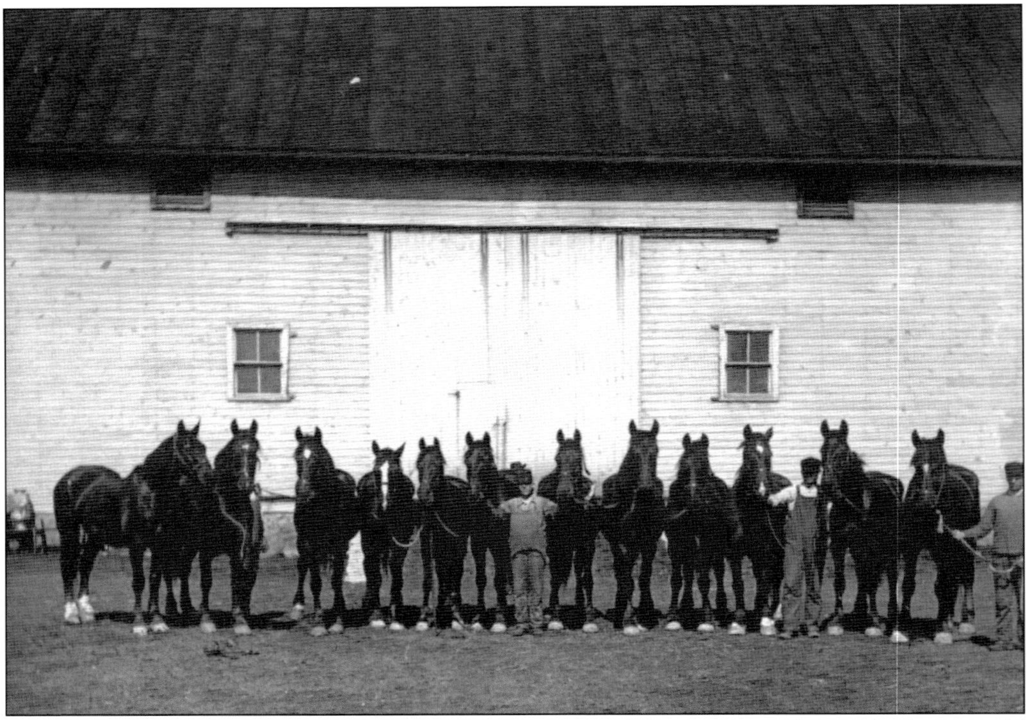

Reformatory workers stand with draught horses in front of the Fox River farm. The farm would later relocate east of the reformatory along the Webster Avenue ridge. (Courtesy Green Bay Correctional Institution.)

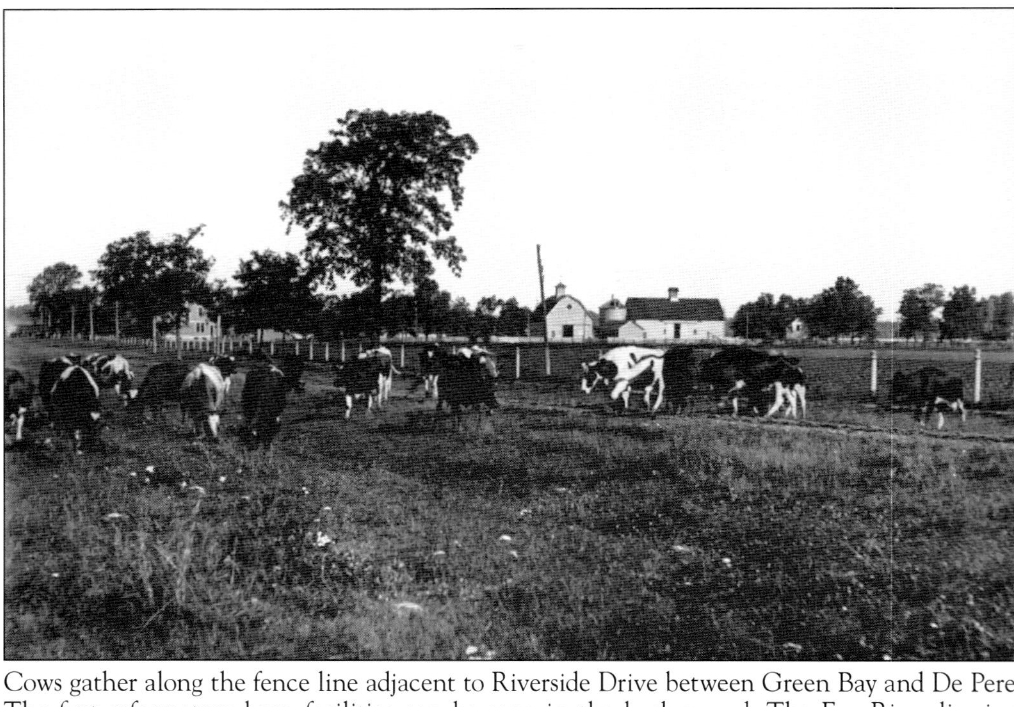

Cows gather along the fence line adjacent to Riverside Drive between Green Bay and De Pere. The first reformatory barn facilities can be seen in the background. The Fox River lies just beyond the buildings. (Courtesy Green Bay Correctional Institution.)

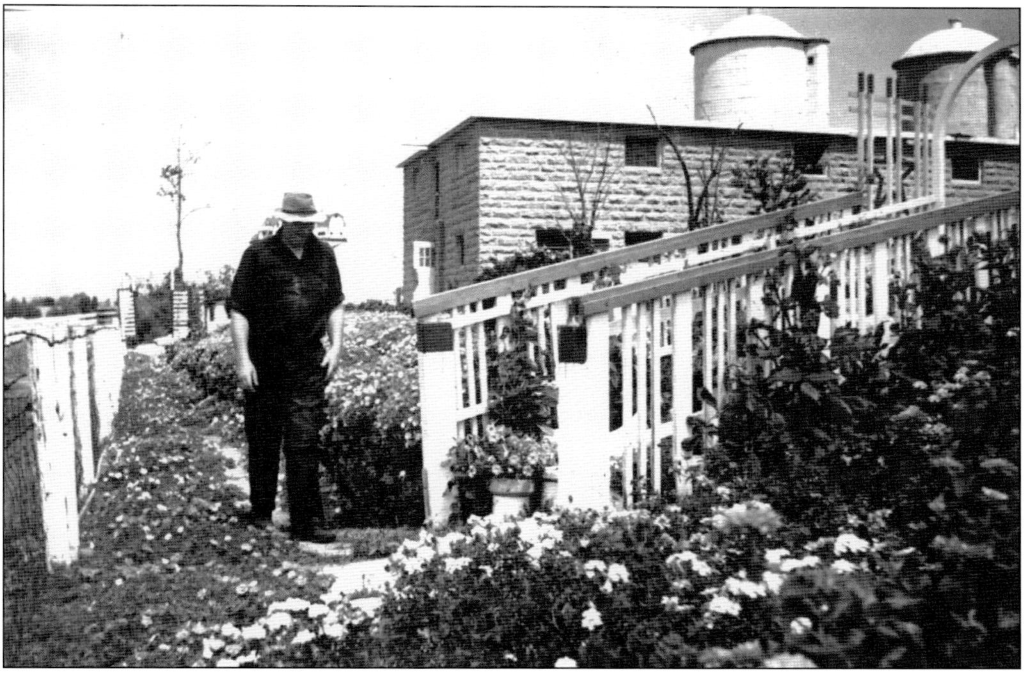

Archie Sandberg oversaw the reformatory's Webster Avenue farm and its award-winning dairy herd. Inmates under Sandberg's supervision cared for the purebred Holstein-Friesian herd, winning recognition at the Wisconsin State Fair and at the National Dairy Congress in Waterloo, Iowa. Sandberg retired in 1956 but not before establishing the finest Holstein-Friesian line in the country.

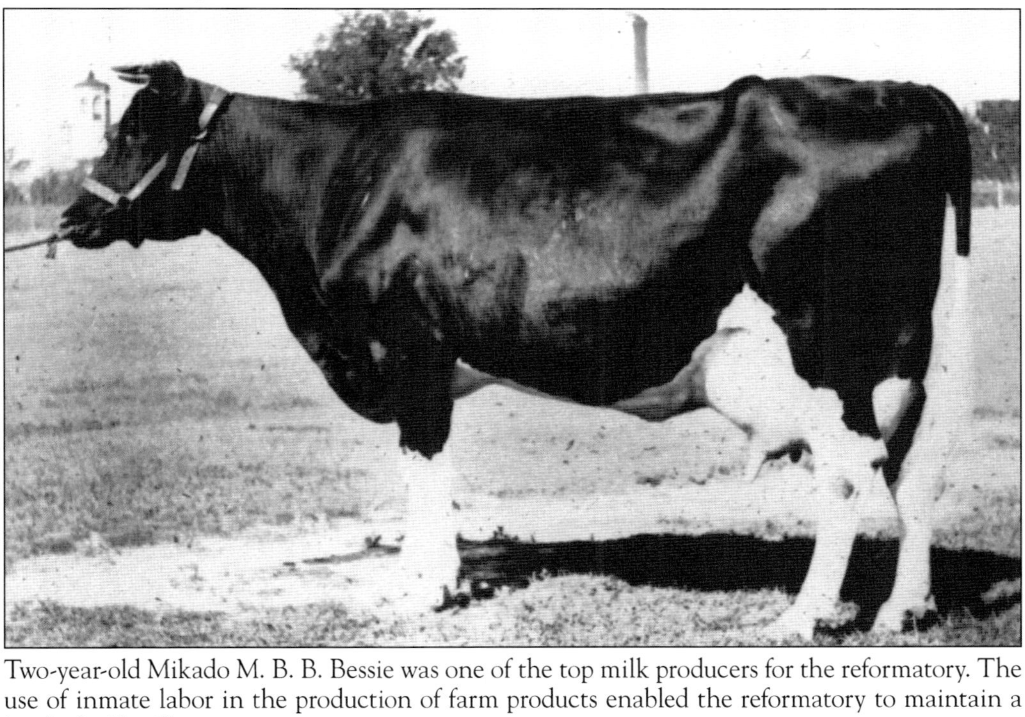

Two-year-old Mikado M. B. B. Bessie was one of the top milk producers for the reformatory. The use of inmate labor in the production of farm products enabled the reformatory to maintain a level of self-sufficiency not common to most state institutions.

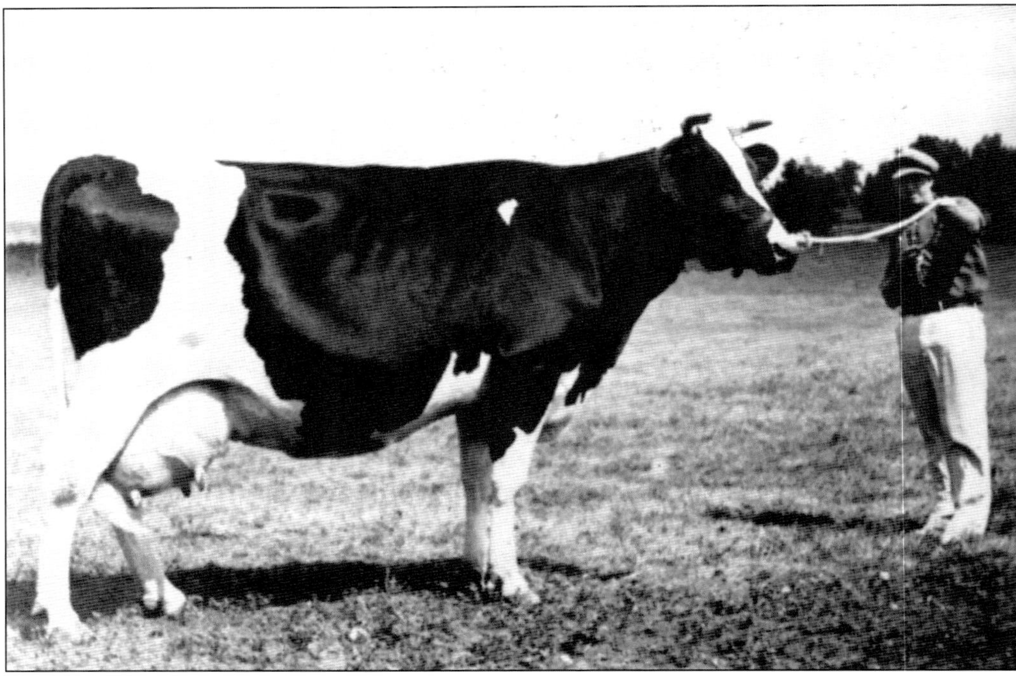

In 1924, the reformatory converted its dairy herd from grades to pure breeds. Officials were once offered $200,000 for a prize bull, but herdsman Archie Sandberg advised them not to sell. Instead, they kept the bull and sold its frozen semen at premium prices. Cows like Wisconsin Gem Pietertje Bess (above) were typical of the herd developed under Sandberg's watchful eye.

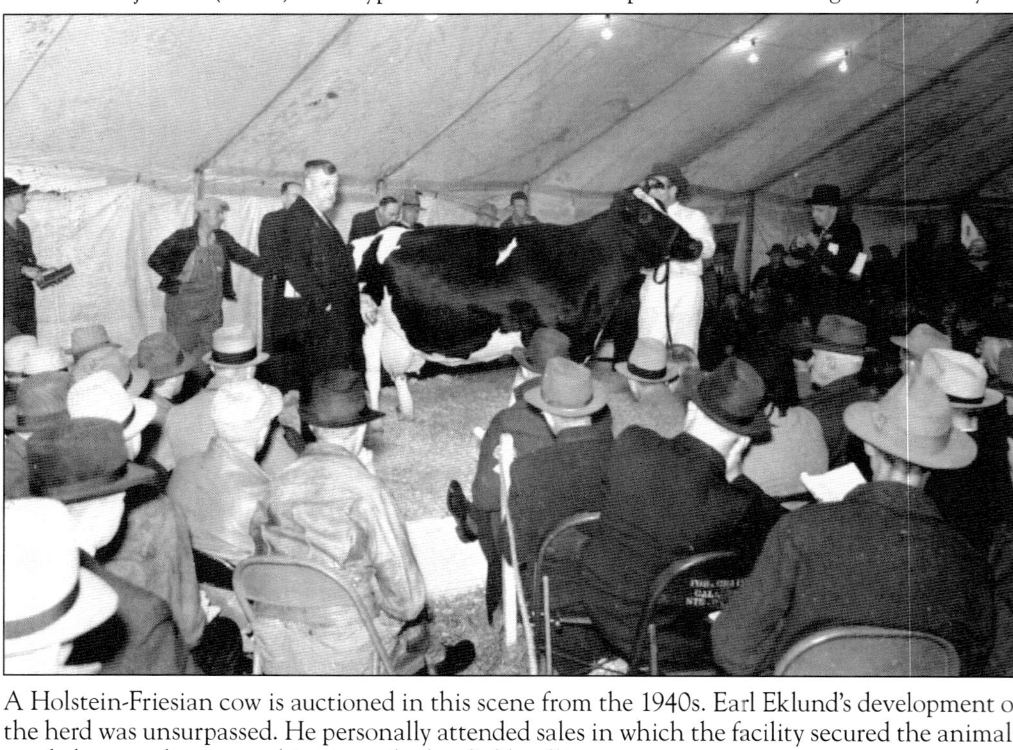

A Holstein-Friesian cow is auctioned in this scene from the 1940s. Earl Eklund's development of the herd was unsurpassed. He personally attended sales in which the facility secured the animals needed to supplement and improve the herd's bloodline.

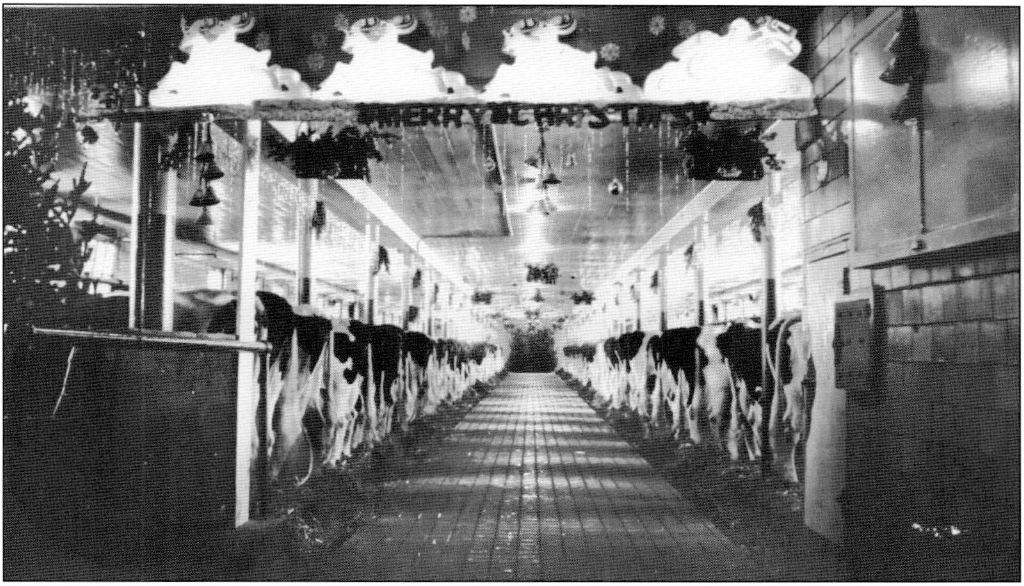

Archie Sandberg took great pride in decorating the Webster Avenue cow barn for Christmas. Reformatory officials often did what they could to lessen the harsh realities of prison life for the inmates.

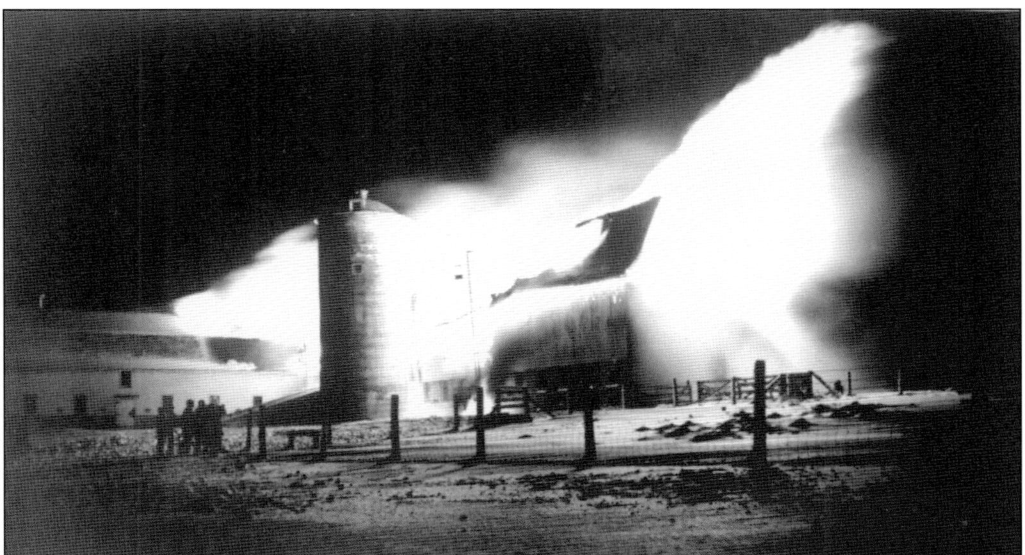

The Webster Avenue farm experienced three fires during its years of operation. Fire ravages the horse barn in this 1938 nighttime photograph.

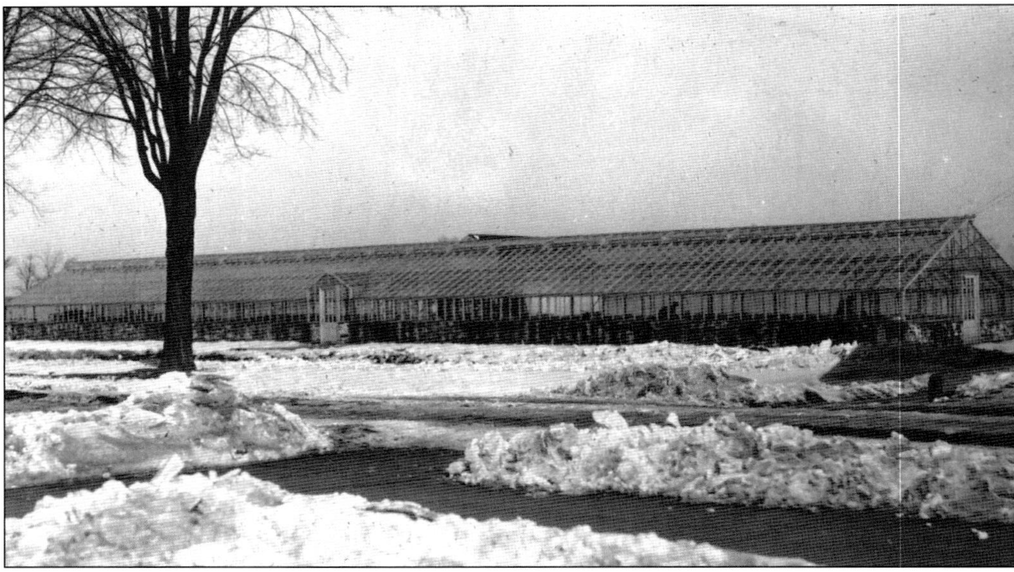

The reformatory also maintained a greenhouse that provided vegetable plants for the farms and flowers for beautification of the prison grounds. The facility was built in 1931 at a cost of $3,197.98, and measured 25 feet by 150 feet. (Courtesy Green Bay Correctional Institution.)

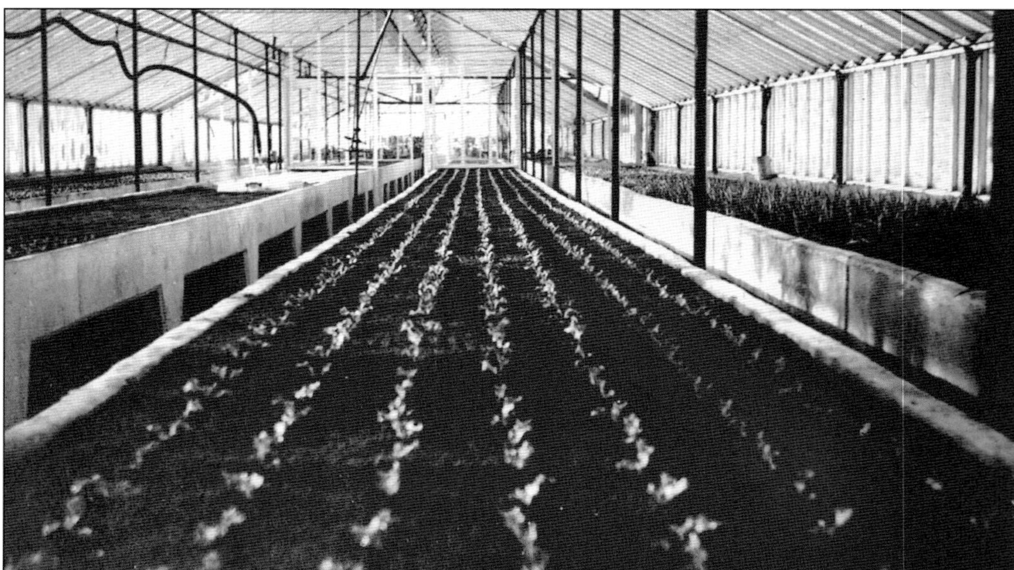

The interior of the greenhouse boasted an elaborate setup. Endeavors like this kept inmates busy and productive even during the winter months. (Courtesy Green Bay Correctional Institution.)

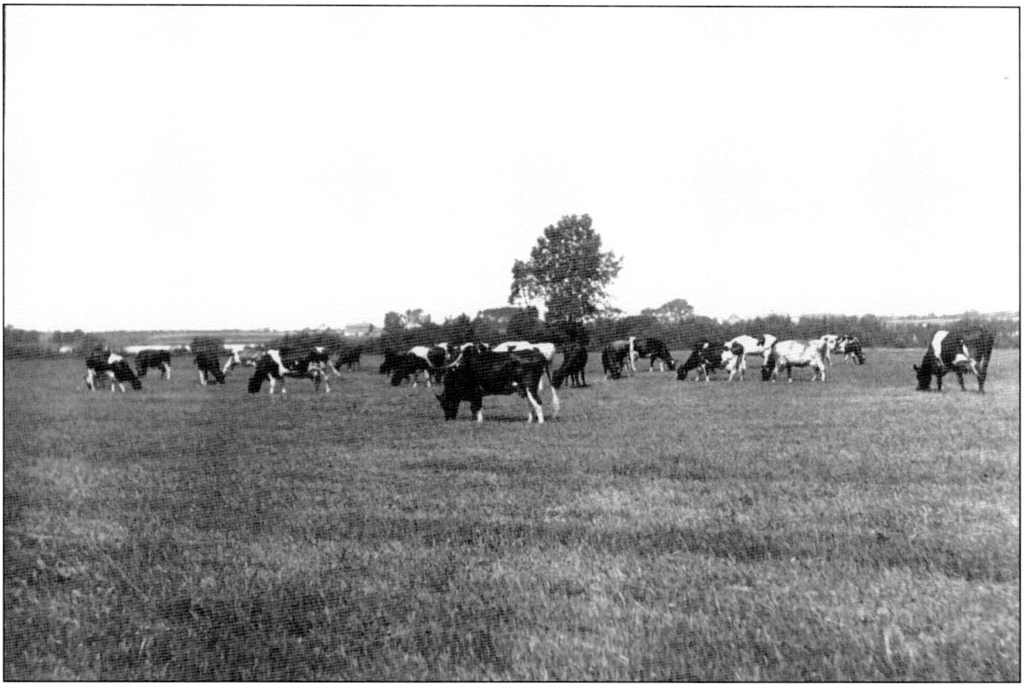

Webster farm cows grazing in the pasture were a common sight for farmers and residents of Allouez.

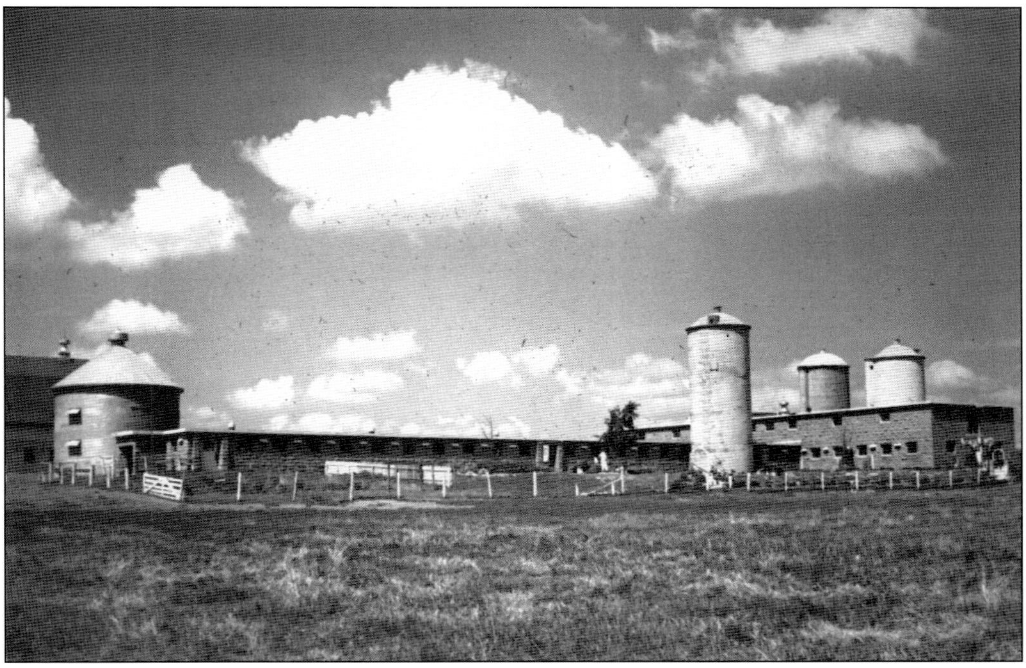

The reformatory's prized purebred Holstein-Friesian herds were kept at the Webster Avenue farm, north and slightly east of the prison. From the beginning, Supt. Earl Eklund ensured that the bloodlines were properly managed in order to supplement the existing herd. Eklund and others in the reformatory hierarchy placed great emphasis on the development of the herd and considered their efforts a service to Wisconsin's dairy industry.

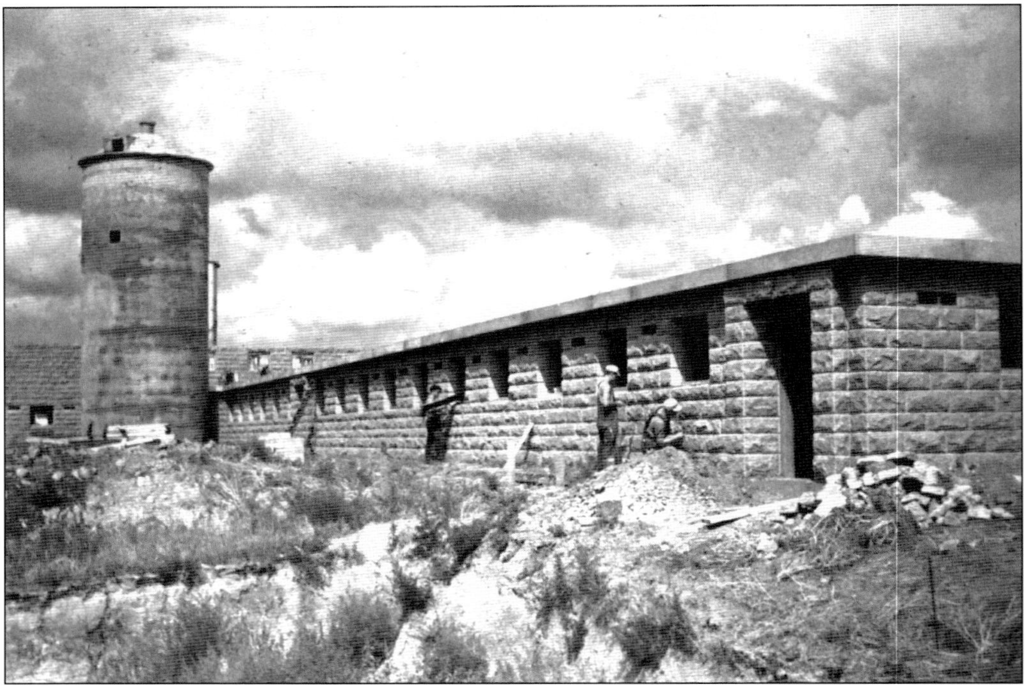

Workman put the finishing touches on a new building located at the Webster Avenue farm site.

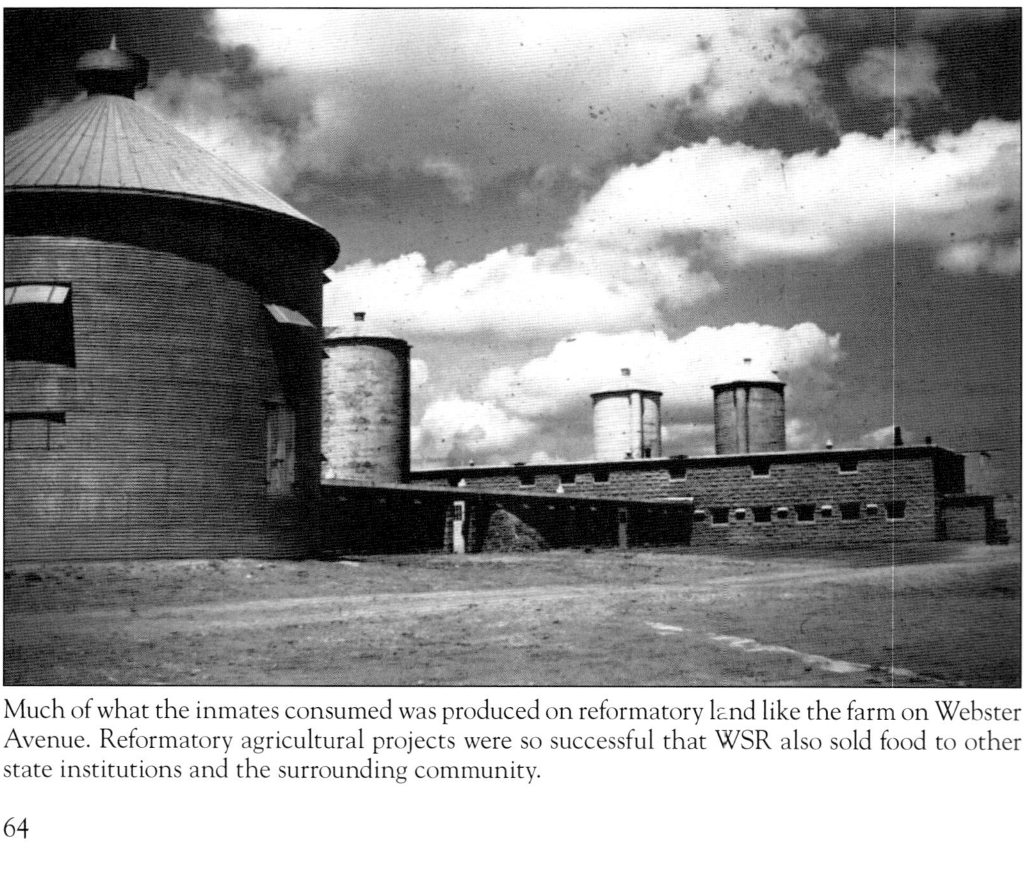

Much of what the inmates consumed was produced on reformatory land like the farm on Webster Avenue. Reformatory agricultural projects were so successful that WSR also sold food to other state institutions and the surrounding community.

Six

The Industrial Era

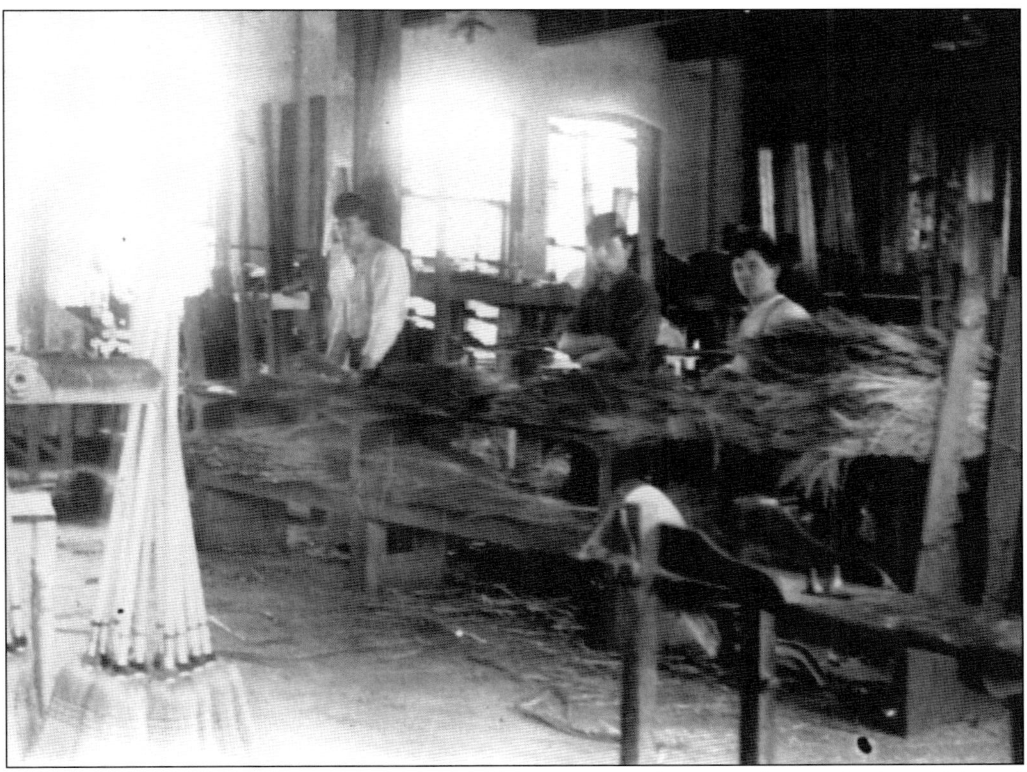

The use of contract labor was common at reformatories and prisons during the late 19th and early 20th centuries. A typical day in the life of an inmate consisted of five hours of labor. The reformatory's broom-making facility, pictured here, was less successful than the garment-making program. The average daily earnings for each inmate employed hovered around 93¢, not much by modern standards but enough to provide a nice savings upon parole.

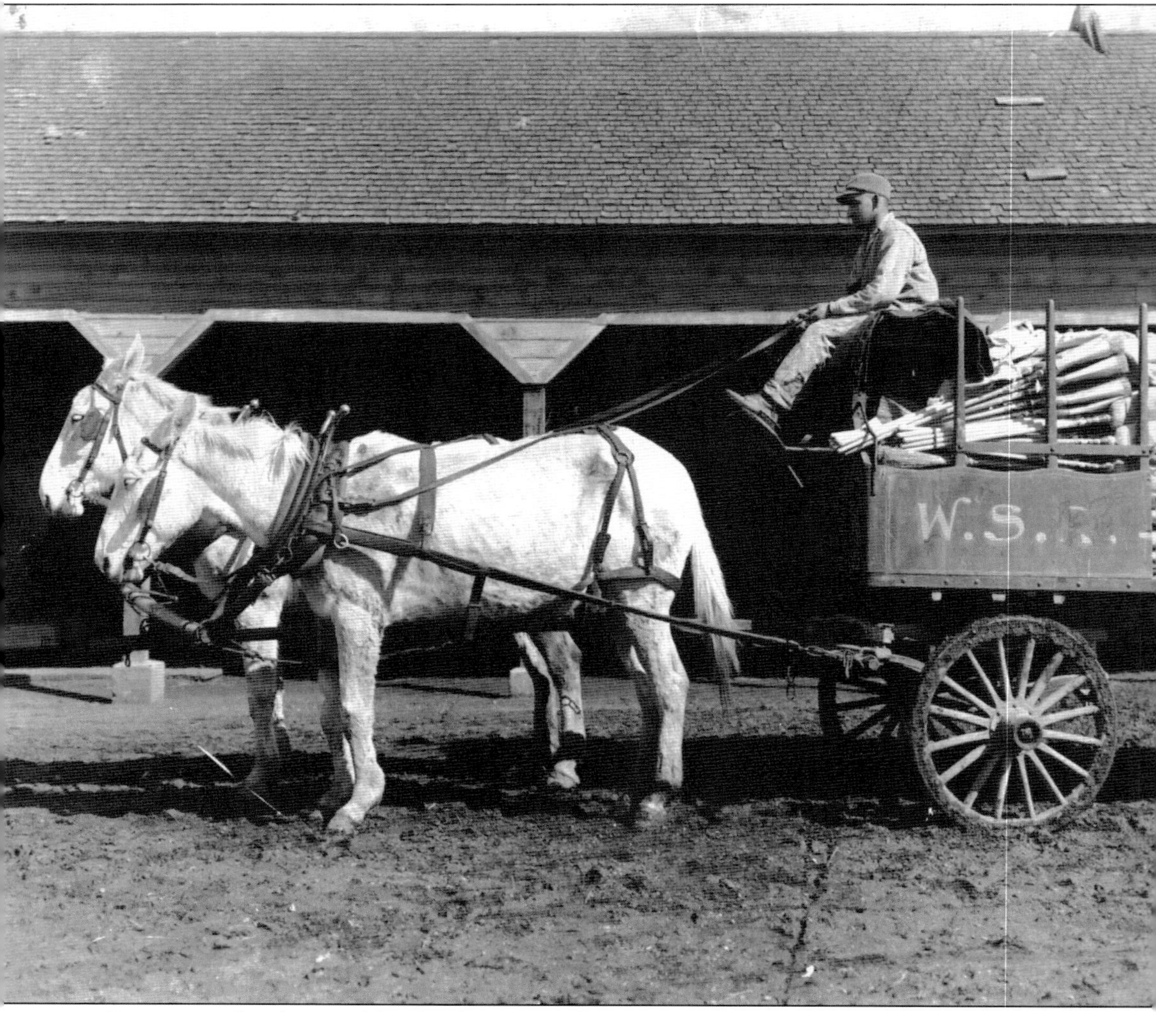

Institutional industries like the farming and granite operations provided significant revenue to the reformatory. The broom shop, however, did not. Production in the shop was so efficient that it produced more brooms than it could sell. In 1907, the reformatory earned $1,817.34 pushing brooms in the open market place. Here an inmate moves completed brooms by horse and wagon. (Courtesy Green Bay Correctional Institution.)

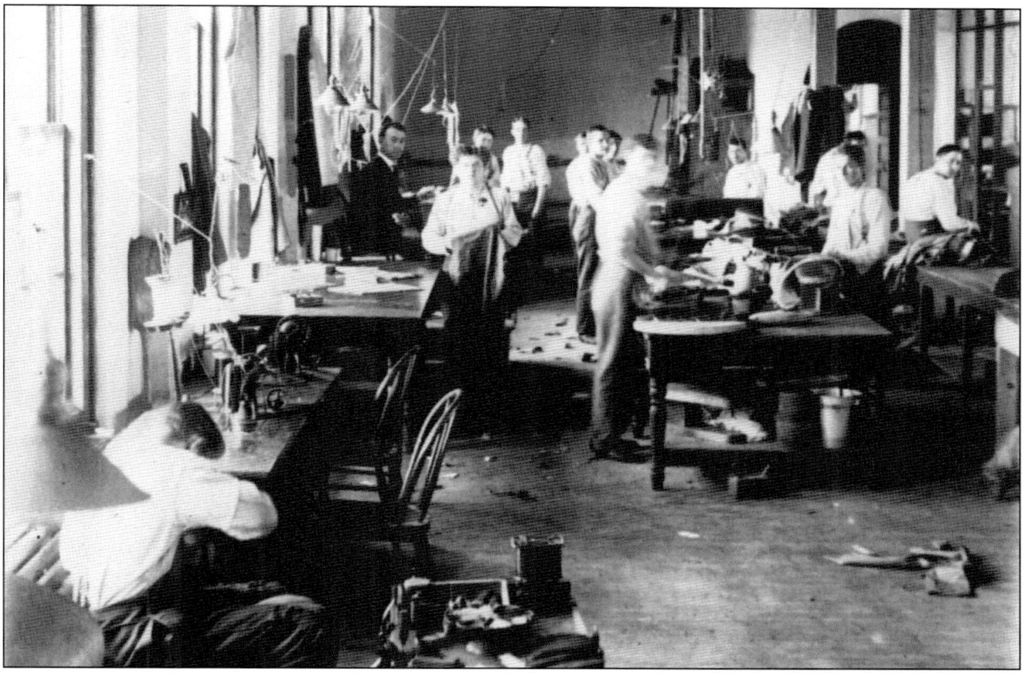

Between 10 and 15 prisoners at a time worked in the prison tailor shop making Big Yank overalls for the Reliance Company of Mattoon, Illinois. Milton F. Goodman of Chicago held the largest labor contract with the WSR. At one time, the production of overalls and jackets for Goodman was the reformatory's main source of income. In 1902, the reformatory factory turned out 713,166 garments and earned more than $30,000.

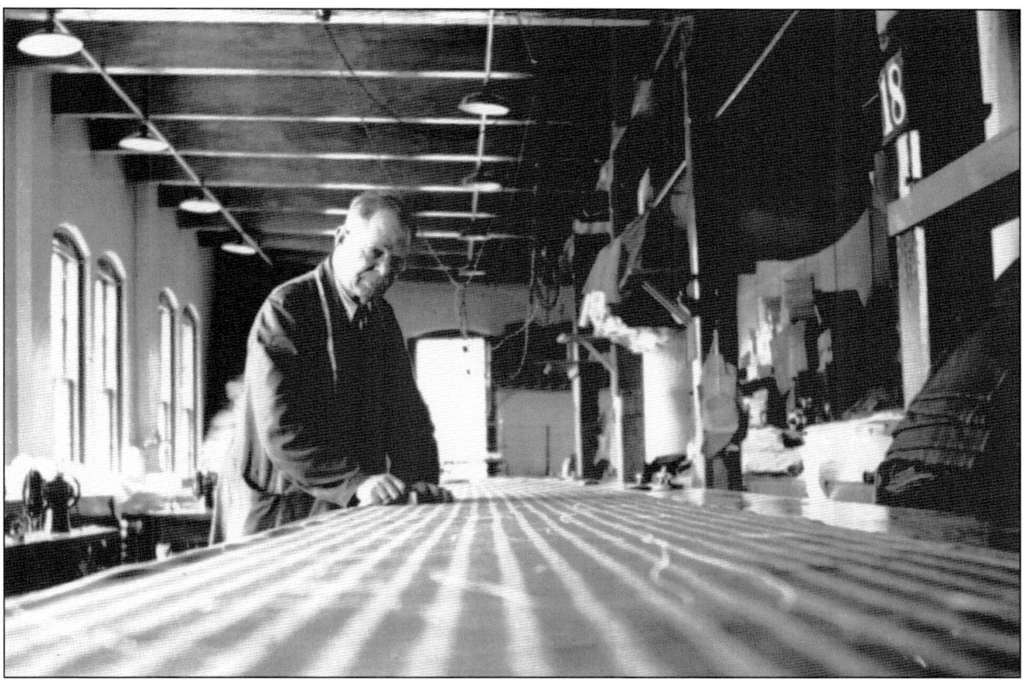

Master tailor "Teddy" Aalbers ran the reformatory garment operation during the industrial era before liberal reformers and federal law put an end to contract prison labor.

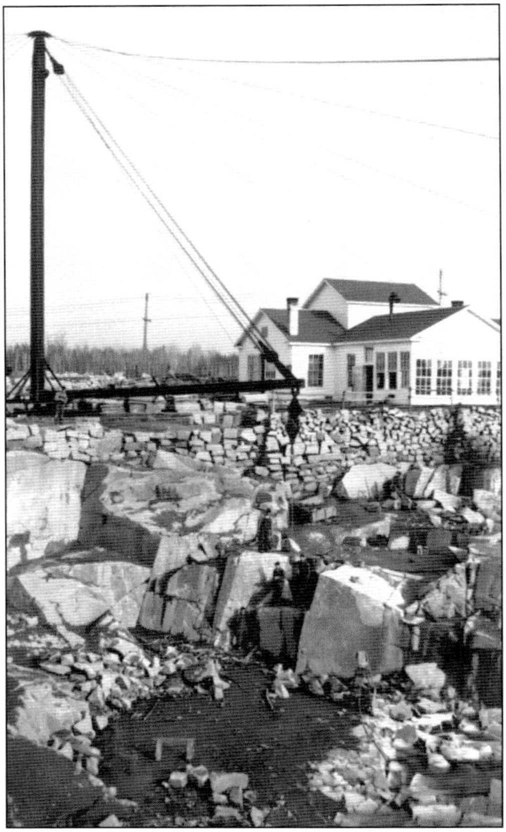

In 1926, the reformatory leased a granite quarry at Amberg and mined it with inmate labor. This quarry provided nearly all of the granite used to construct the State Capitol Annex in Madison and much of the later WSR building projects.

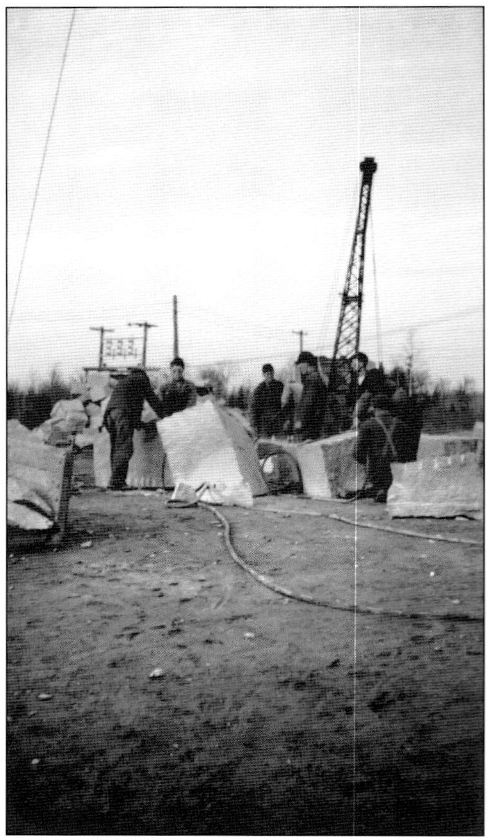

Inmate laborers perform the arduous task of cutting and preparing granite blocks at the Camp Amberg quarry in this 1930s photograph by J. Emory Temple. (Courtesy Green Bay Correctional Institution.)

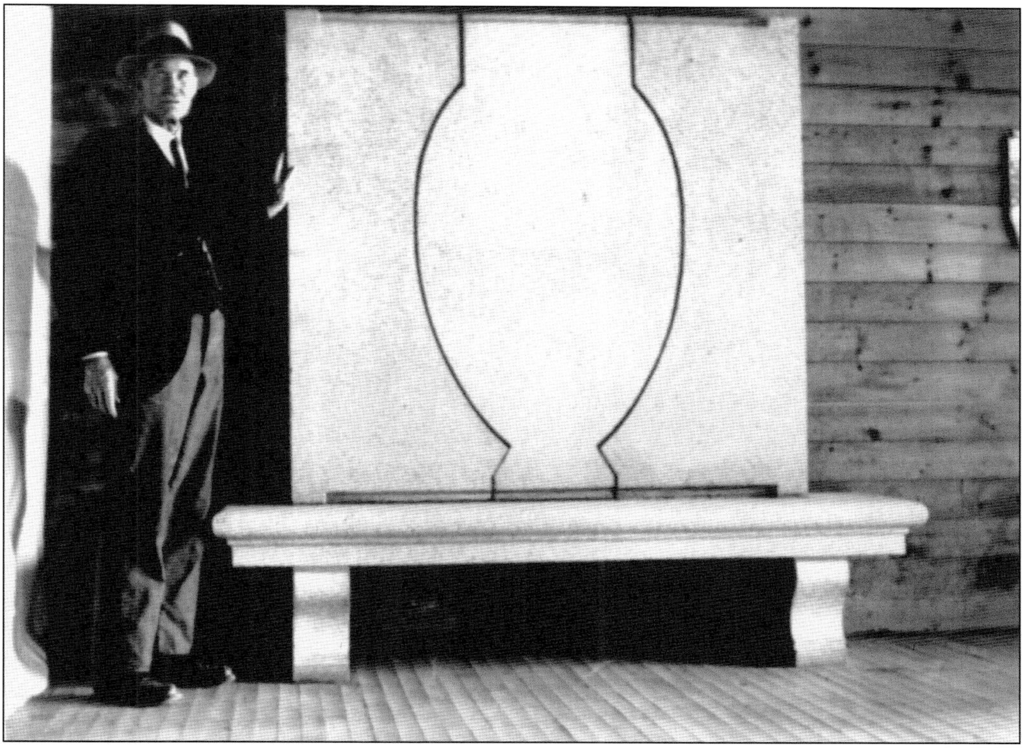

The lease of the Amberg granite quarry gave rise to a brisk business in stone cutting and monument production at the reformatory. Barney Bailey, granite foreman under Earl Eklund, stands next to the work done by one of his "boys."

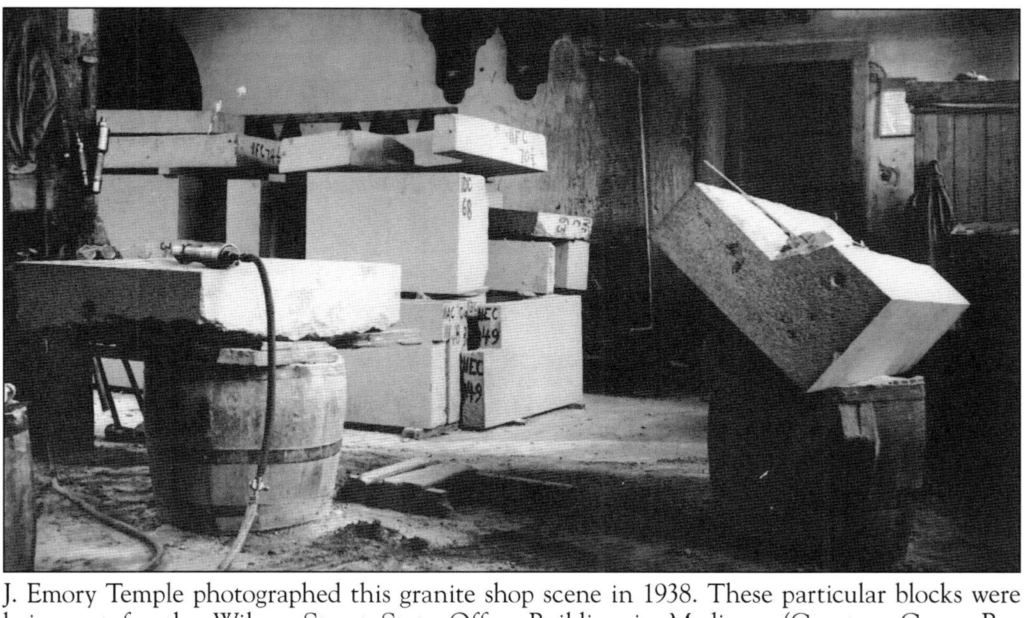

J. Emory Temple photographed this granite shop scene in 1938. These particular blocks were being cut for the Wilson Street State Office Building in Madison. (Courtesy Green Bay Correctional Institution.)

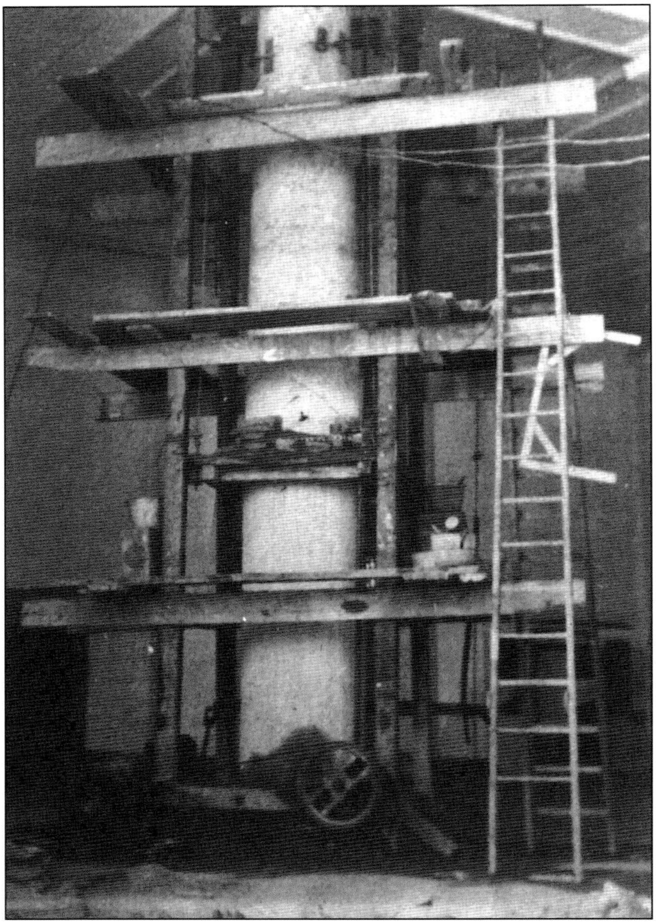

Barney Bailey devised this ingenious contraption that polished the four enormous columns that grace the center of the rotunda—the most dramatic architectural feature of the facility. (Courtesy Green Bay Correctional Institution.)

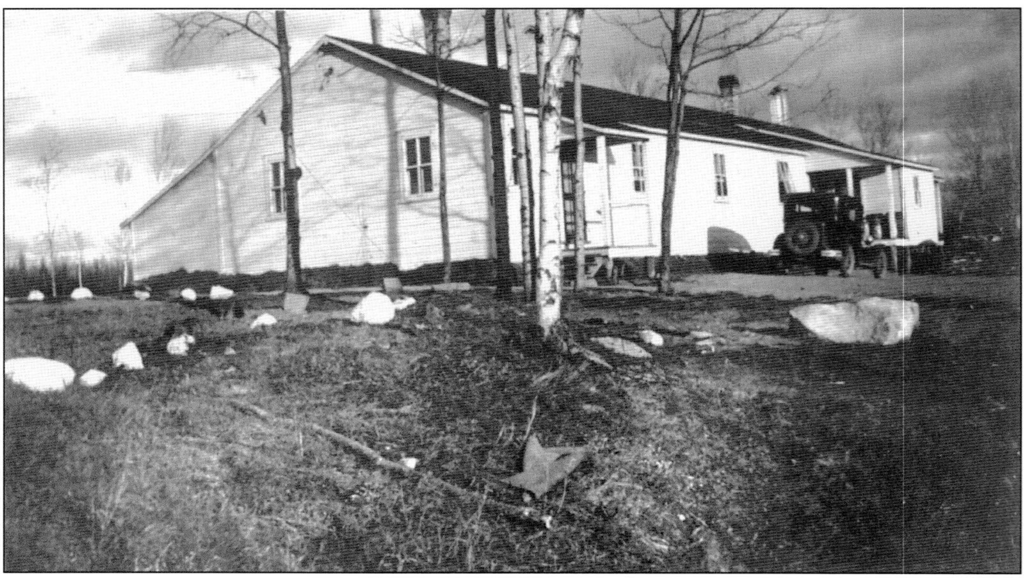

Reformatory granite miners and cutters lived in this frame bunkhouse constructed on site at the 120-acre Camp Amberg.

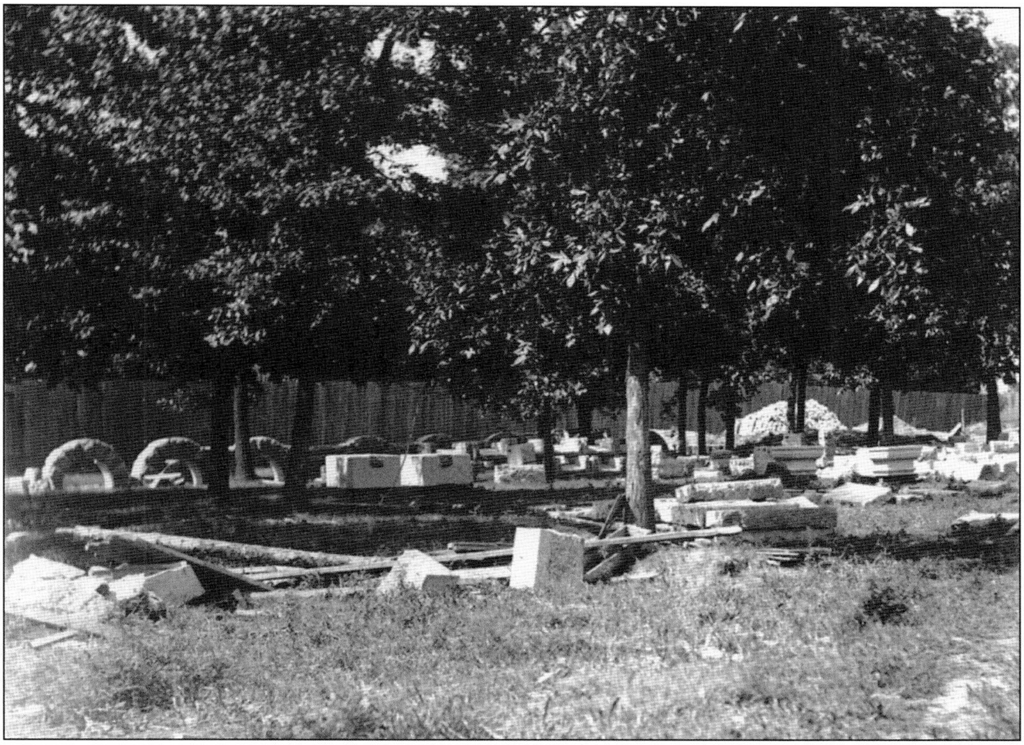

Blocks of granite await use in the yard at WSR. The old stockade wall is visible in the background of this photograph that predates 1921. (Courtesy Green Bay Correctional Institution.)

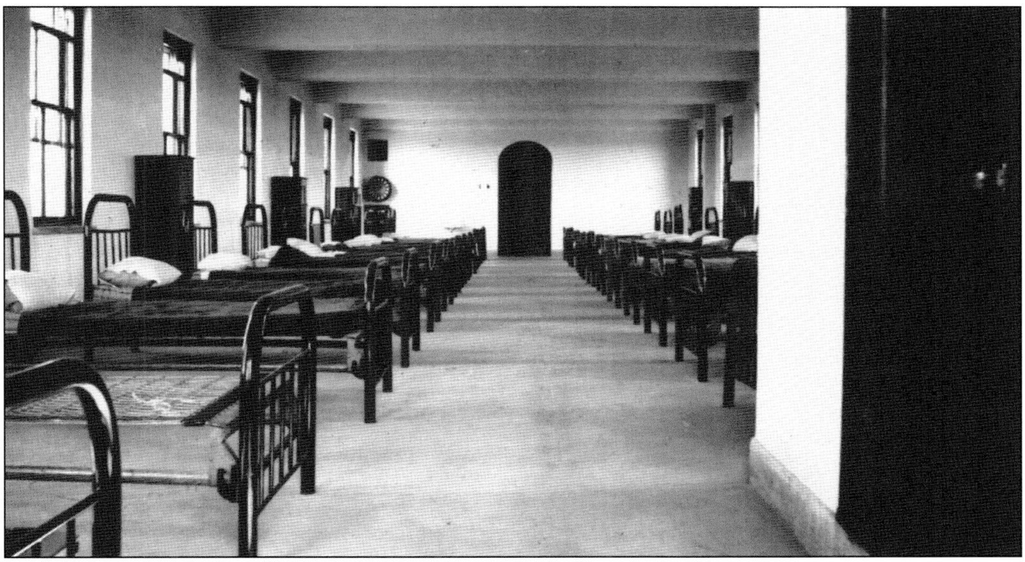

Rows of beds line the interior of one of the dormitory areas at the Oneida Honor Farm. Working on the farm gave trusted inmates a break from the drudgery of life inside prison walls.

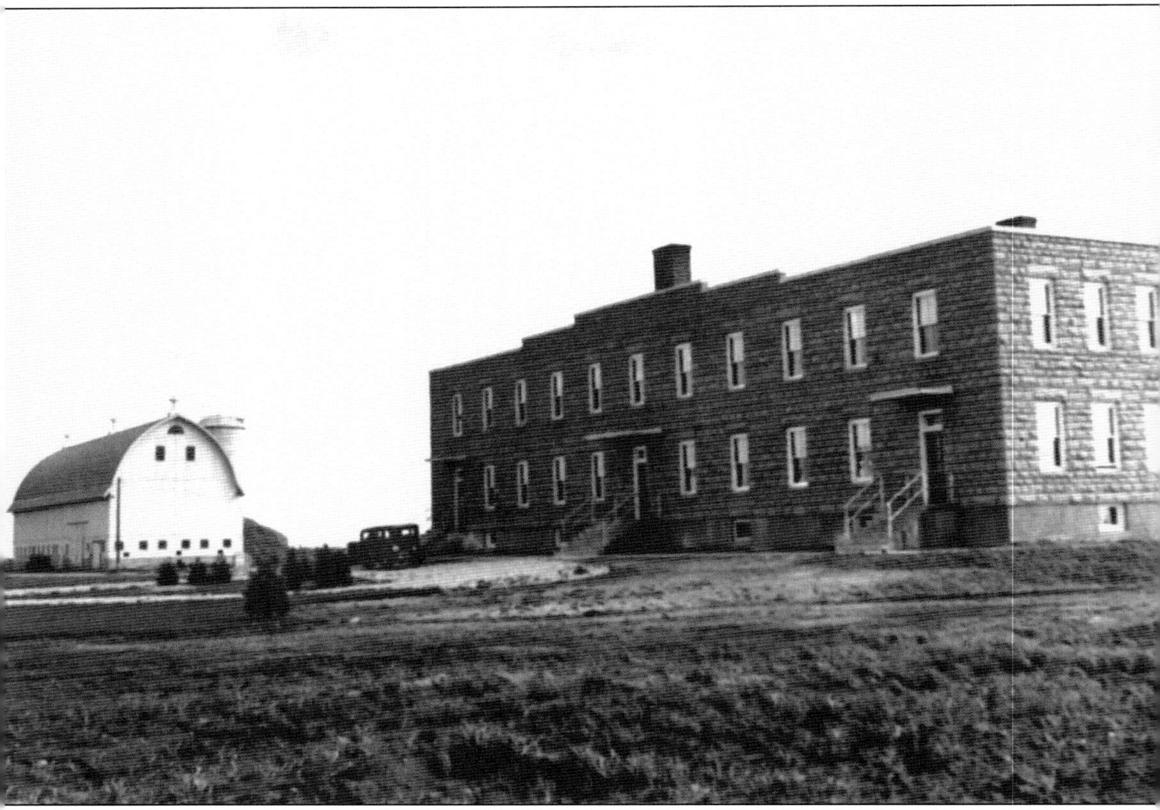

In 1921, the reformatory increased its farming capacity by purchasing 306 acres of land about 20 miles west of the facility near Oneida in Outagamie County. Prison trustees, sometimes numbering 60 at a time, worked this highly productive site and lived in this 118,195-cubic-foot granite dormitory. In 1952, the reformatory earned $184,847.18 in the transfer of farm commodities, including the sale of young dairy bulls to breeders in Wisconsin. Most of the other commodities were sold to the reformatory or to other state institutions.

Seven

LIFE IN THE CAN

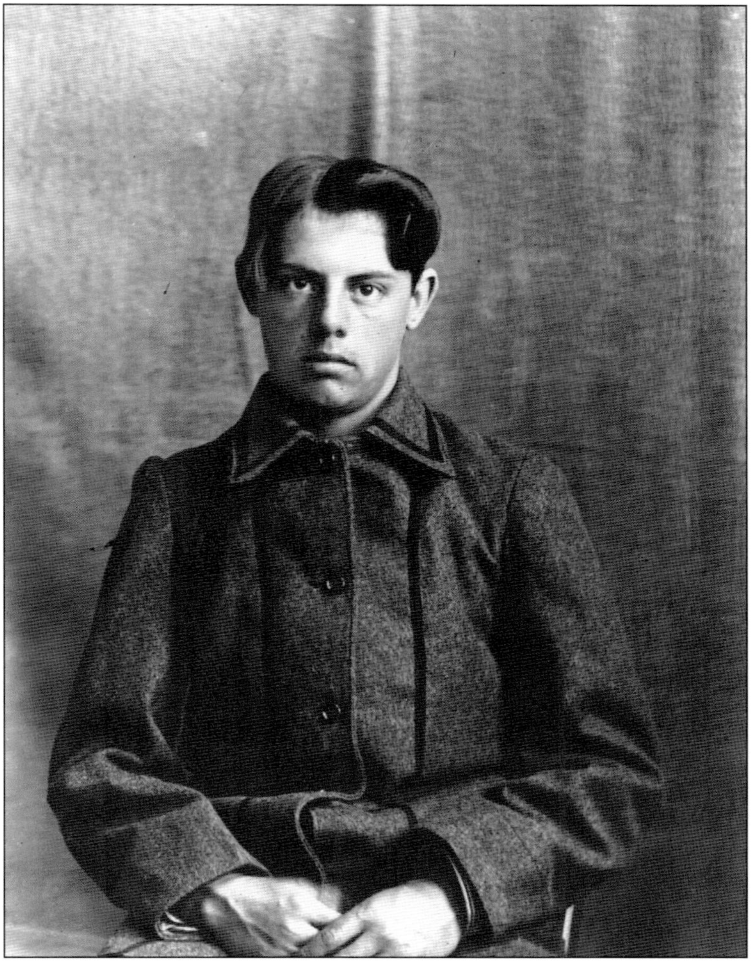

William Graf, the reformatory's 45th prisoner, was photographed the day he arrived at the prison on May 19, 1899. The first inmates, all between the ages of 17 and 28, arrived from the state prison at Waupun on August 31, 1898, and took up residence in a temporary cell house. Like Graf, most were first-time offenders. According to James E. Heg's report to the state in 1900, all but 3 of the original 24 prisoners had been paroled and were living "honest and upright" lives. Graf's sentence expired November 23, 1900.

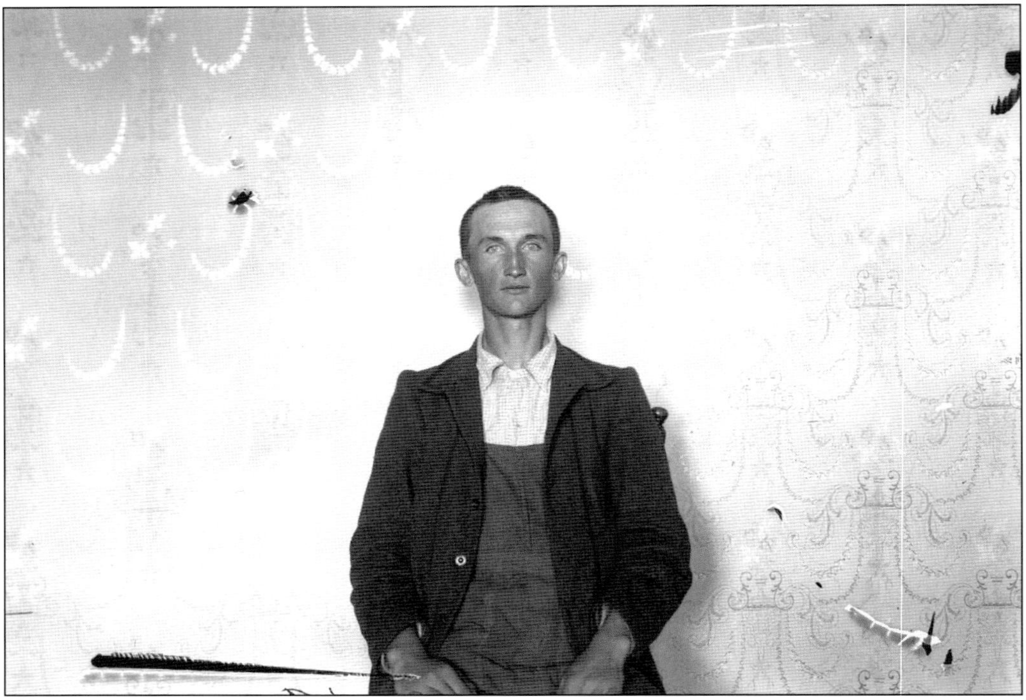

Inmate Elmer Feagel was the 19th prisoner admitted to WSR. Feagel would have been introduced to a world in which inmate labor, military drill, and vocational training dominated his daily routine. A typical day for Feagel and his comrades in crime consisted of five hours of labor, four and a half hours of vocational and academic training, and one hour devoted to military drill.

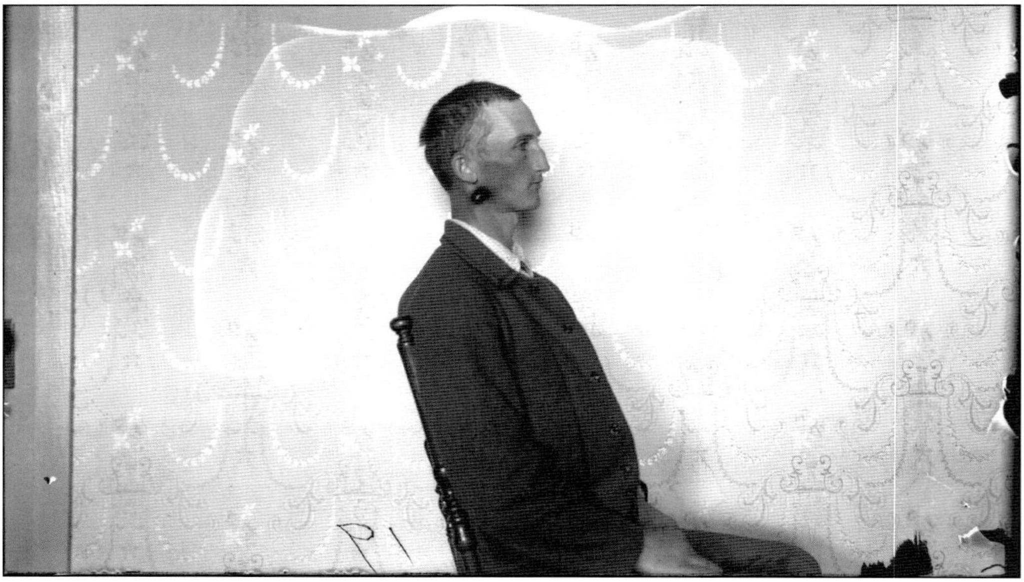

In 1900, James E. Heg, superintendent, wrote, "The design of the Reformatory, in short, is to give every one within it a chance, by good conduct and his own efforts, to shorten his stay herein; to give proper schooling; to teach industrious and honest habits; and, by all available means to advance his material, mental and moral interests." Feagel disappeared while on parole and was never heard from again.

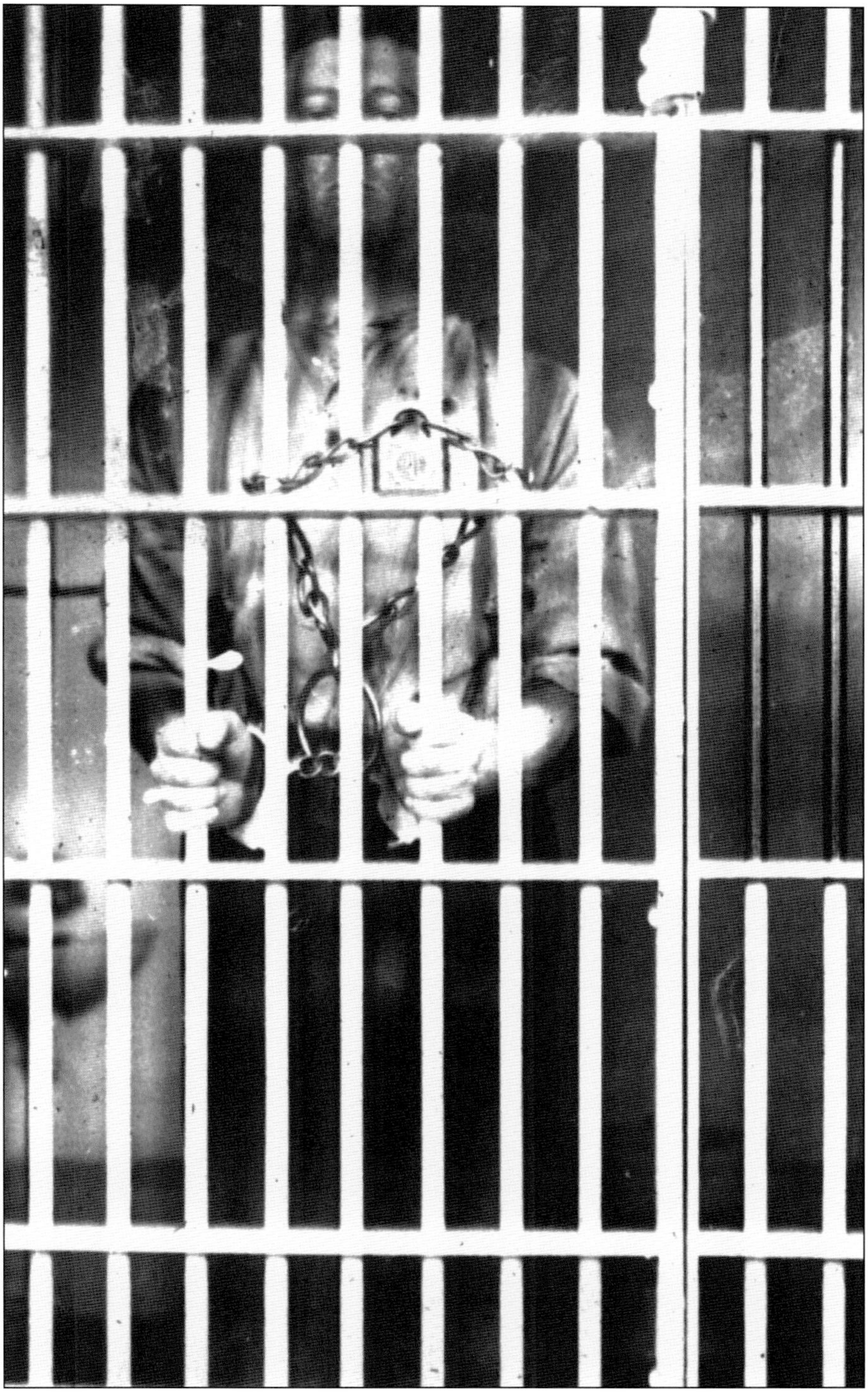

Chained to his cell door in 1908, prisoner No. 1308 likely suffered reduced rations as punishment for committing a serious offense. Methods to punish inmates for offenses involved various types of corporal punishments. Something as seemingly harmless as laughing in the dining hall typically resulted in a $5 fine. Assaulting an officer might earn the offender reduced rations and a week handcuffed to his cell door.

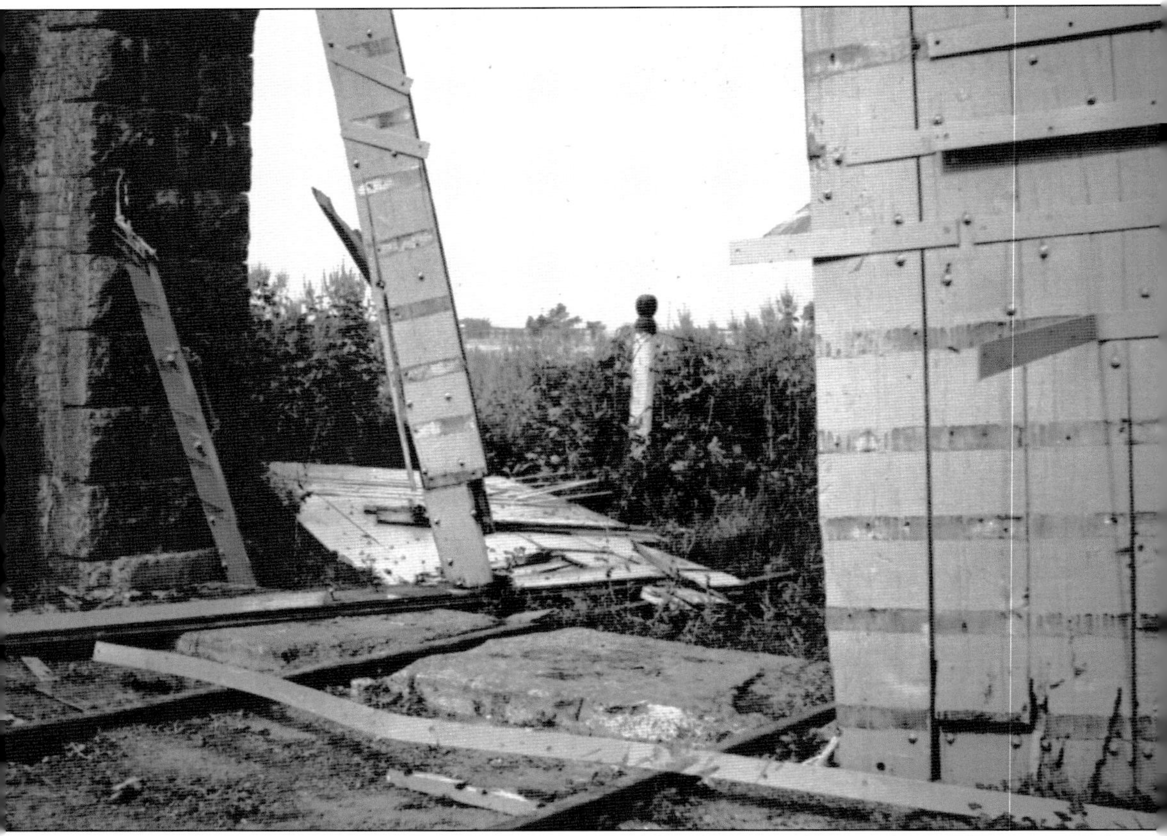

The only thing between two daring inmates and freedom was this sturdy wooden gate on the south end of the reformatory. After absconding with Supt. Benjamin Kramer's four-year-old Cadillac, two inmates attempted to make a break by using the car as a battering ram. The gate was breached, but extensive damage to the automobile prevented escape to the field and beyond. The effects of a failed escape attempt are shown clearly in this photograph. It is not known what sort of punishment was handed out to the two would-be escape artists.

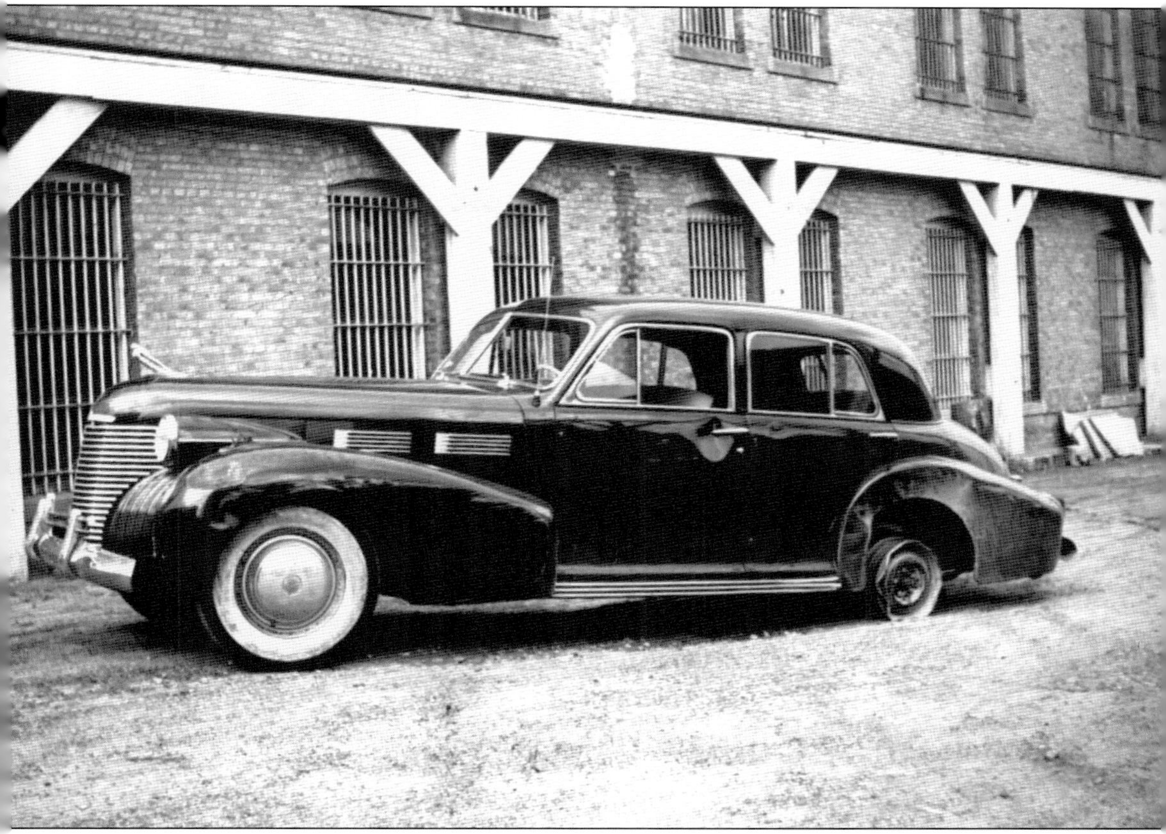

Destroyed by gate-crashing inmates, this damaged Cadillac rests just inside the reformatory's west side railroad gate. The Chicago, Milwaukee, & St. Paul Railroad Company ran a spur through this gate for delivery of coal and other materials.

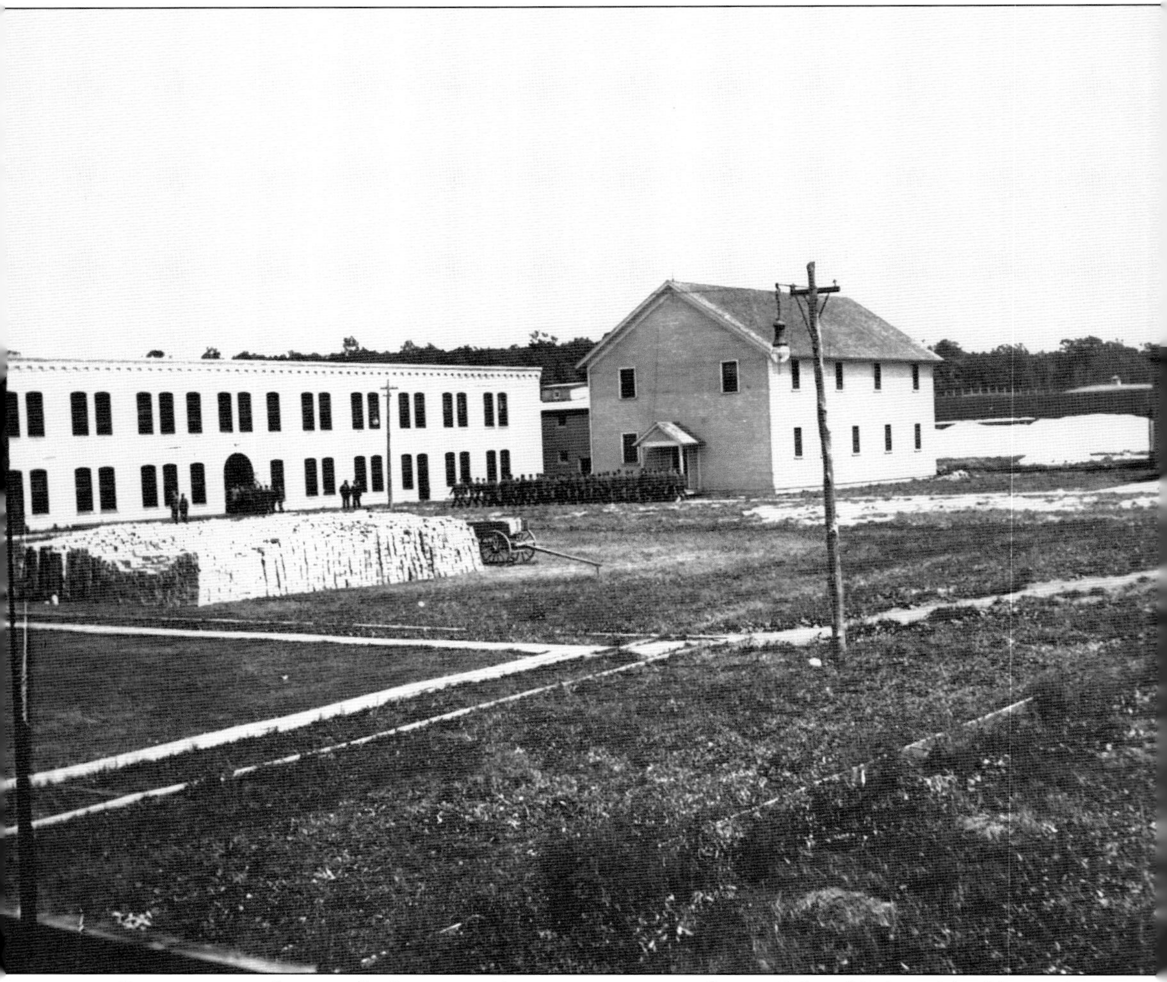

Prisoners marching in lockstep can be seen moving in front of the old chapel building adjacent to the power plant and North Cell Hall. Marching in lockstep was a vestigial remnant of the days when discipline and order dominated the organizational approach at American prisons. The two-story structure with paired arched windows is the dormitory and shop. Built in 1901, it is one of the oldest structures at Green Bay Correctional Institution.

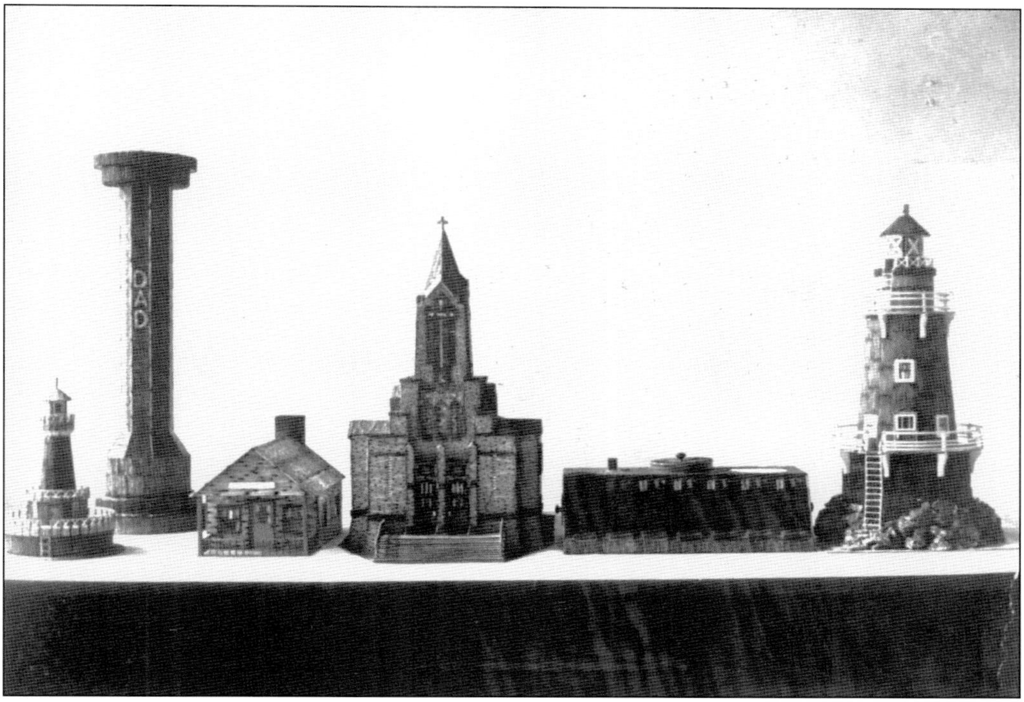

Craft work kept inmates busy and gave them a sense of satisfaction. With time on their hands, inmates often produced beautiful and intricate creations.

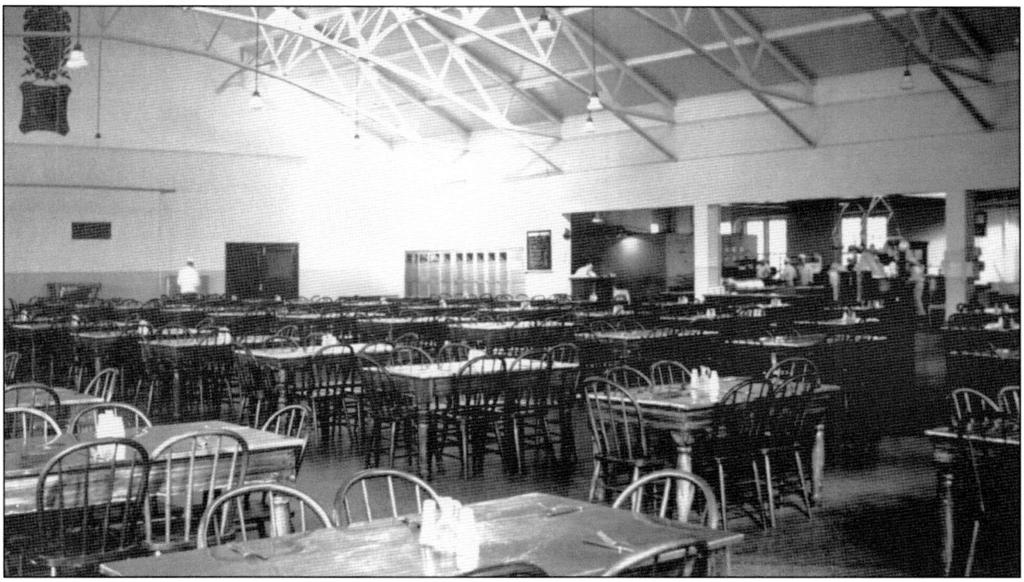

The dining room was one of the few places inmates could engage in idle conversation—but only for a few minutes. The rule of silence ordered their daily routines until Sanger Powers granted the privilege of talking during the entire morning and evening meals.

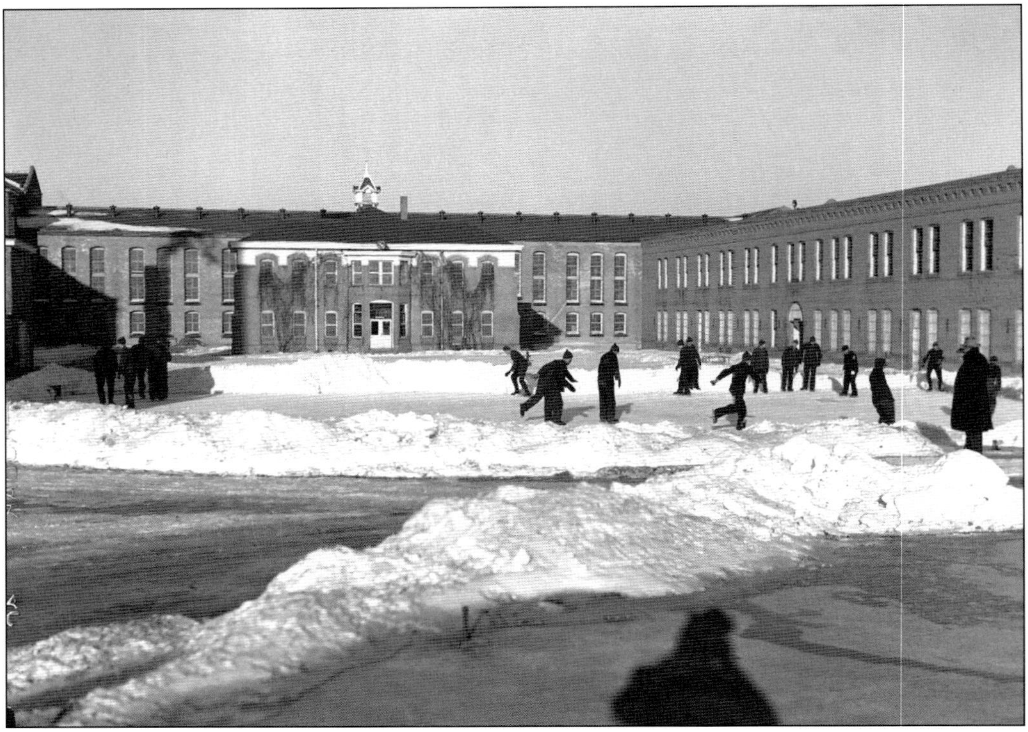

Inmates enjoy a bit of relaxation on a makeshift skating rink during Sanger B. Powers's regime. His relaxation of old rules coupled with an increase in recreational activities made life easier for inmates. Many longtime reformatory employees, however, felt that some of Powers's changes went too far.

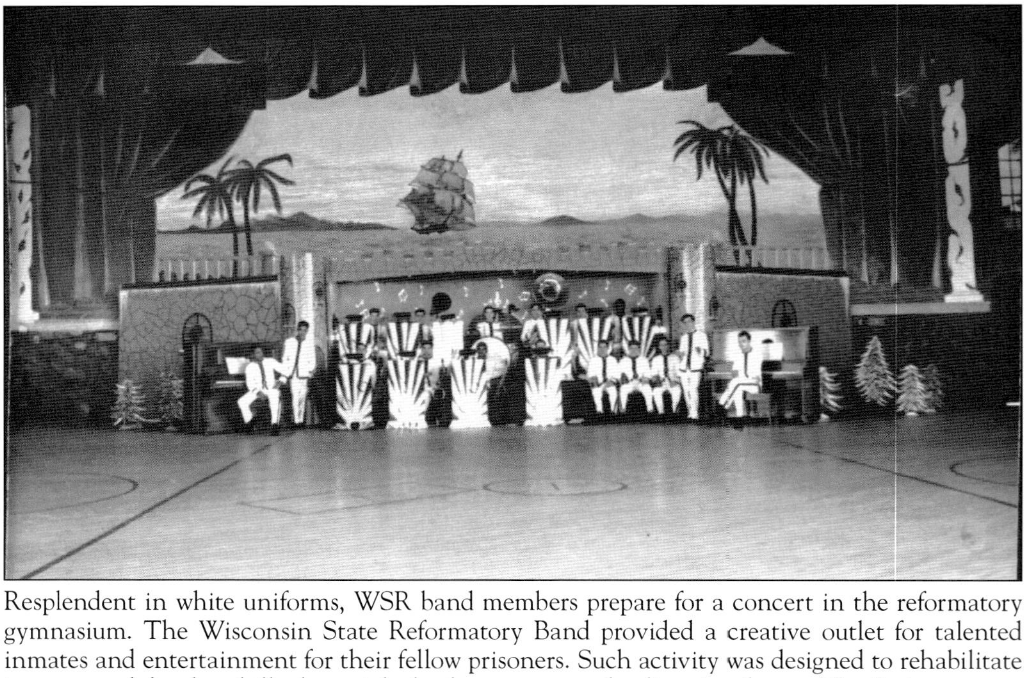

Resplendent in white uniforms, WSR band members prepare for a concert in the reformatory gymnasium. The Wisconsin State Reformatory Band provided a creative outlet for talented inmates and entertainment for their fellow prisoners. Such activity was designed to rehabilitate inmates and develop skills that might lead to success and a diversion from a life of crime.

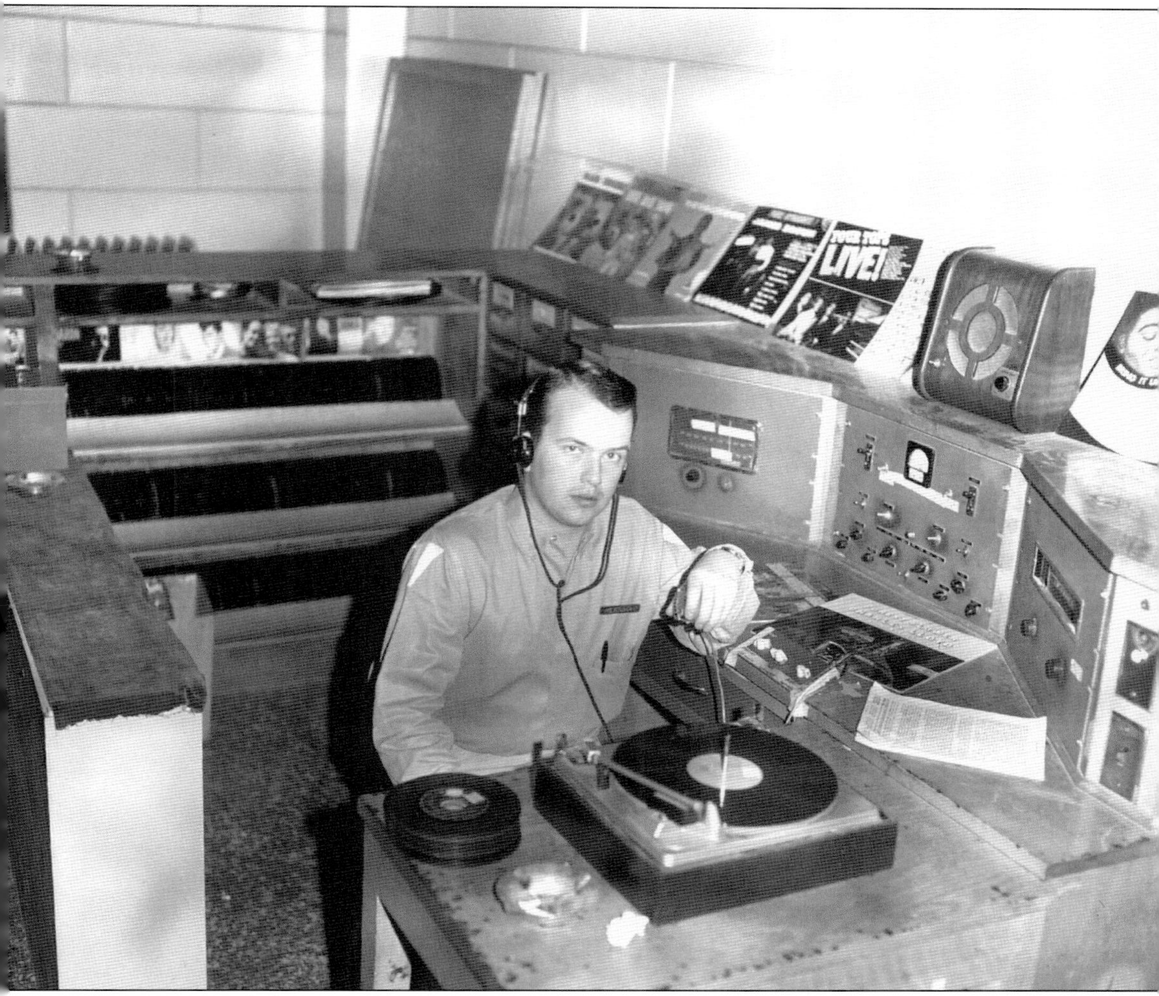

Inmates imprisoned during Sanger B. Powers's reform era enjoyed freedoms and amenities unheard of in previous times. Powers did away with the oppressive silent rule, allowed inmates to publish a prison journal, and approved the installation of a two-channel radio receiver connected to individual receivers in each cell. Here a prison deejay spins the latest hits on vinyl. The identification patch on his left shoulder indicates that he is a "runner" and enjoyed the privilege of movement throughout the prison without the need for a typical pass.

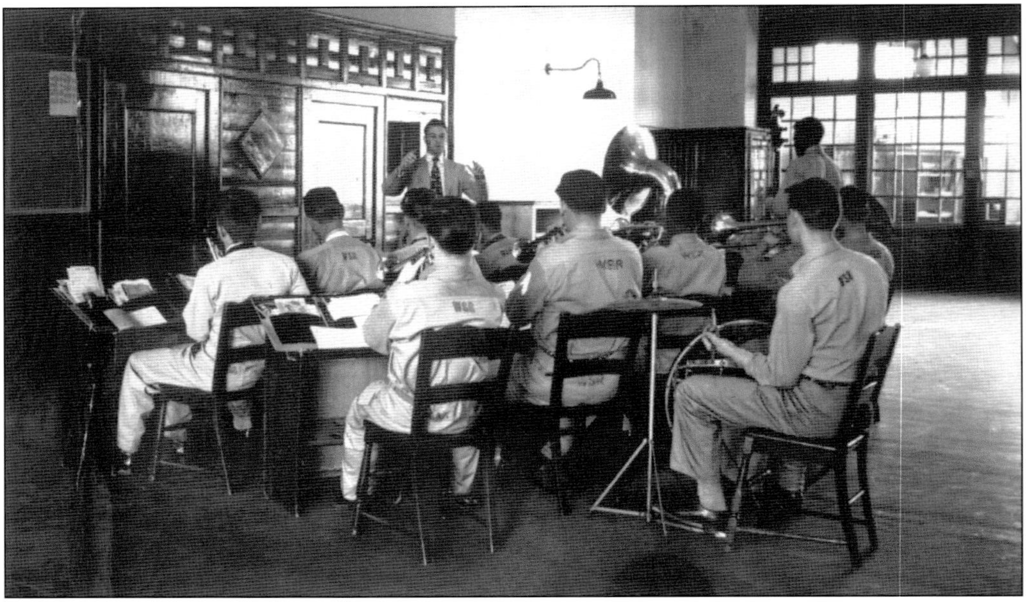

Music played a major role in the rehabilitative efforts at WSR. In this photograph, Carl Sturdevant directs the inmate orchestra sometime during the 1950s.

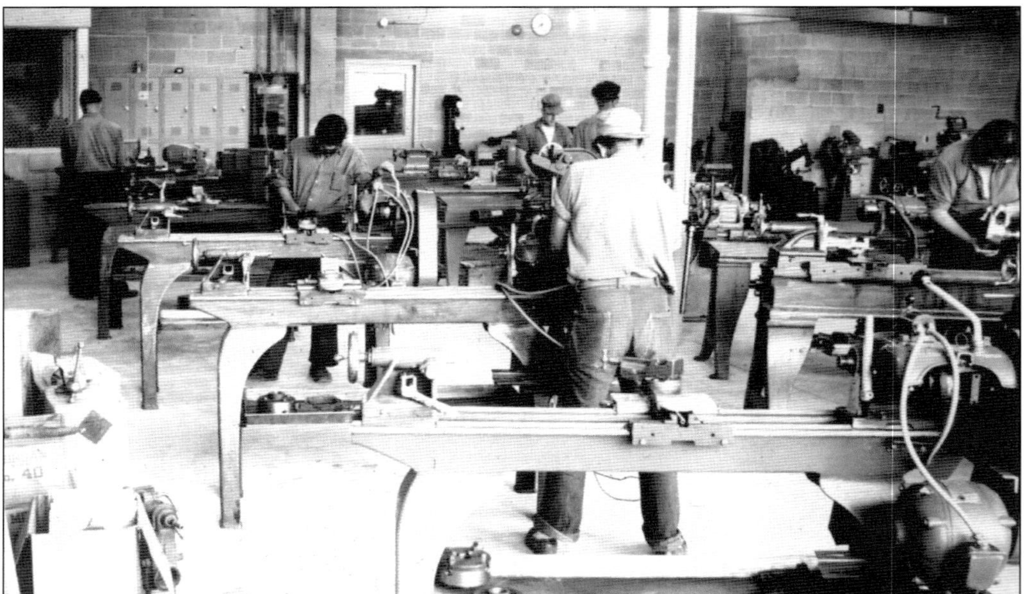

When not in the classroom, inmates spent much of their time working in one of the reformatory shops, or at one of the outlying camps. Here a group of youthful cffenders work in concert to complete an assigned task.

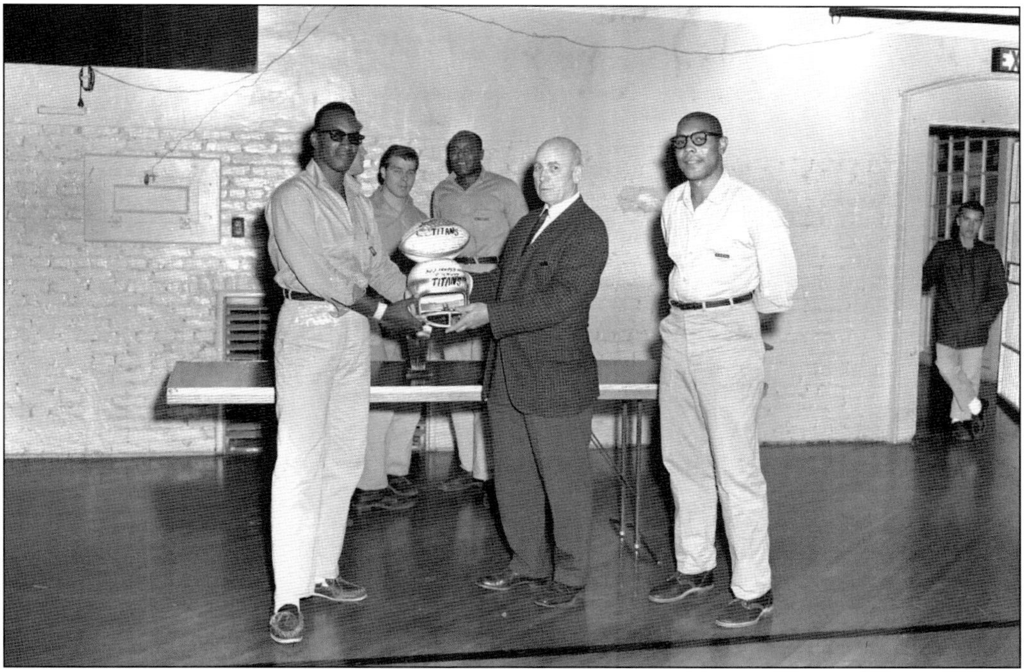

Bill Baye, the reformatory's athletic director, was highly regarded as a mentor and coach by inmates and staff alike. Here he poses with members of the institution's intramural football team.

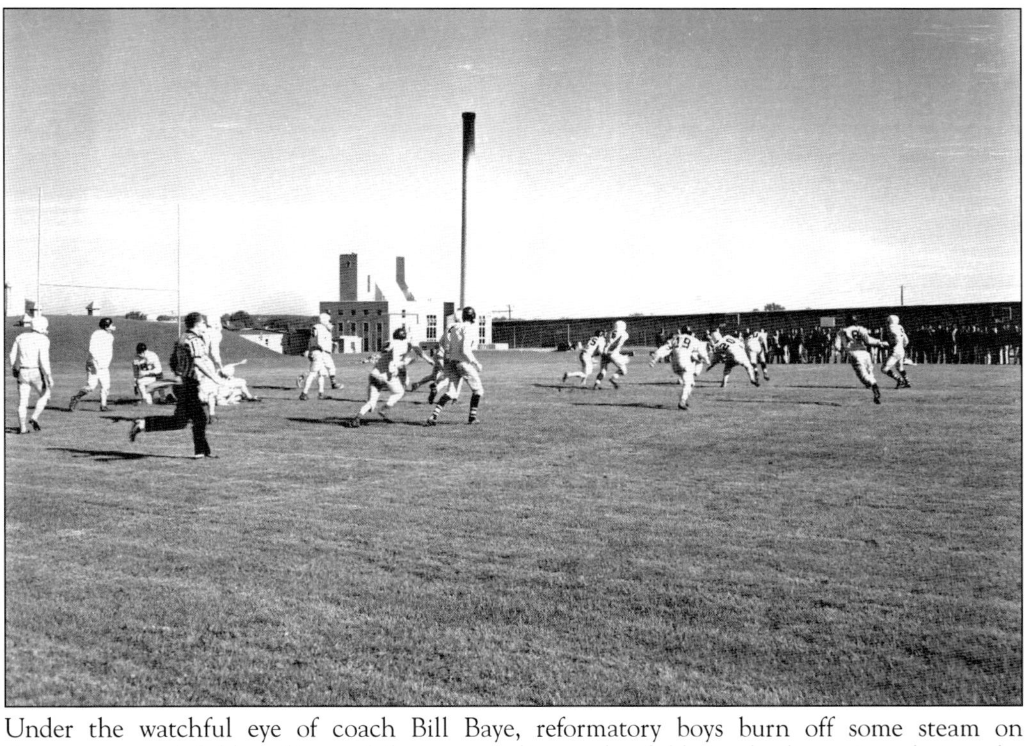

Under the watchful eye of coach Bill Baye, reformatory boys burn off some steam on the recreational field gridiron while inmates lining the field watch the action during the early 1960s.

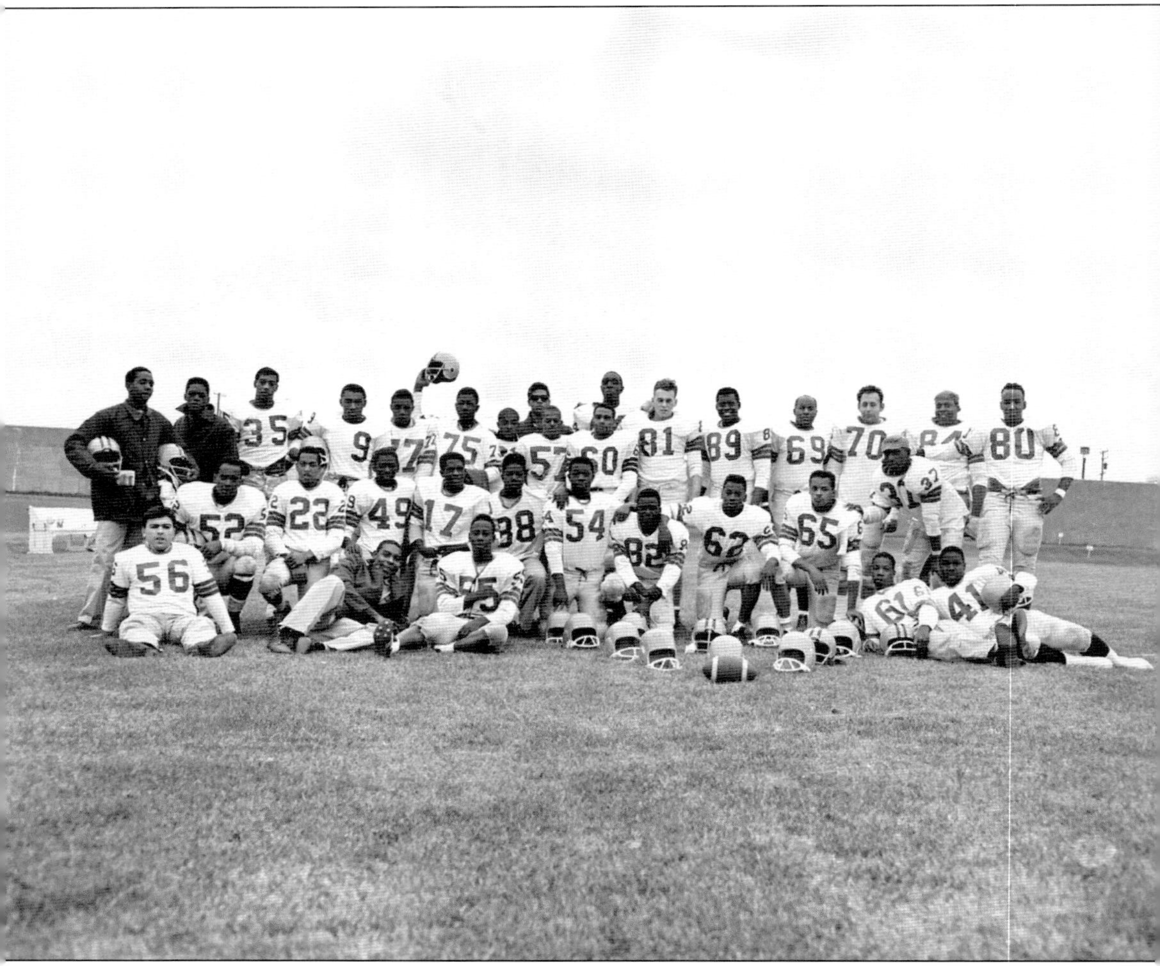

Bill Baye's intramural football team wore uniforms donated by the Green Bay Packers. Sports activities provided a diversion from the routine of prison life and an outlet for youthful energy.

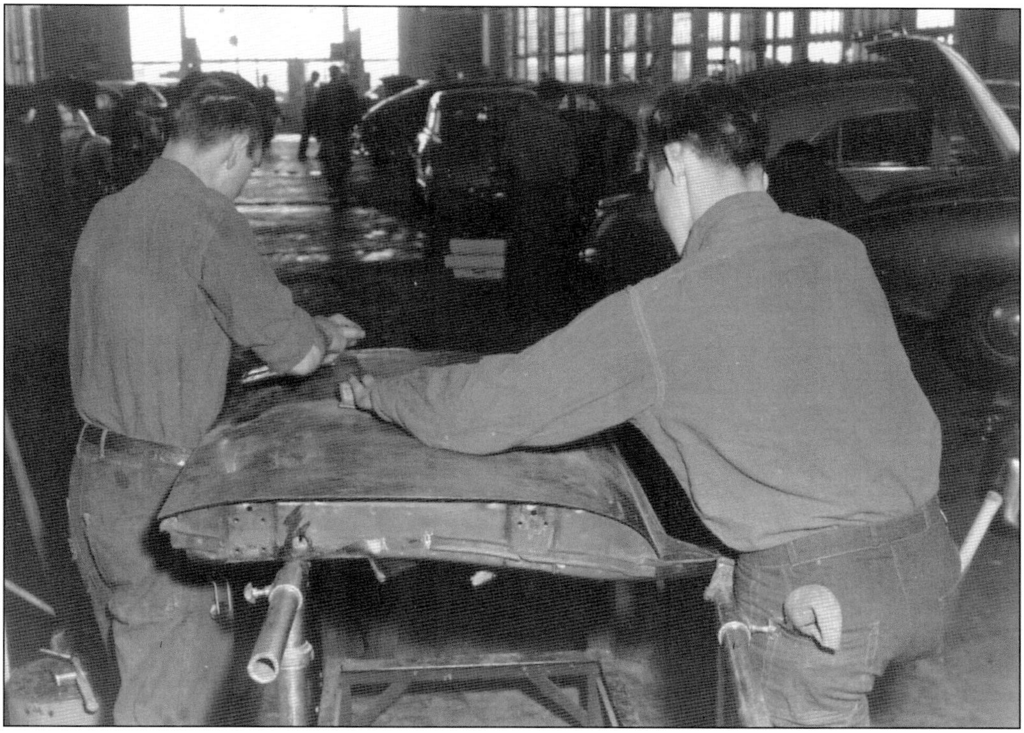

In 1953, a new auto body shop was built at WSR. Special legislative authority allowed the reformatory to service cars for automobile dealers. Two inmates perform auto body repair. Note the number of cars present in the shop—a testament to the level of activity the shop enjoyed in its heyday.

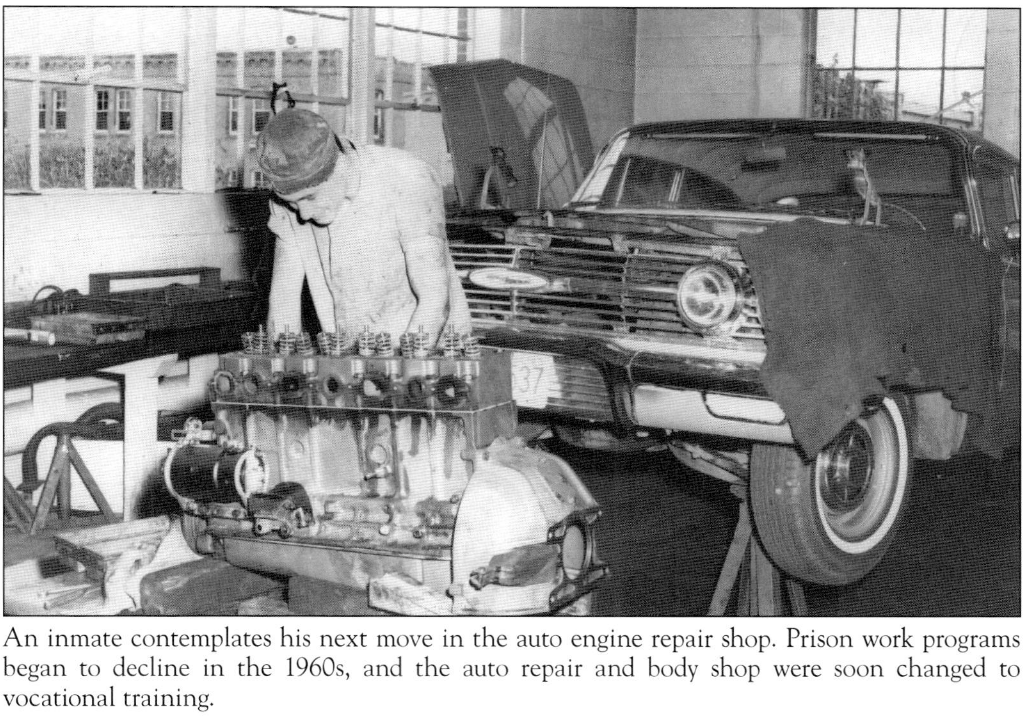

An inmate contemplates his next move in the auto engine repair shop. Prison work programs began to decline in the 1960s, and the auto repair and body shop were soon changed to vocational training.

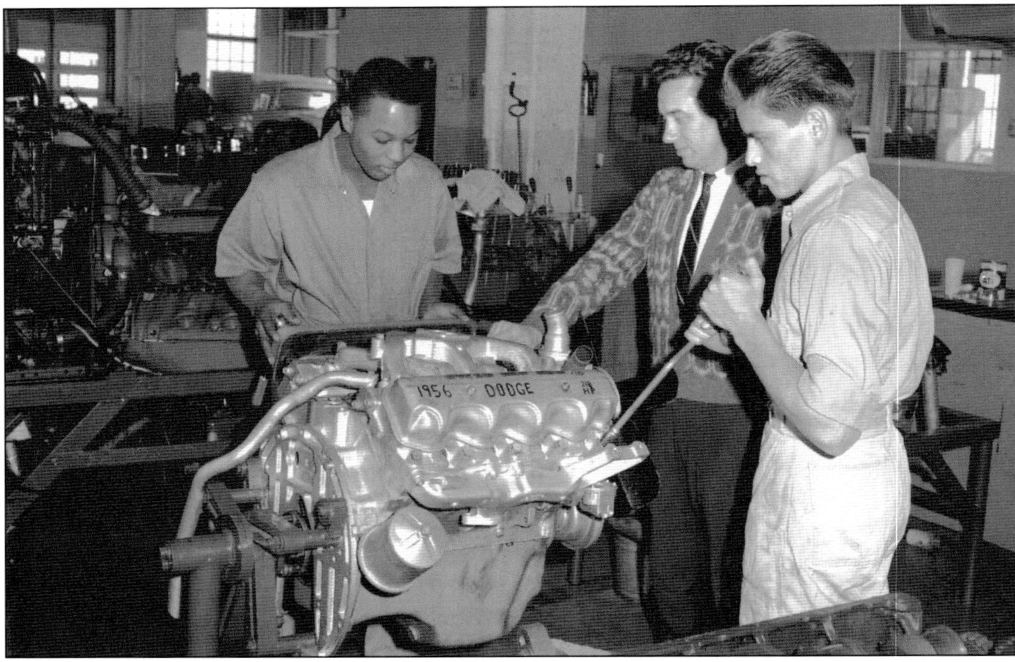

Auto body repair and mechanics were two of the most popular vocational programs at WSR. The quality of work was such that local automobile dealers often brought their vehicles to the prison for work. Here Herman Bader, a reformatory instructor, helps two inmates learn the fine points of an eight-cylinder 1956 Dodge engine.

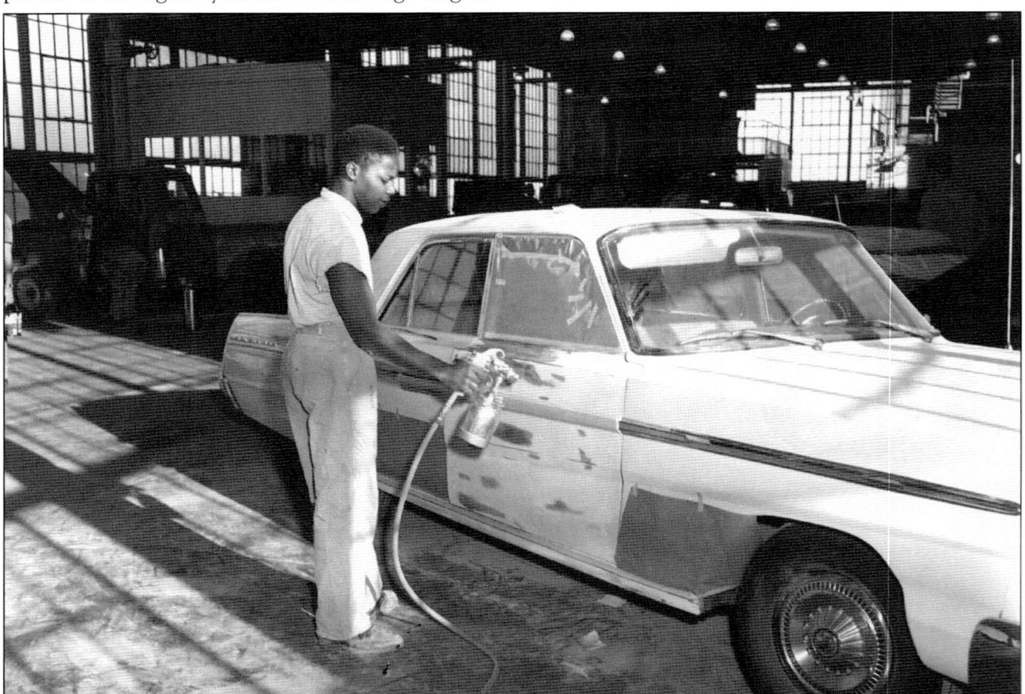

The abolition of contract labor in 1924 forced prison officials to increase the amount of time devoted to vocational training.

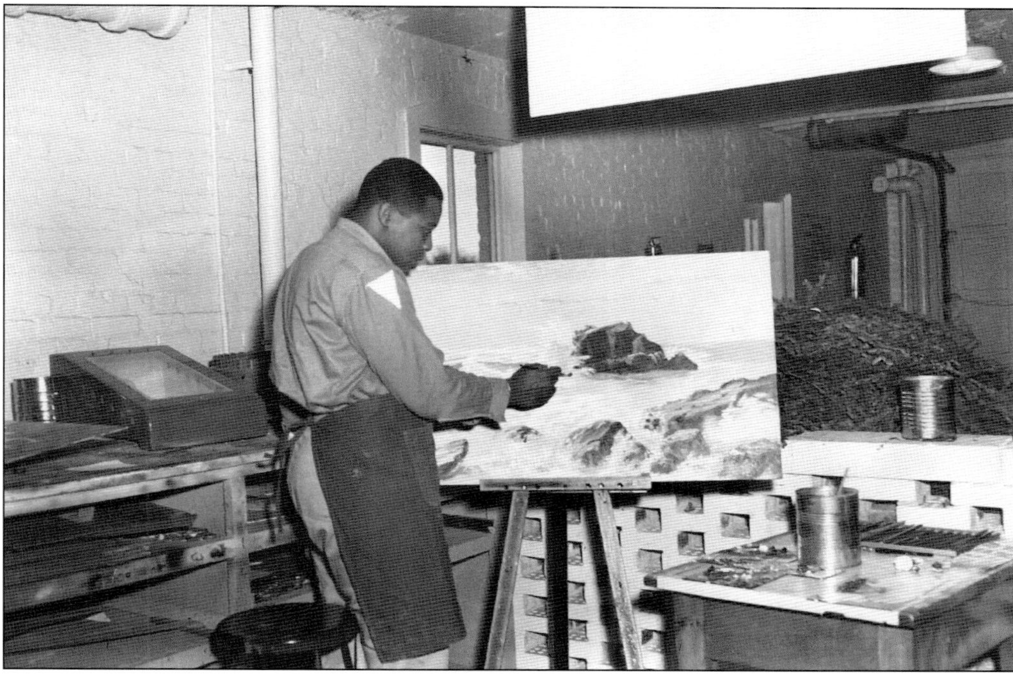

Inmates like this budding artist took advantage of the reformatory's liberal vocational training programs and classes during Sanger B. Powers's tenure as superintendent. The restriction of contract prisoner labor compelled reformatory officials to bolster their vocational programs as early as 1940. While other institutions were reducing programs, WSR officials were adding programs ranging from automobile repair to cabinet making.

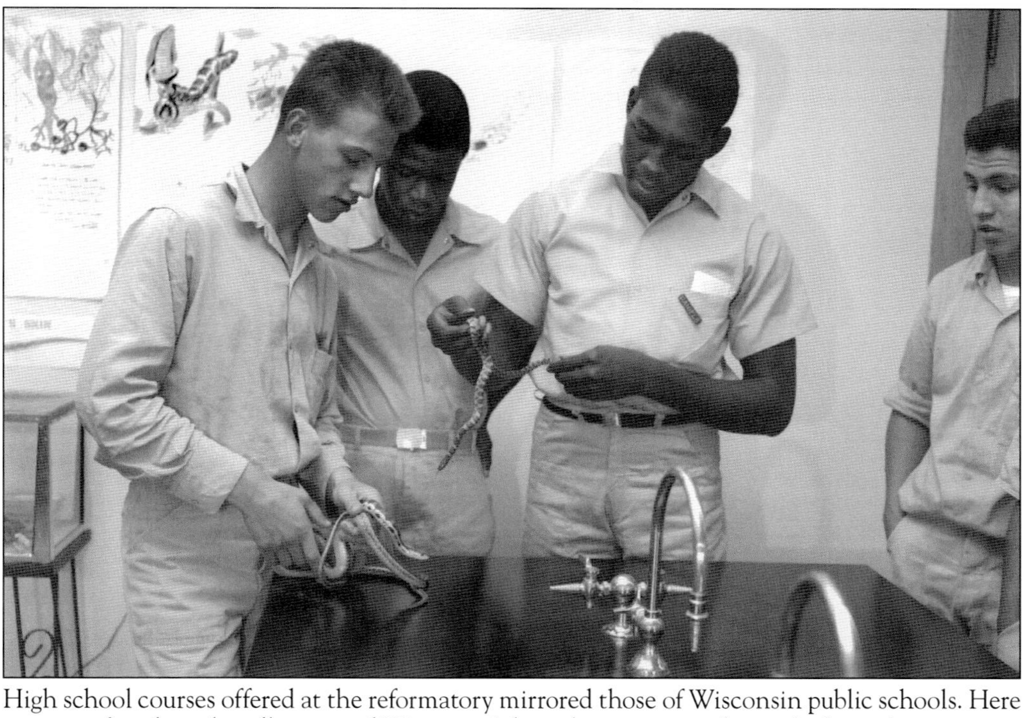

High school courses offered at the reformatory mirrored those of Wisconsin public schools. Here a group of students handle some of Wisconsin's harmless native snakes in biology class.

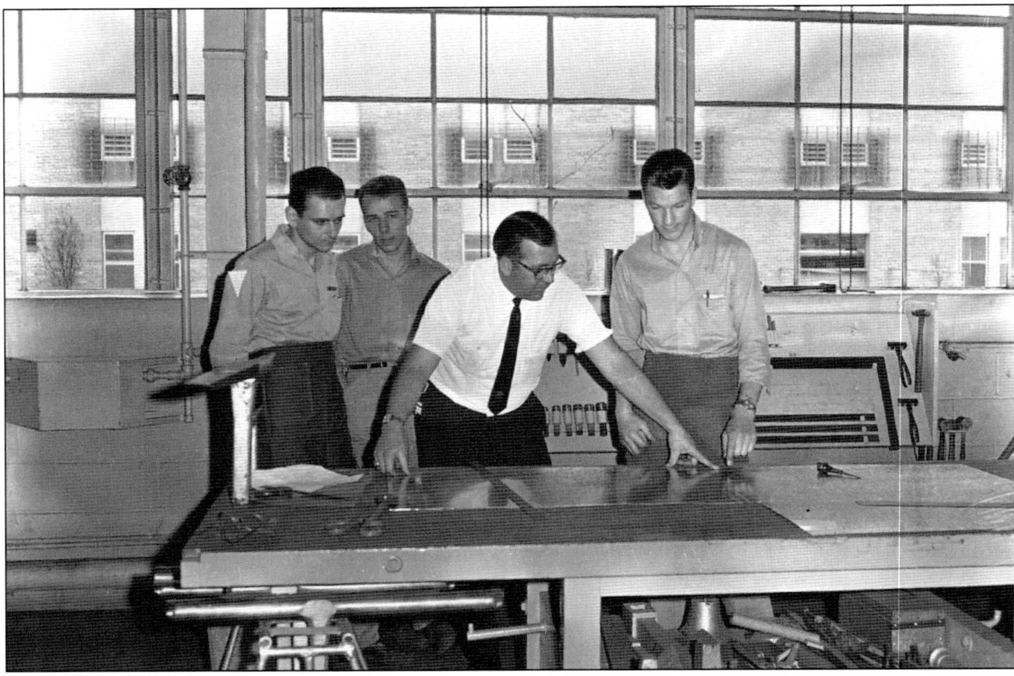

Harry Krysiak, reformatory high school principal, instructs students in sheet metal fabrication. Even today, the Green Bay Correctional Institution tries to retain a philosophical link to its reformatory by providing reentry programs for inmates.

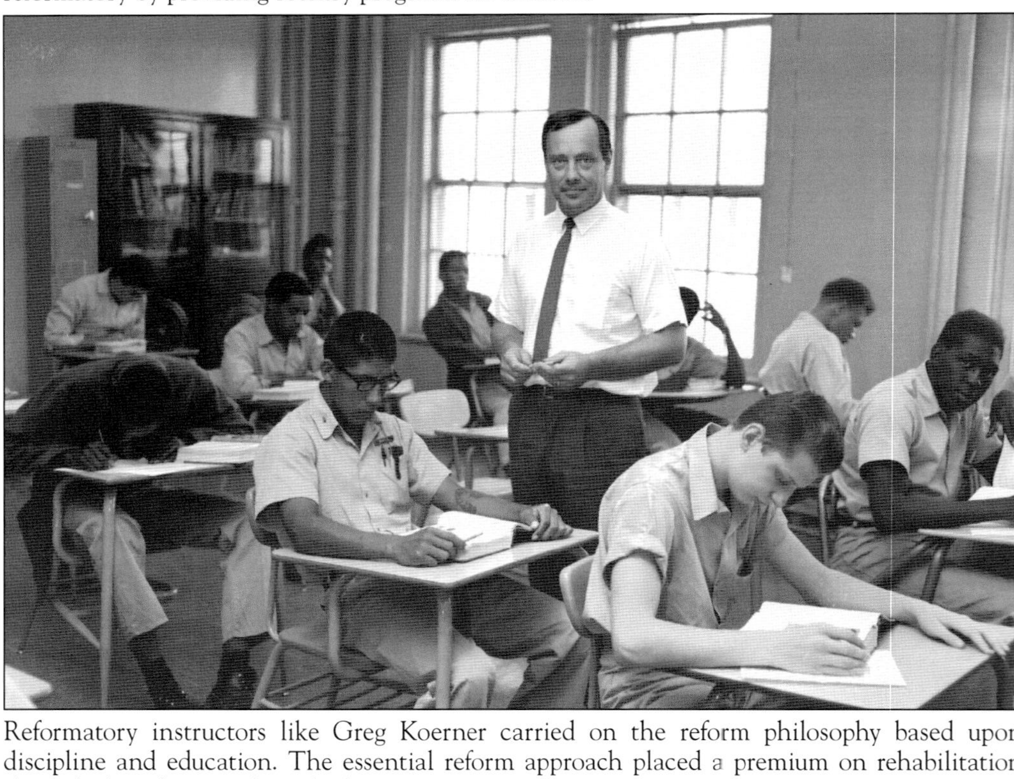

Reformatory instructors like Greg Koerner carried on the reform philosophy based upon discipline and education. The essential reform approach placed a premium on rehabilitation through discipline, work, and education.

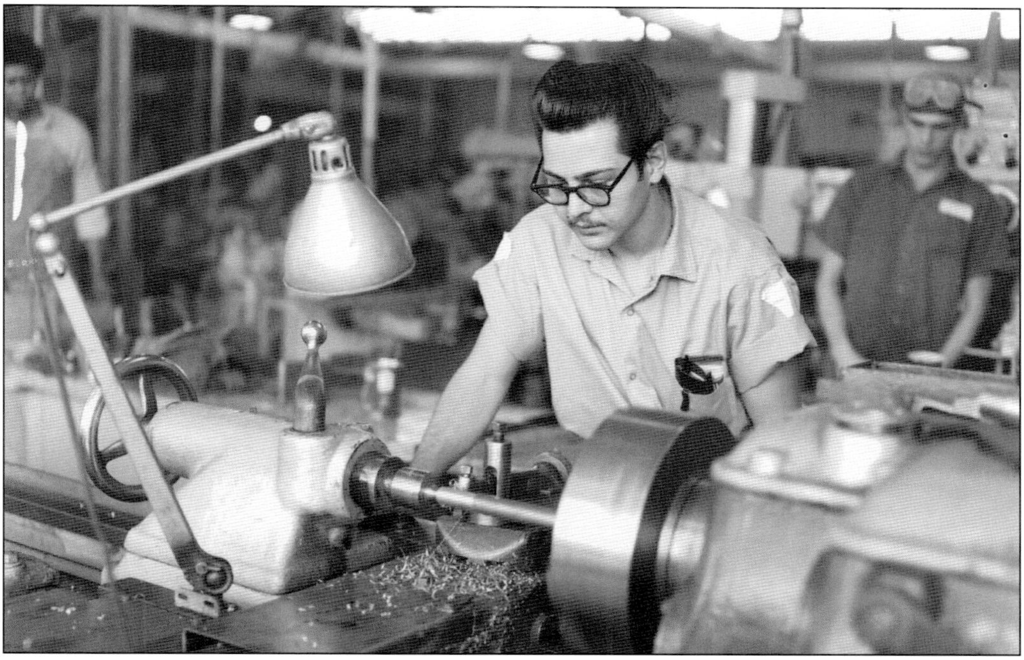

Vocational students were offered an array of opportunities, including sheet metal and machine work. This student was photographed in the early 1950s during Sanger Powers's regime. Powers experimented liberally and abolished the requirement that inmates keep their top shirt button secured, and the wearing of caps was made optional. Powers's methods gained national recognition and established Wisconsin as a model of progressive corrections reform.

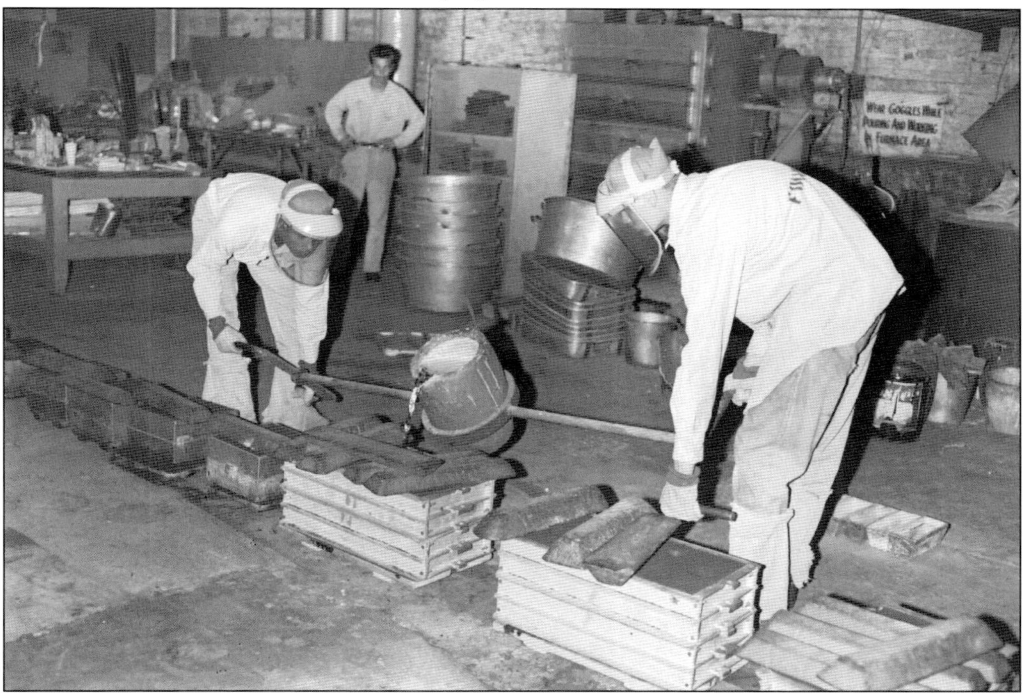

Vocational training was beneficial, but it was work. Equipped with proper safety gear, two hardworking inmates pour molten lead into moulds in the reformatory's foundry.

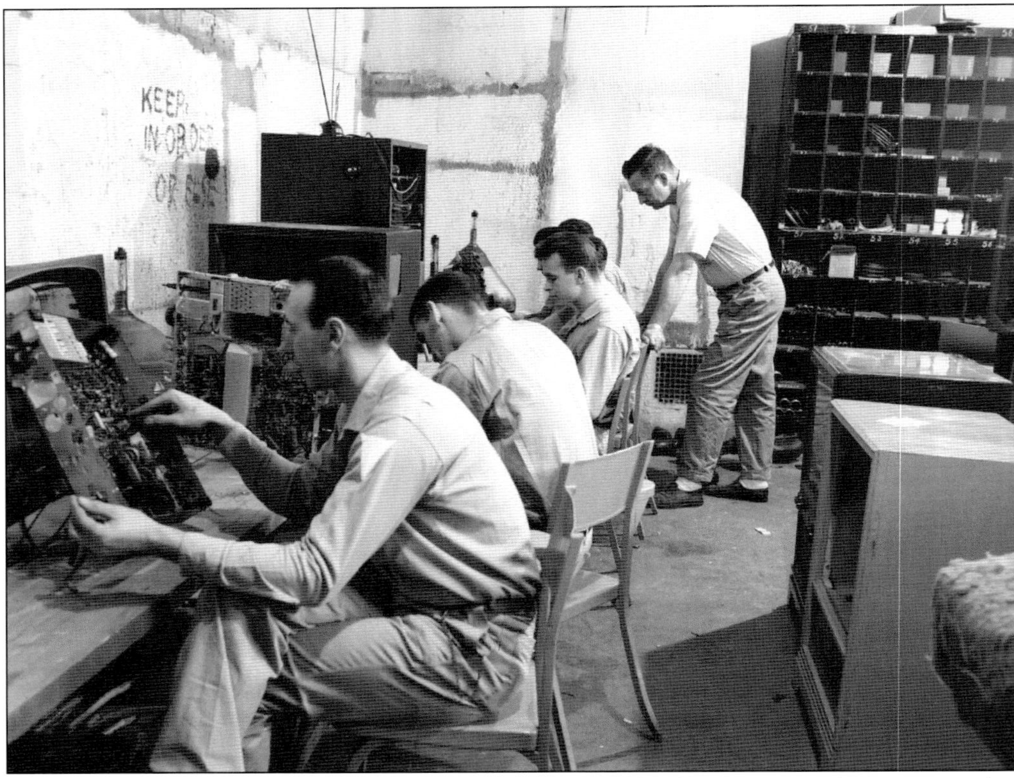

Khaki-clad inmates perfect their skills in the reformatory radio shop. Vocational training reached its peak in the 1950s.

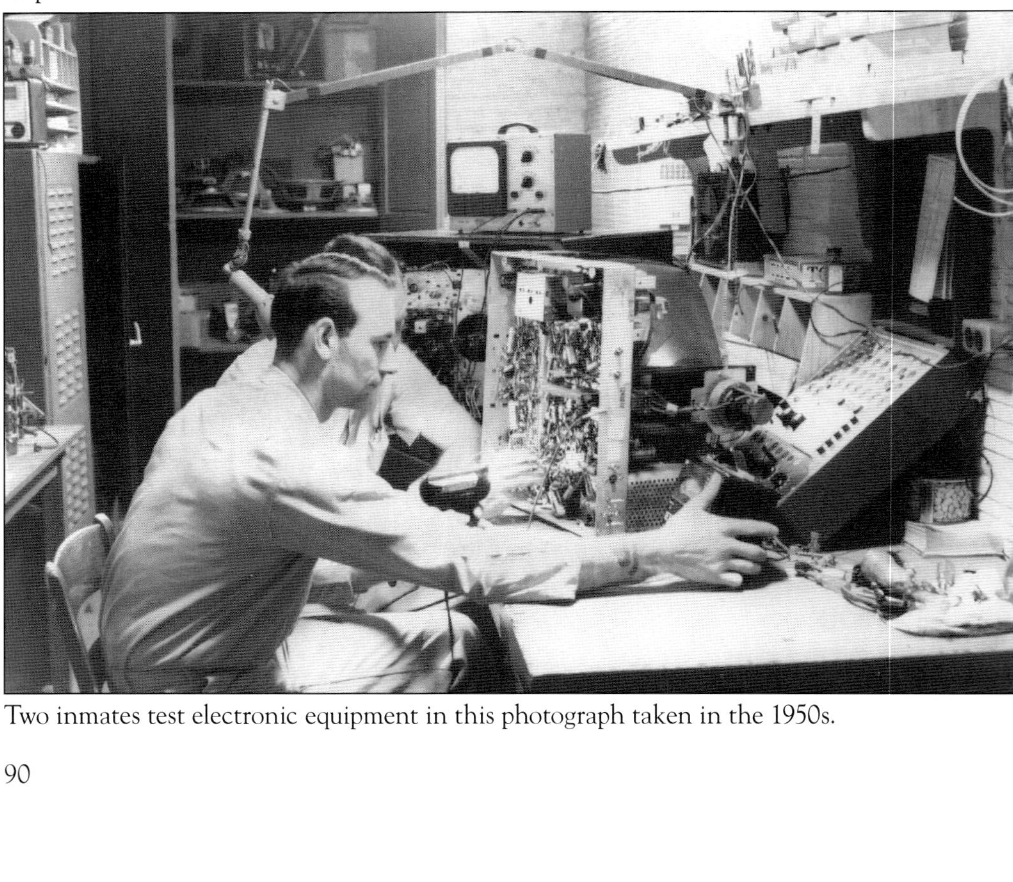

Two inmates test electronic equipment in this photograph taken in the 1950s.

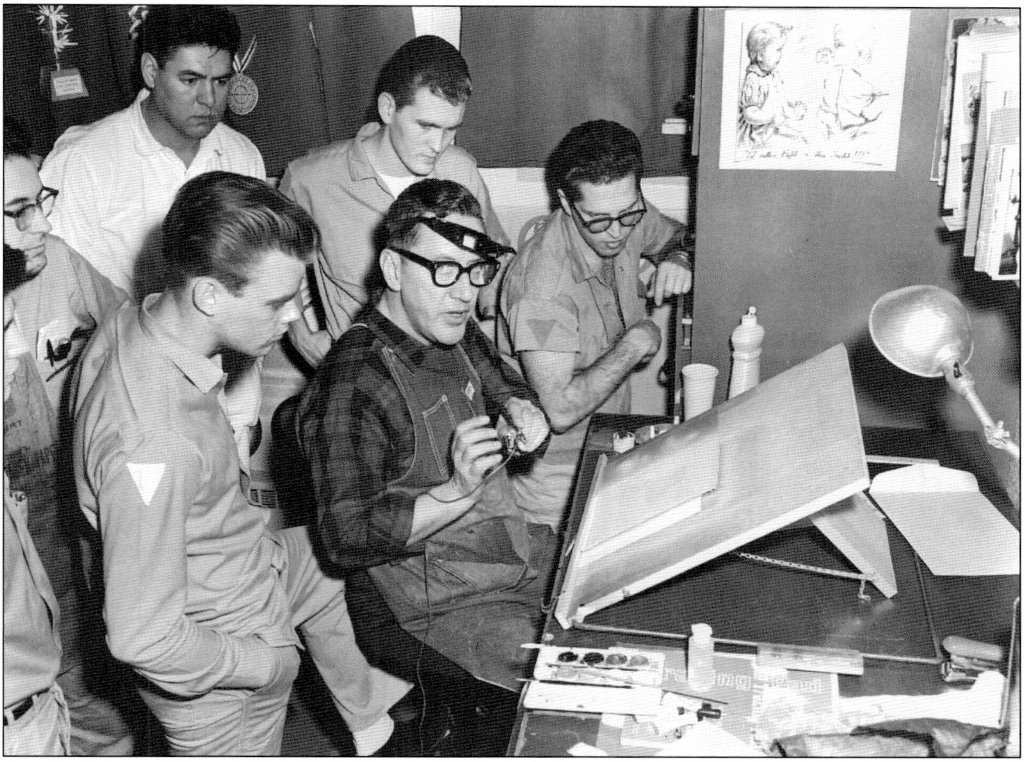

Attentive students gather around their graphics instructor in the 1950s. Vocational training has been a major part of the rehabilitative process at WSR for over 100 years. In 1968, the state-certified vocational-technical training program was staffed by 13 full-time instructors with bachelor's degrees in vocational education.

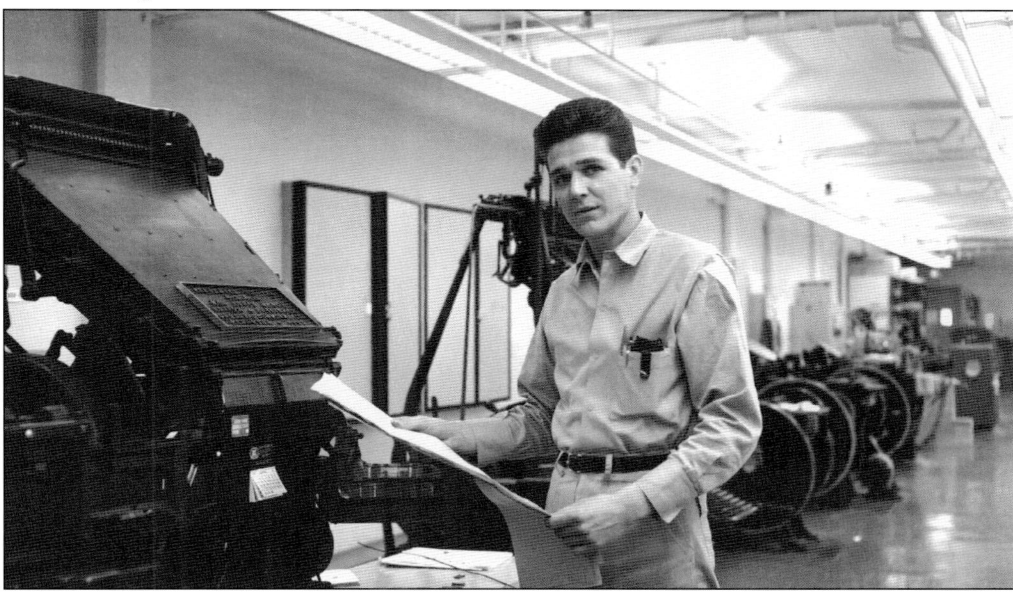

The reformatory print shop produced work for use in the facility and beyond. In 1951, Sanger Powers approved the publication of an inmate publication entitled *Bay Banner*. A print shop inmate checks his work in this *c.* 1960 photograph.

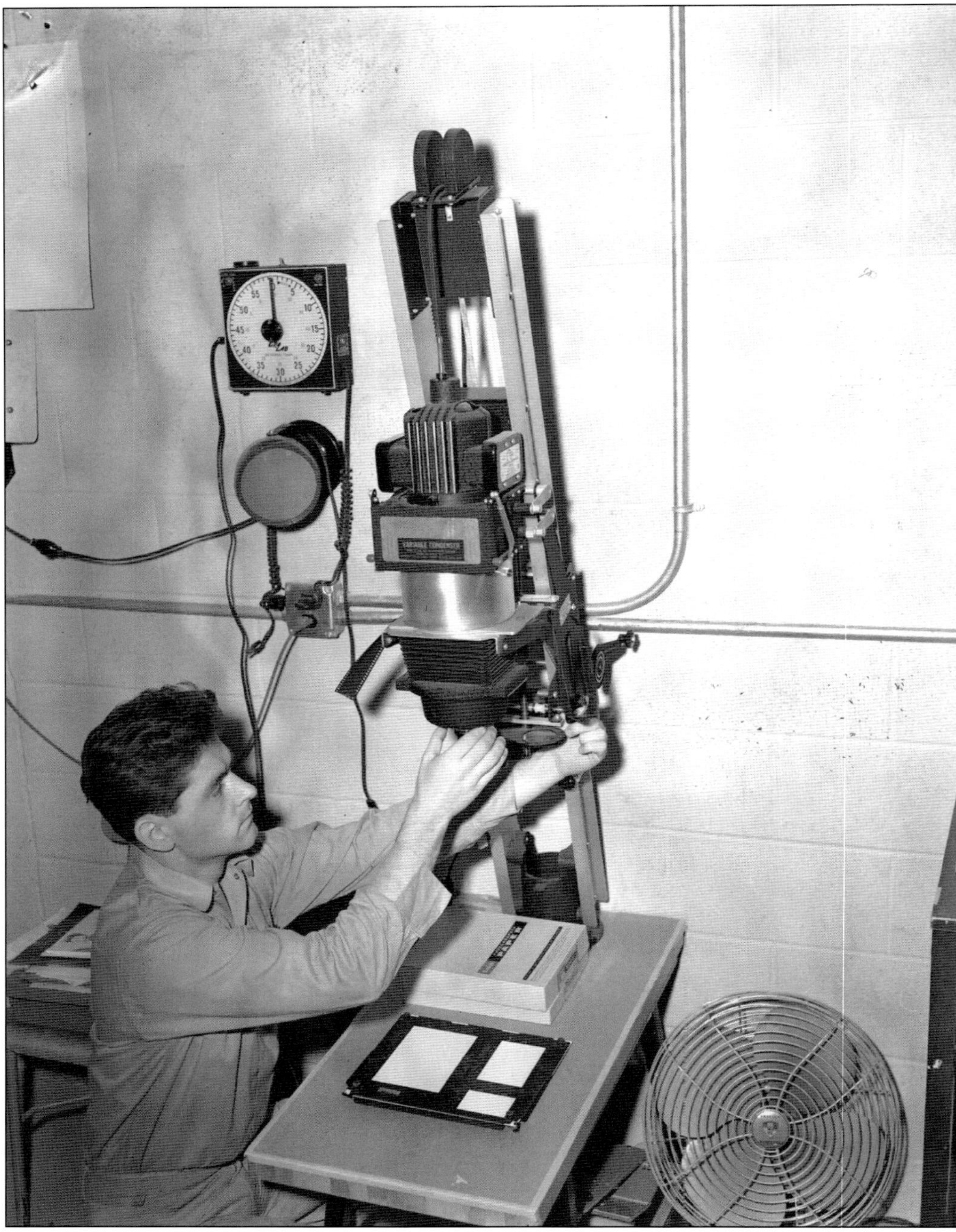

Many inmates took advantage of the opportunities offered at WSR. This inmate works with a copy stand and photograph enlargement equipment. In 1968, the reformatory offered classes in machine shop, barbering, foundry, auto mechanics, sheet metal, woodworking, printing, masonry, drafting, small engine repair, welding, and painting.

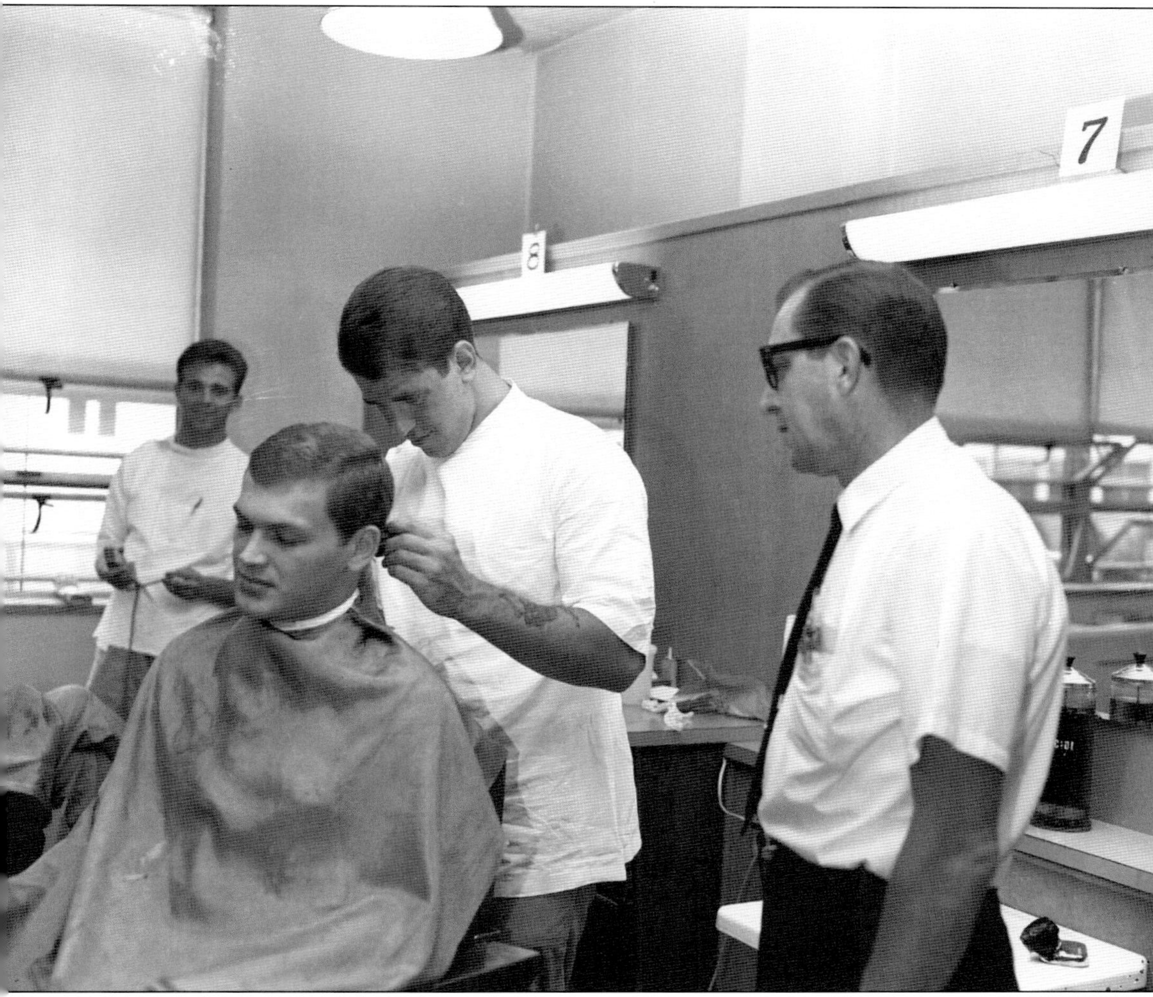

Instructor Merlin Rohloff watches an inmate demonstrate his technique in this photograph taken in the early 1960s. Barbering was one of the most popular vocational programs offered at WSR.

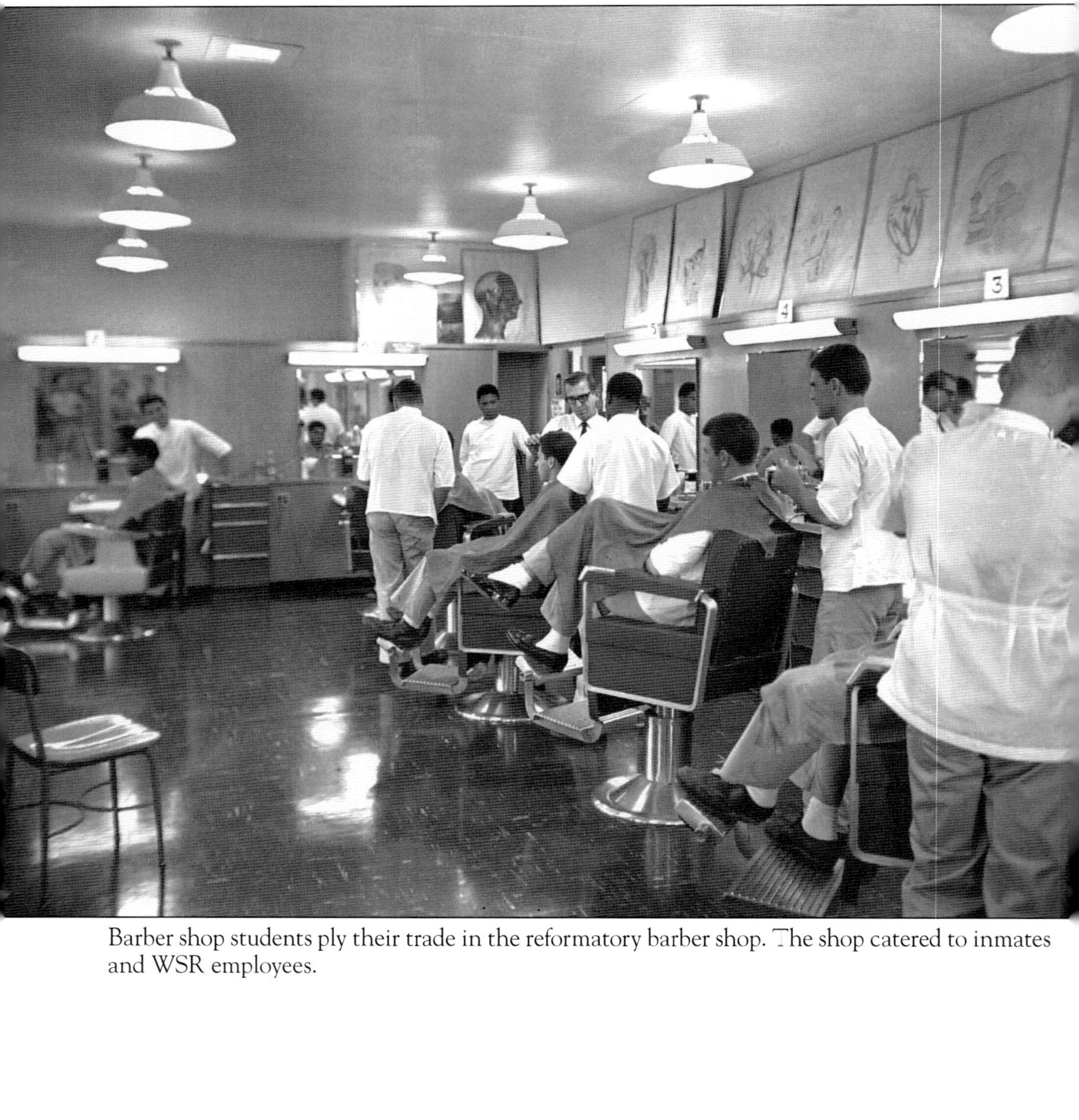

Barber shop students ply their trade in the reformatory barber shop. The shop catered to inmates and WSR employees.

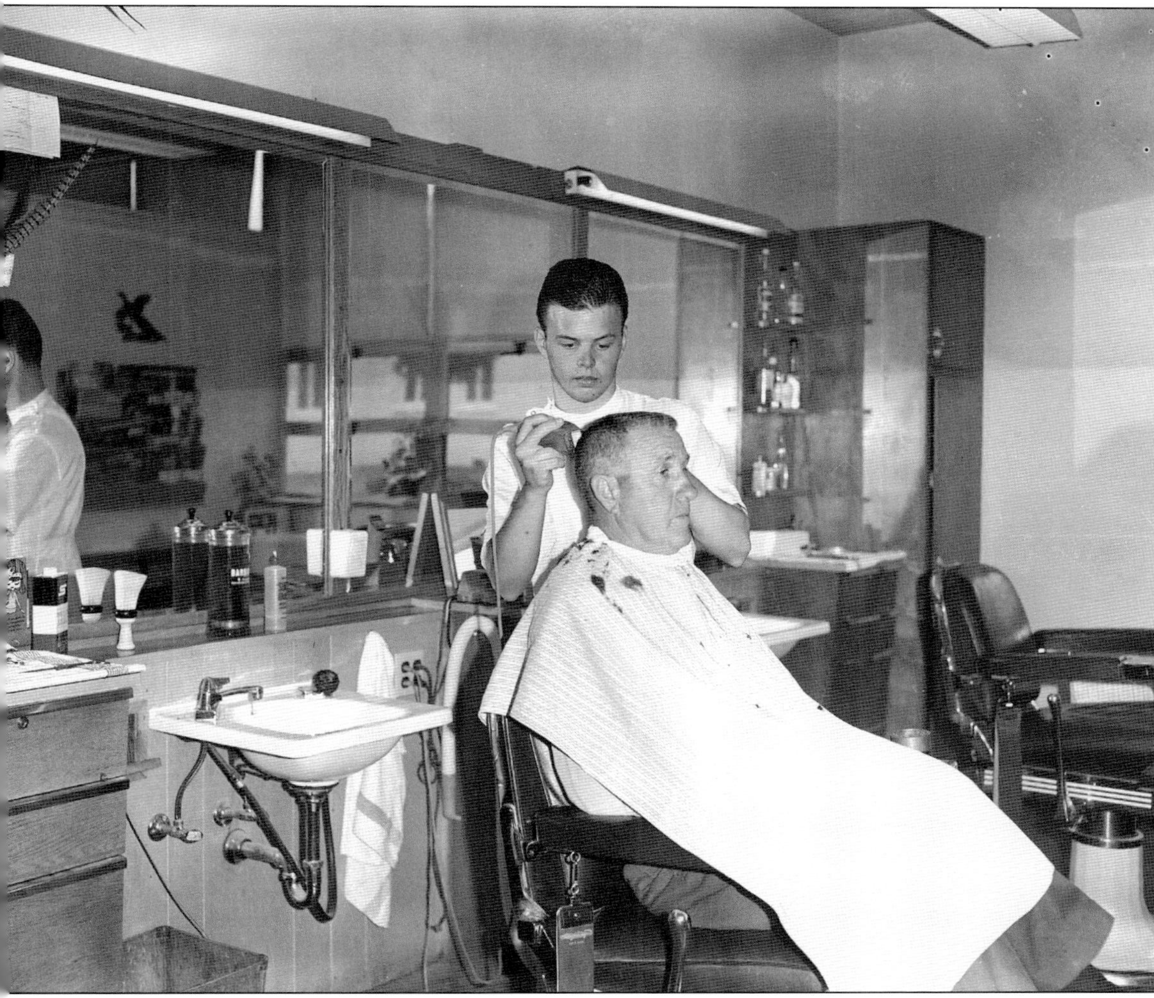

WSR employee Dick Vandewalle enjoys a close haircut in the reformatory barbershop. Inmates learning the trade provided the service under the direction of trained barbers.

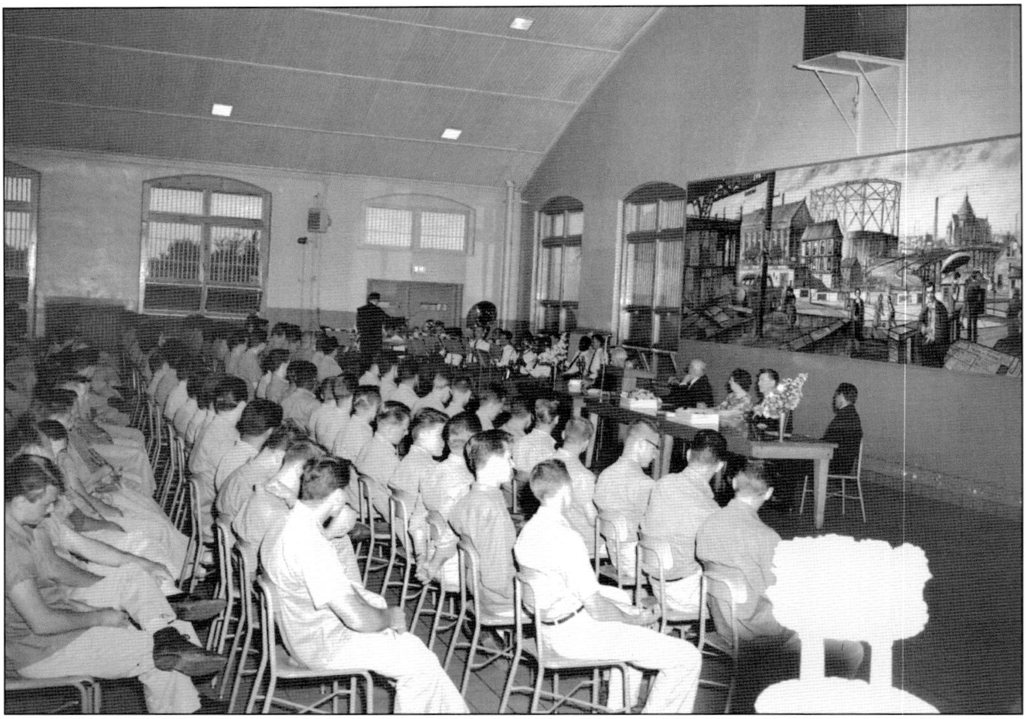

The reformatory band, school dignitaries, and inmates assembled in preparation for an awards ceremony.

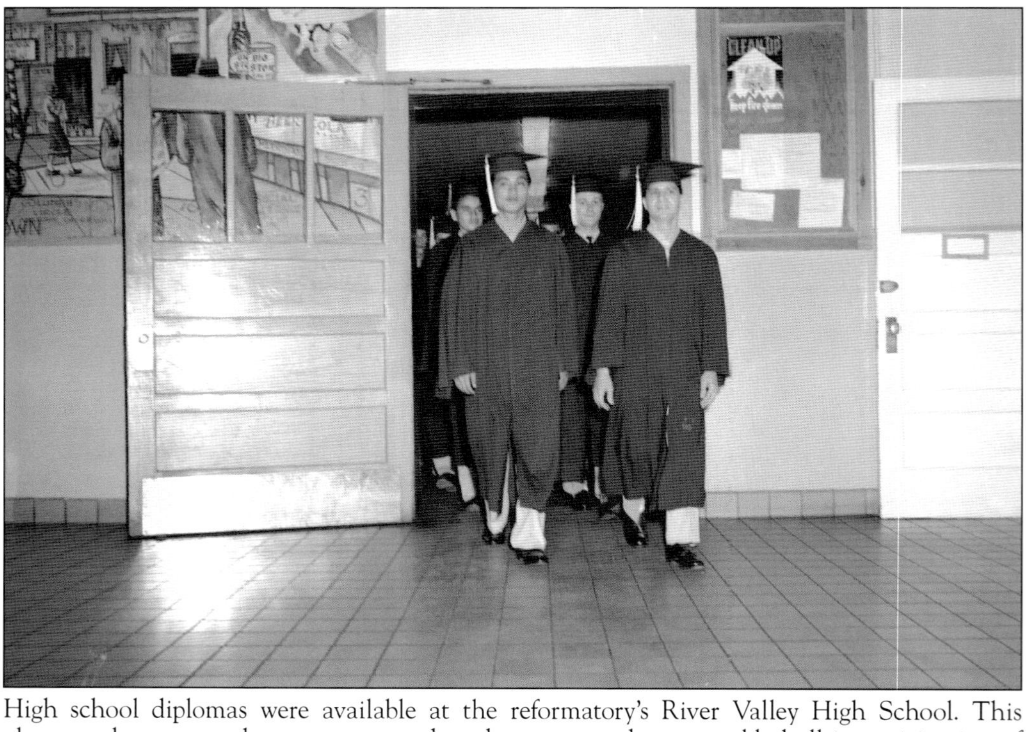

High school diplomas were available at the reformatory's River Valley High School. This photograph captures the moment proud graduates entered an assembly hall in anticipation of receiving their diplomas.

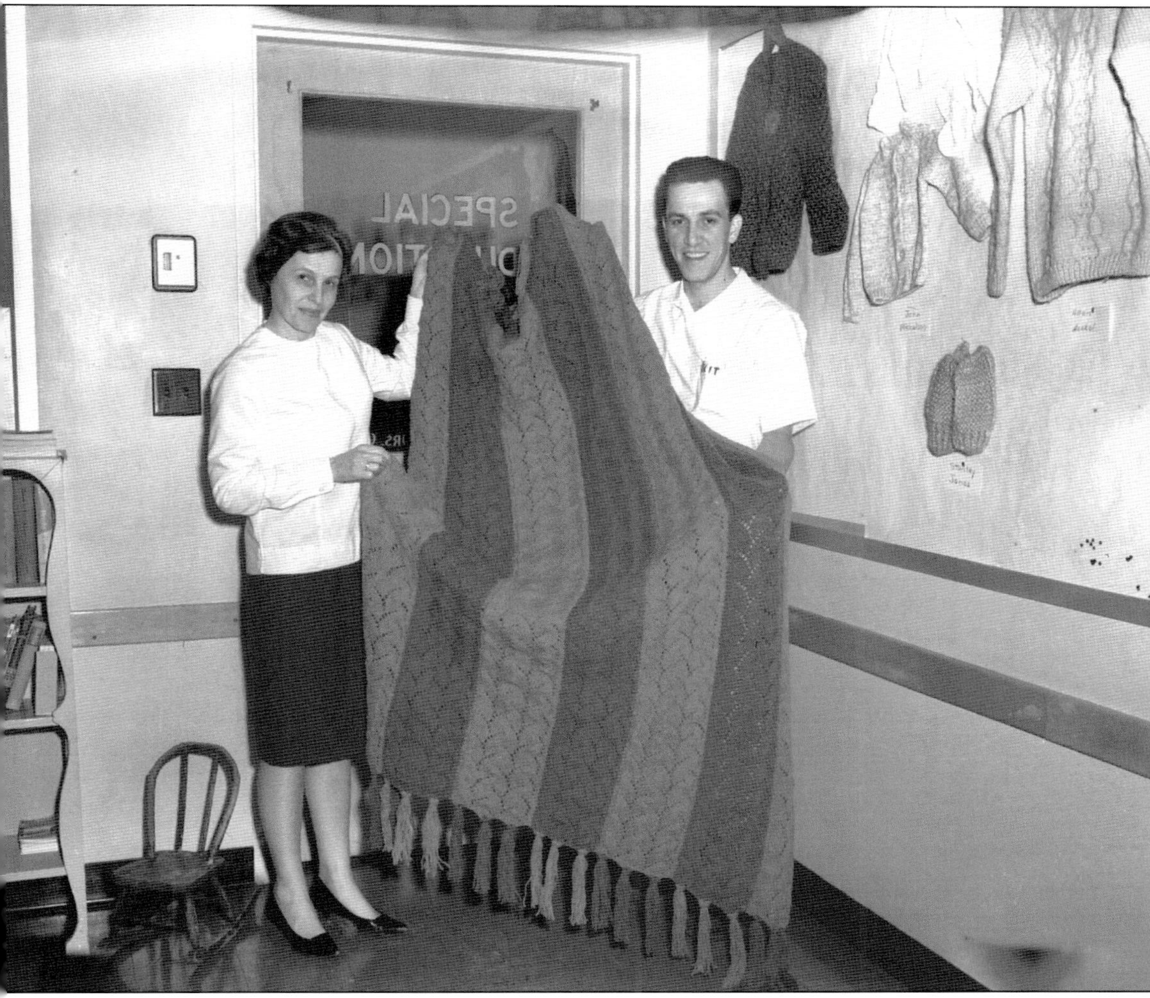

In the 1950s, the WSR witnessed an explosion in vocational and educational activity. Instructor Carol Van Roy introduced a knitting course into the curriculum. A proud inmate shows his latest creation assisted by Van Roy.

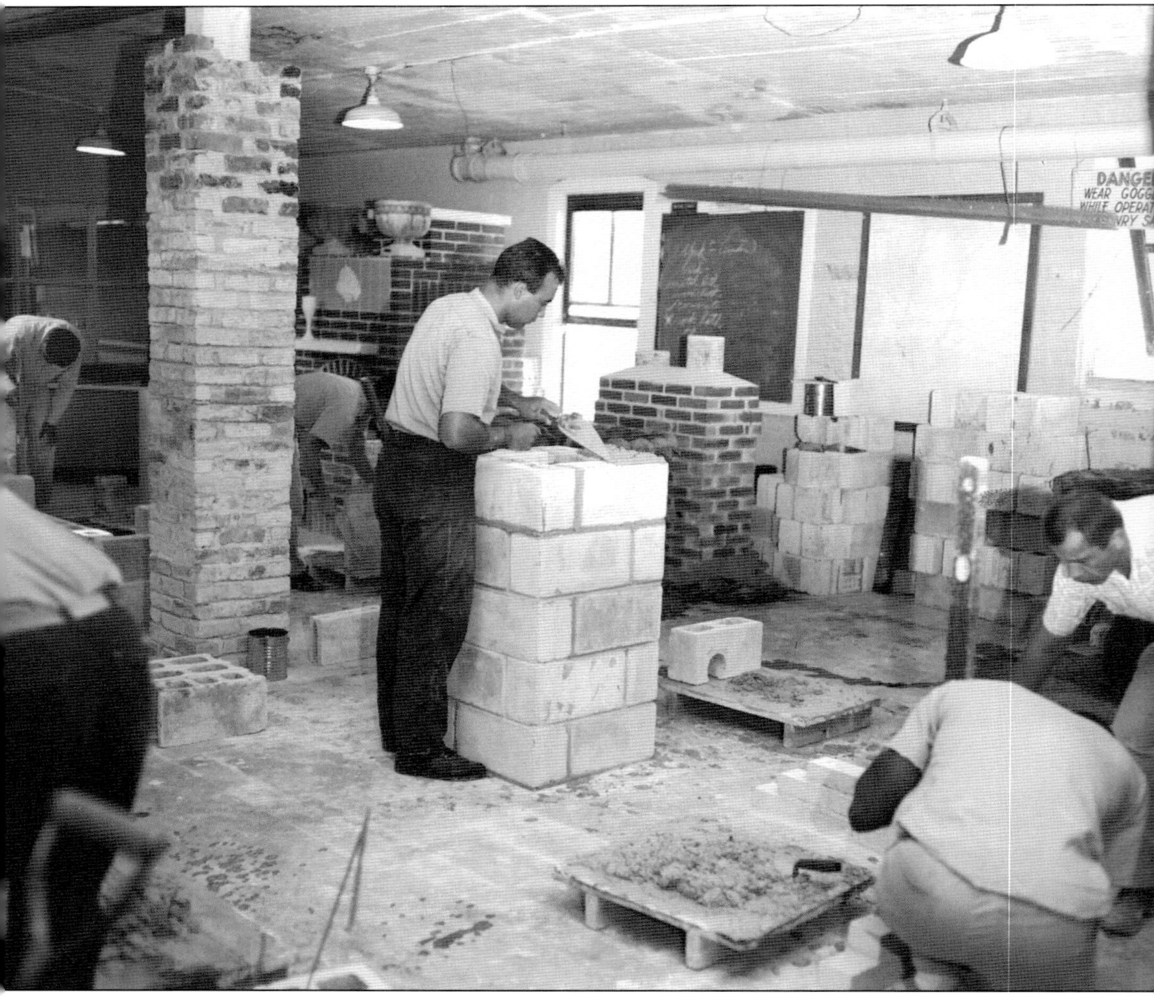

Stonemason Stanley Van Hoff ran the masonry program when this photograph was taken. Programs like this provided inmates with the opportunity to learn a skill and perhaps avoid the return to a life of crime after release.

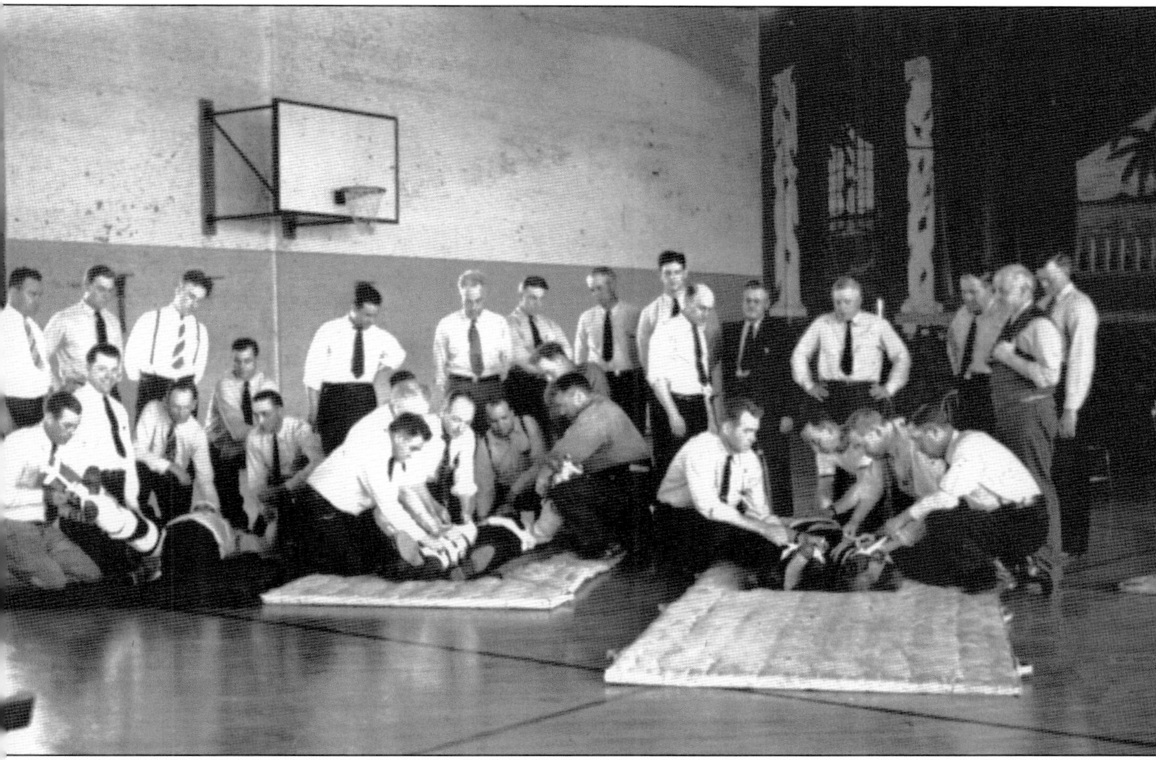

World War II brought many changes to the reformatory. Inmate populations dropped as would-be offenders were recruited for service in increasing numbers. In this photograph taken during the war, reformatory employees practice home defense first aid techniques.

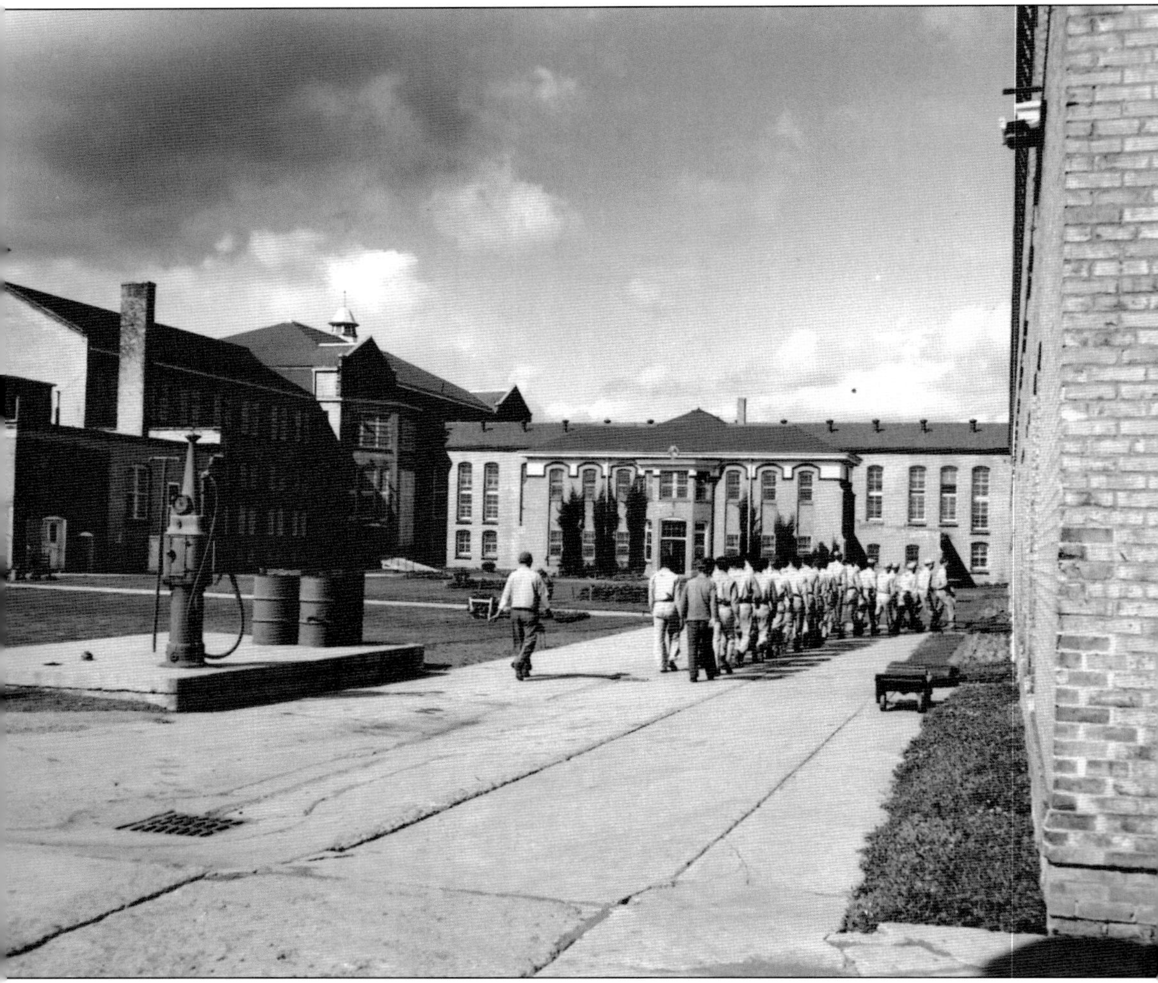

Inmates march on their way to the dormitory and shop building in 1948. At that time, much of the original structures still remained, including the old hospital pictured in the center of the photograph. (Courtesy Green Bay Correctional Institution.)

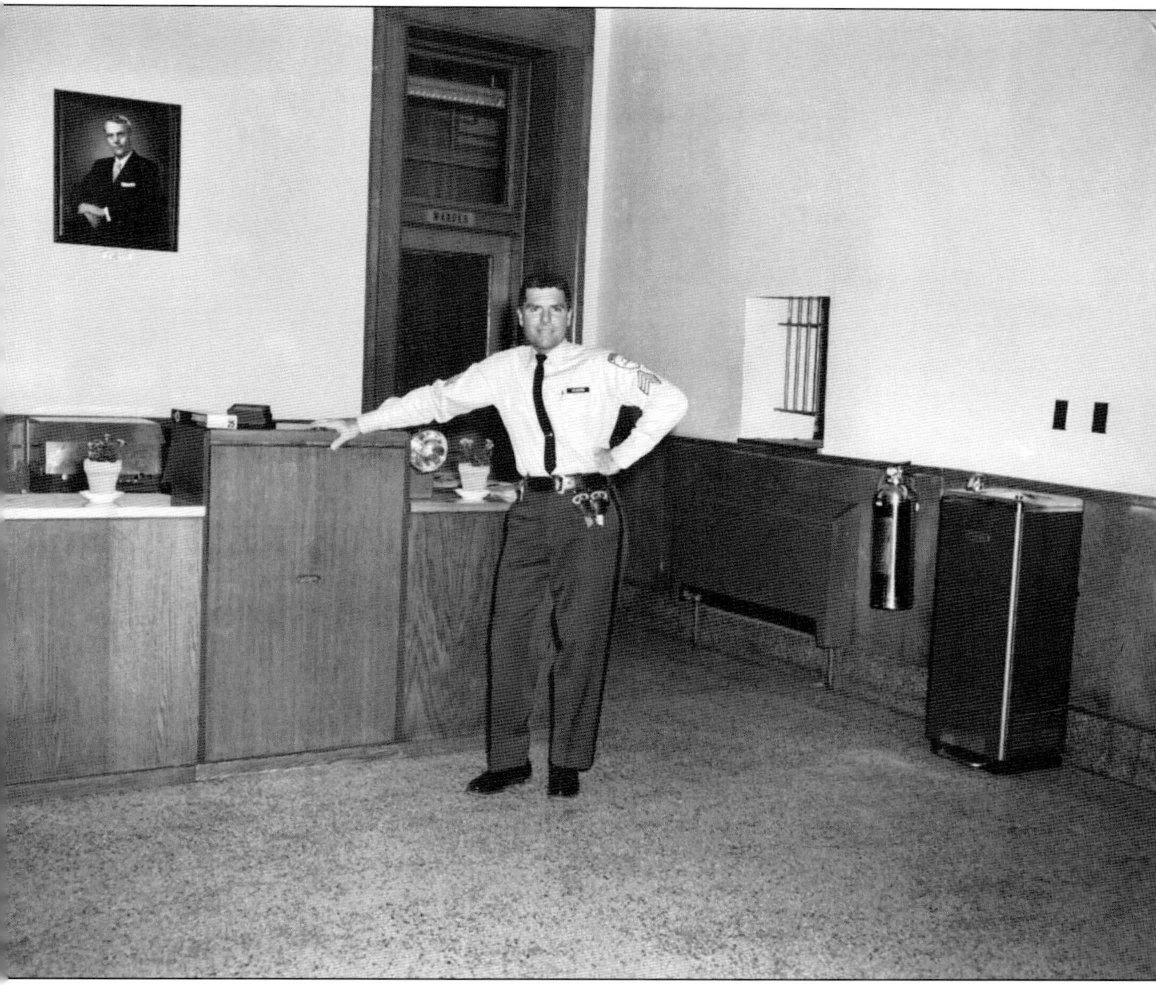

Guards and officers like Sgt. Dick Zegers have always formed the backbone of the reformatory staff. Here Sergeant Zegers poses at the front gate area just below a portrait of Supt. Sanger B. Powers.

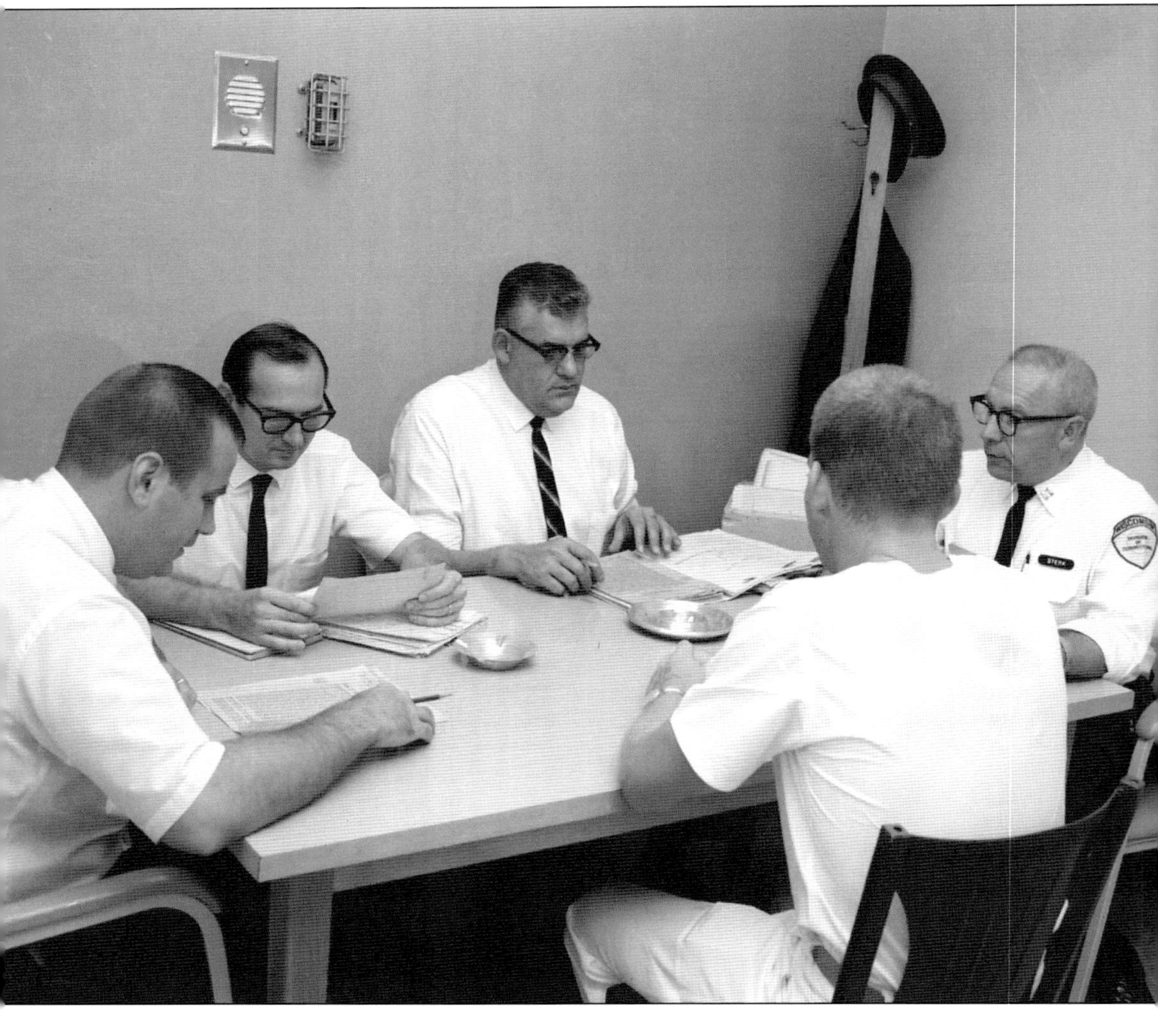

Held every day at 1:00 p.m., the institution court dealt with inmate disciplinary issues. Clockwise starting second from left are reformatory employees Phil Slinger, Don Donlevy, and Jake Sterk. The inmate is unidentified.

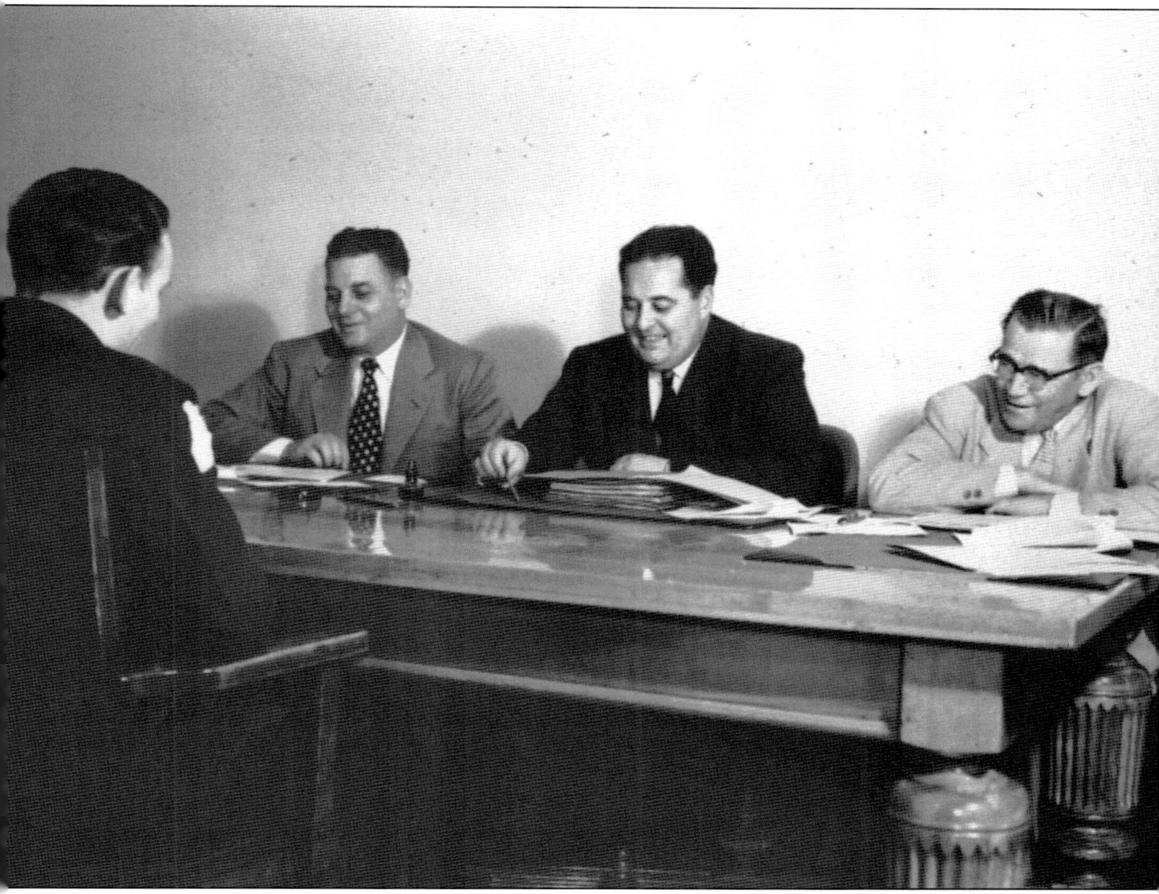

Department of Correction officials Quentin Fern (left), Russell Oswald (center), and B. D. Odegaard interview a potential parolee sometime in the 1950s. The reformatory system was designed to give an inmate a chance to shorten his stay by exhibiting good behavior and academic progress. Those that maintained a satisfactory record became eligible for parole.

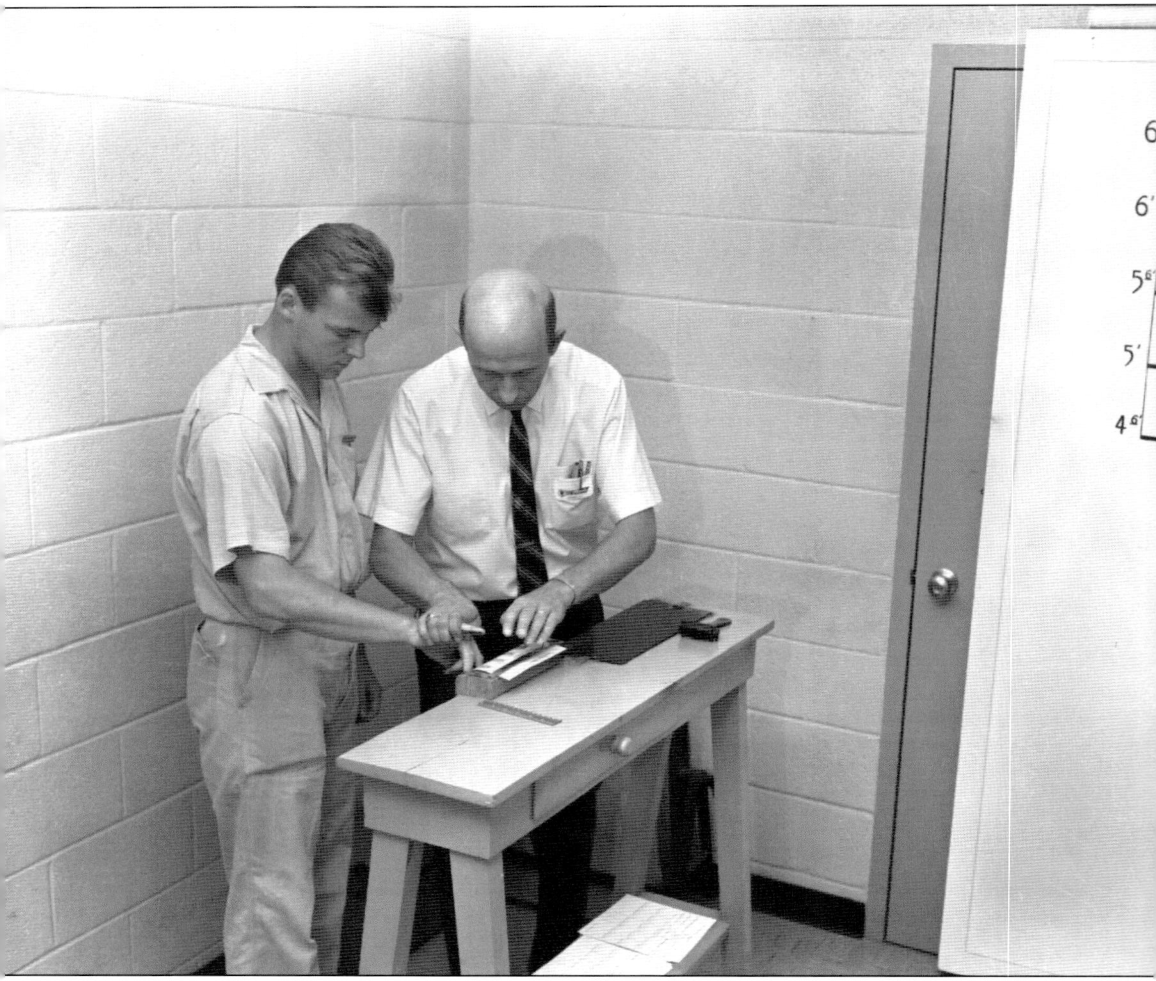

Following procedural routine, Tedd Thomas, fingerprint and records specialist, processes an incoming prisoner. Fingerprint technology replaced an earlier system of criminal identification developed by Alphonse Bertillon that relied on head and body measurements.

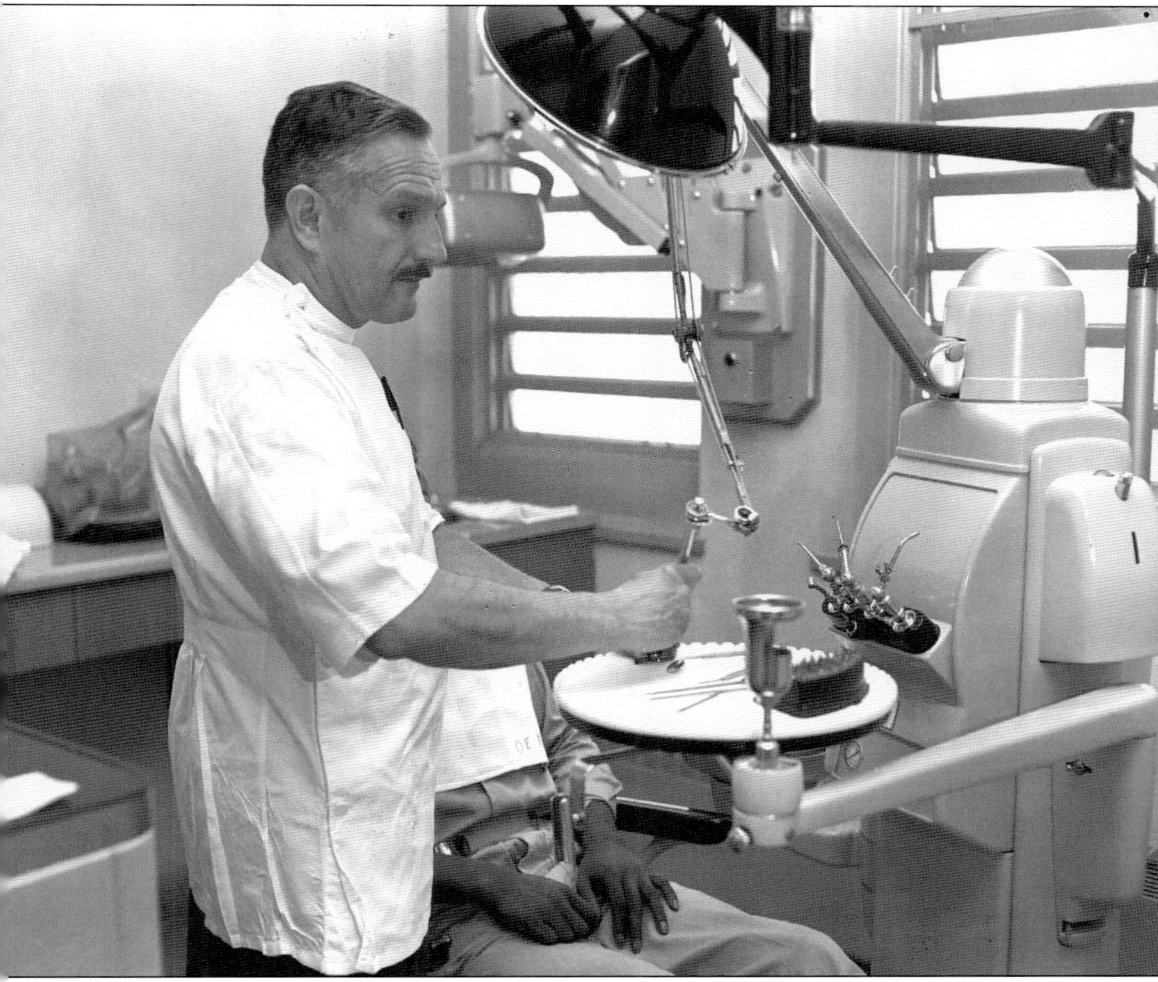

The reformatory dentist tends to an inmate during the 1950s. Inmates received excellent medical care while serving time at WSR.

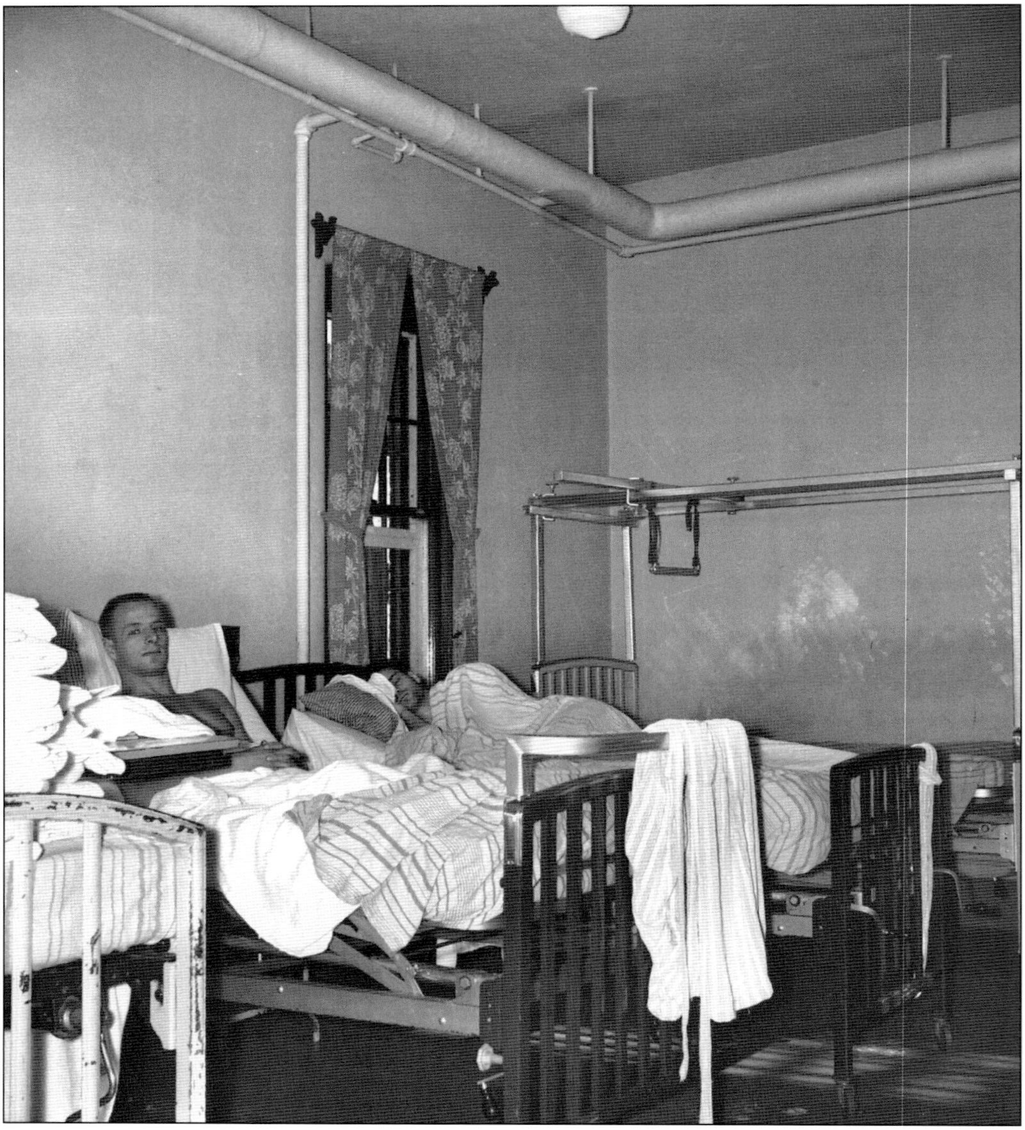

Inmates recovering from illness rest in their beds in the old hospital building. A new treatment center that included the hospital, segregation units, and clinical services was built in the 1960s.

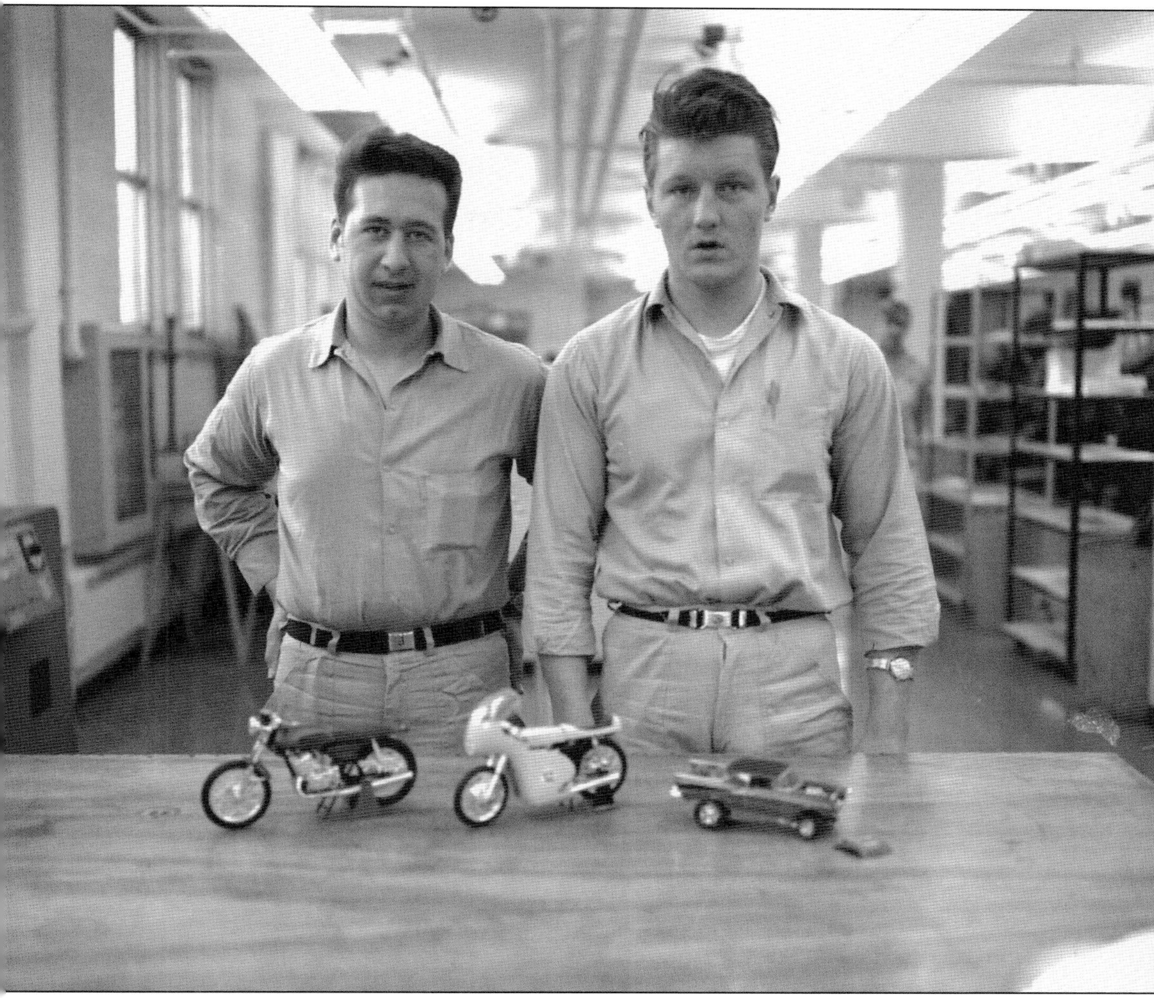

Until the 1970s, most of the inmates at WSR were mere teenage boys or young men in their 20s. Here two young men display their latest model creations. Activities such as this brought a level of humanity to the institution.

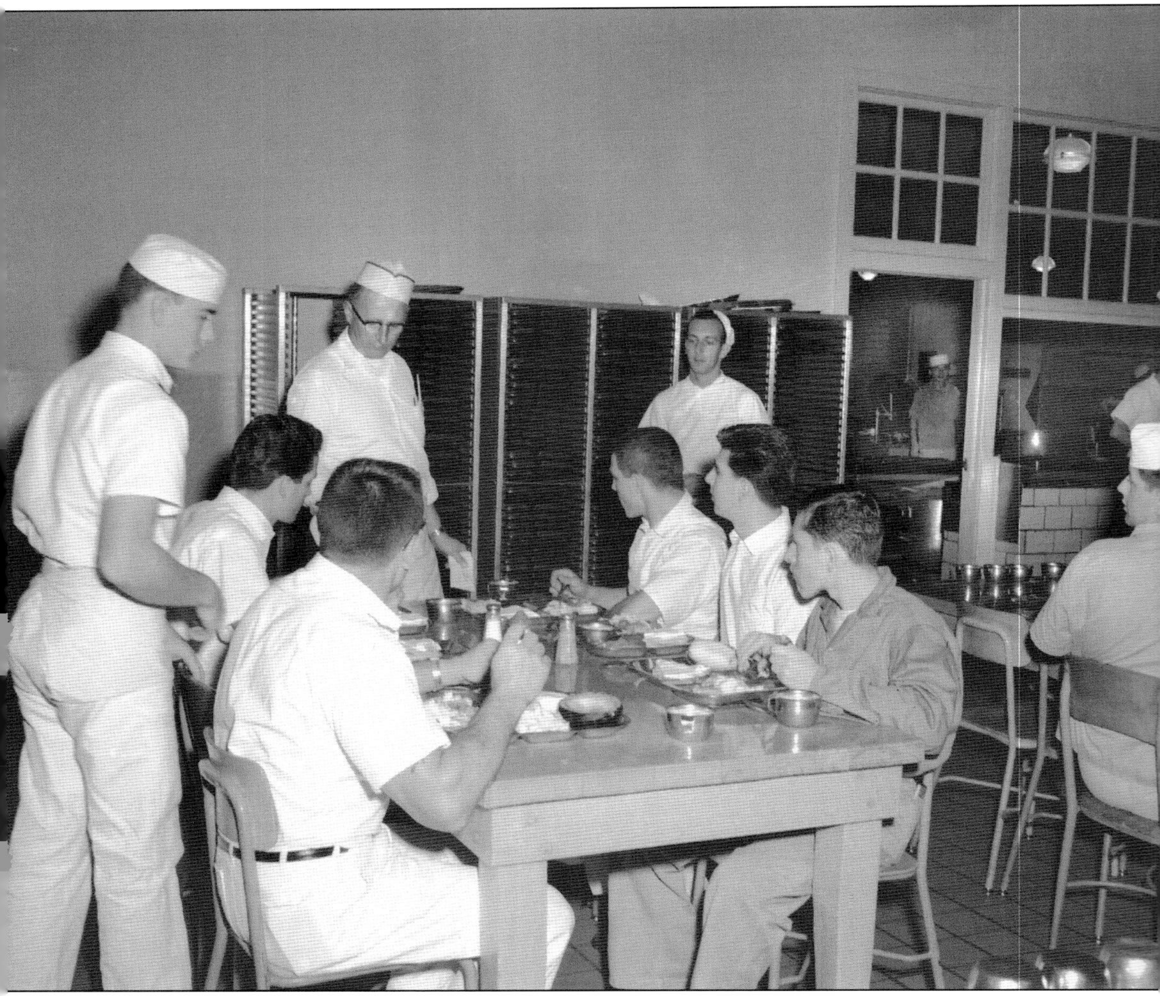

Kitchen staff members gather at a table during meal time. It was Sanger Powers who introduced cafeteria-style dining to the institution. He also abolished the use of food deprivation as a tool of punishment. Both initiatives were understandably popular with the inmates and did much to improve their self-image as men rather than simply "cons."

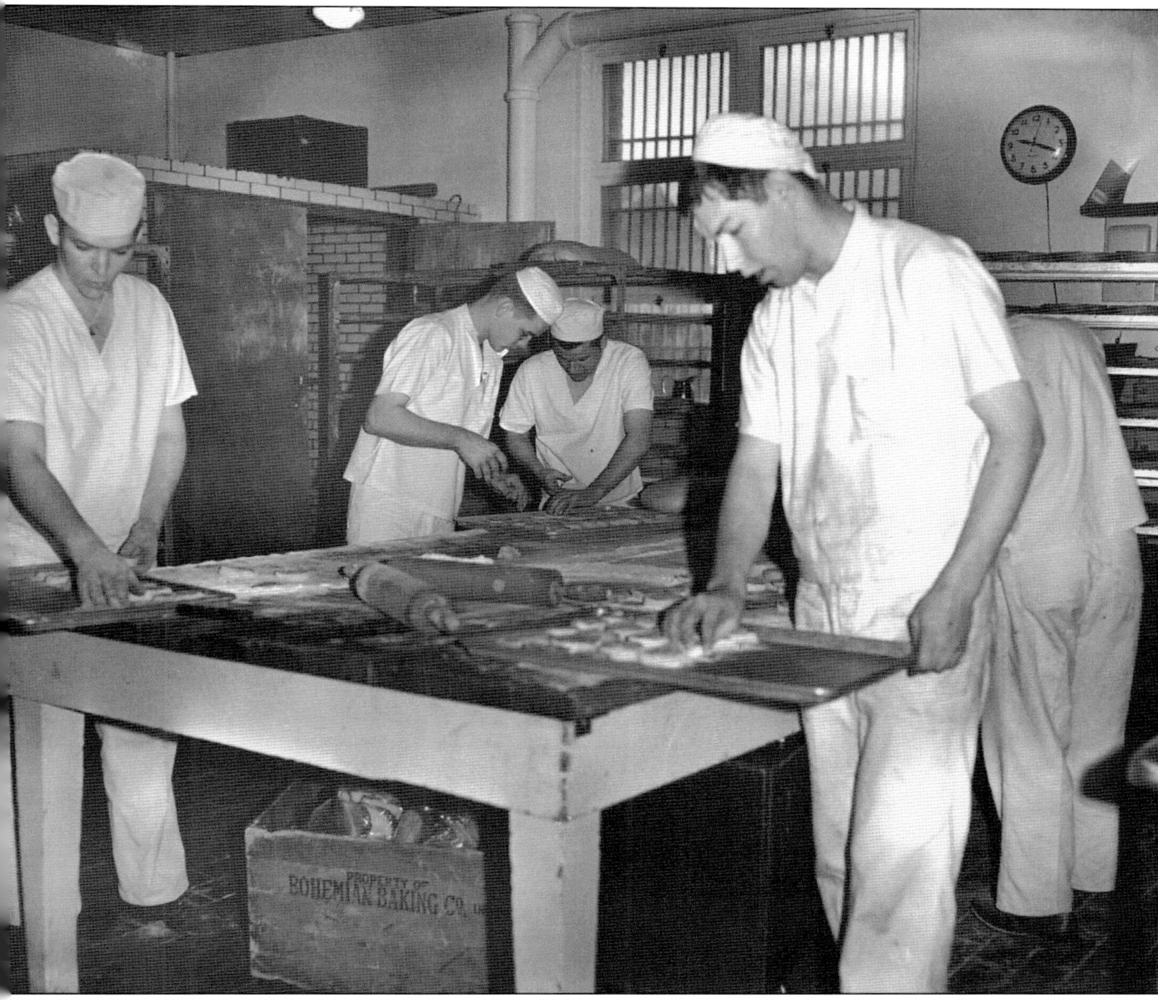

Inmates roll out dough in preparation for the noon meal in this photograph taken in the late 1950s. The opportunity to learn a trade and contribute to the self-sufficiency of the institution was often a great source of pride for many inmates.

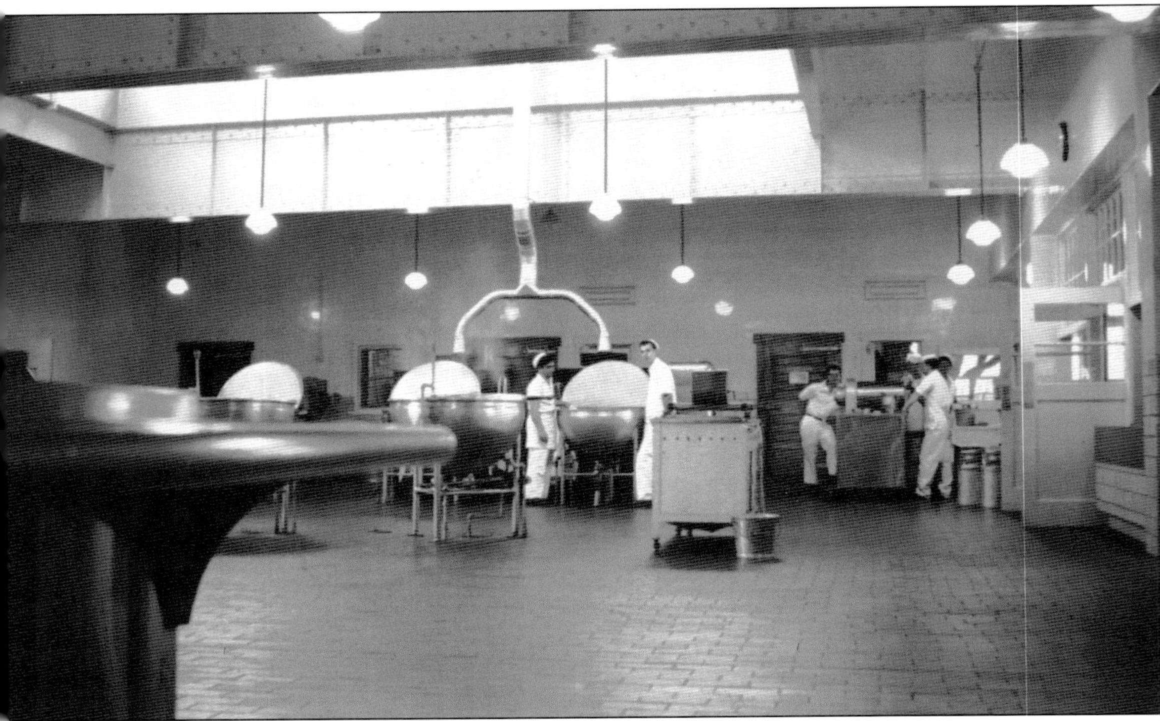

Although the site still retains much of its early appearance, many of the old buildings and room layouts have been destroyed or replaced. The old food service area is shown here. A new dining facility was built in 1982.

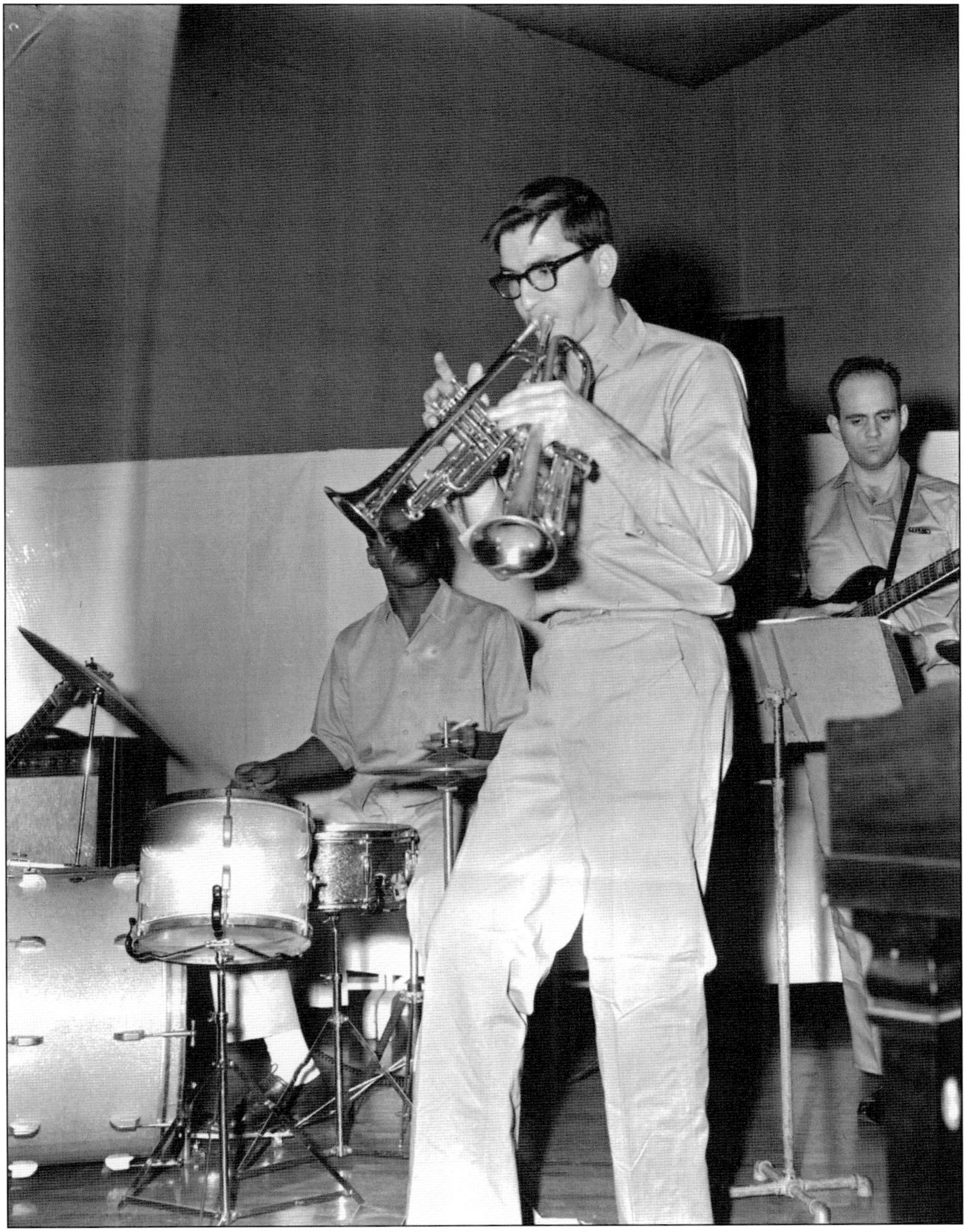

An inmate demonstrates his musical skill during a reformatory performance in the 1960s. Diversionary activities that included musical performances for the benefit of the general prison population helped inmates cope with life behind bars.

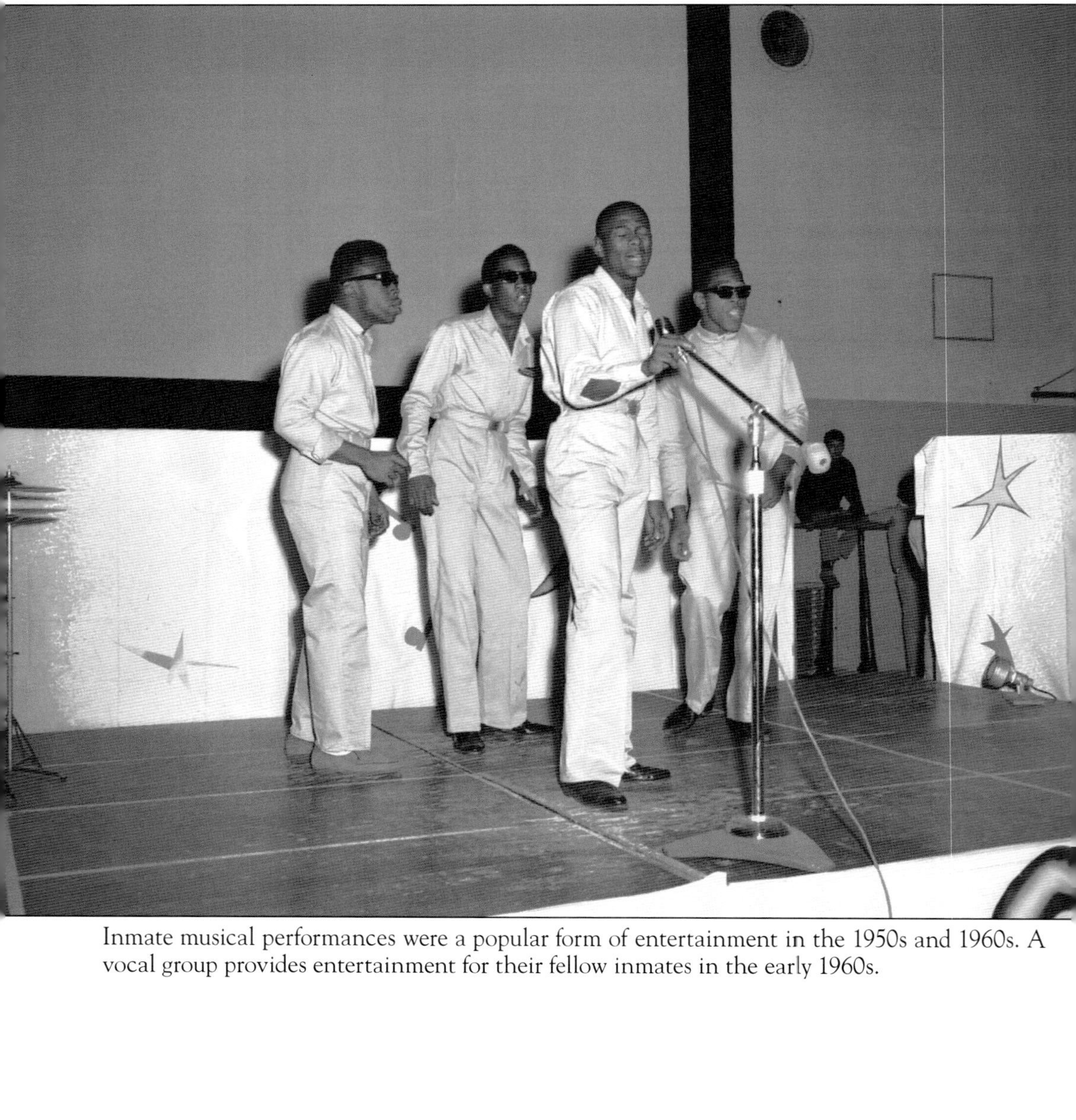

Inmate musical performances were a popular form of entertainment in the 1950s and 1960s. A vocal group provides entertainment for their fellow inmates in the early 1960s.

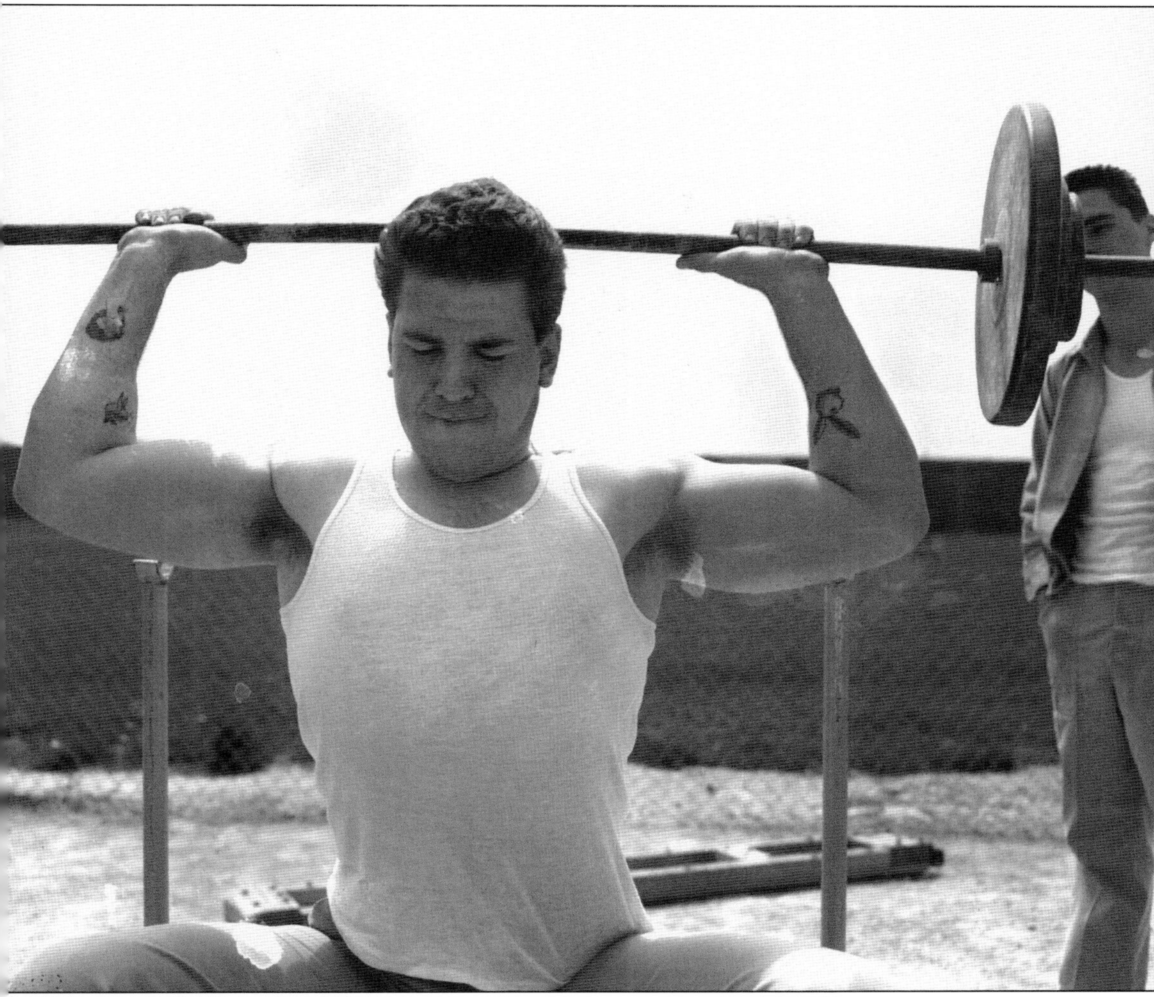

An inmate exercises with weights in the recreation yard sometime during Sanger Powers's tenure as superintendent. Weight lifting, baseball, football, and swimming were a part of the recreational activities offered to inmates, particularly during the progressive era following the 1940s.

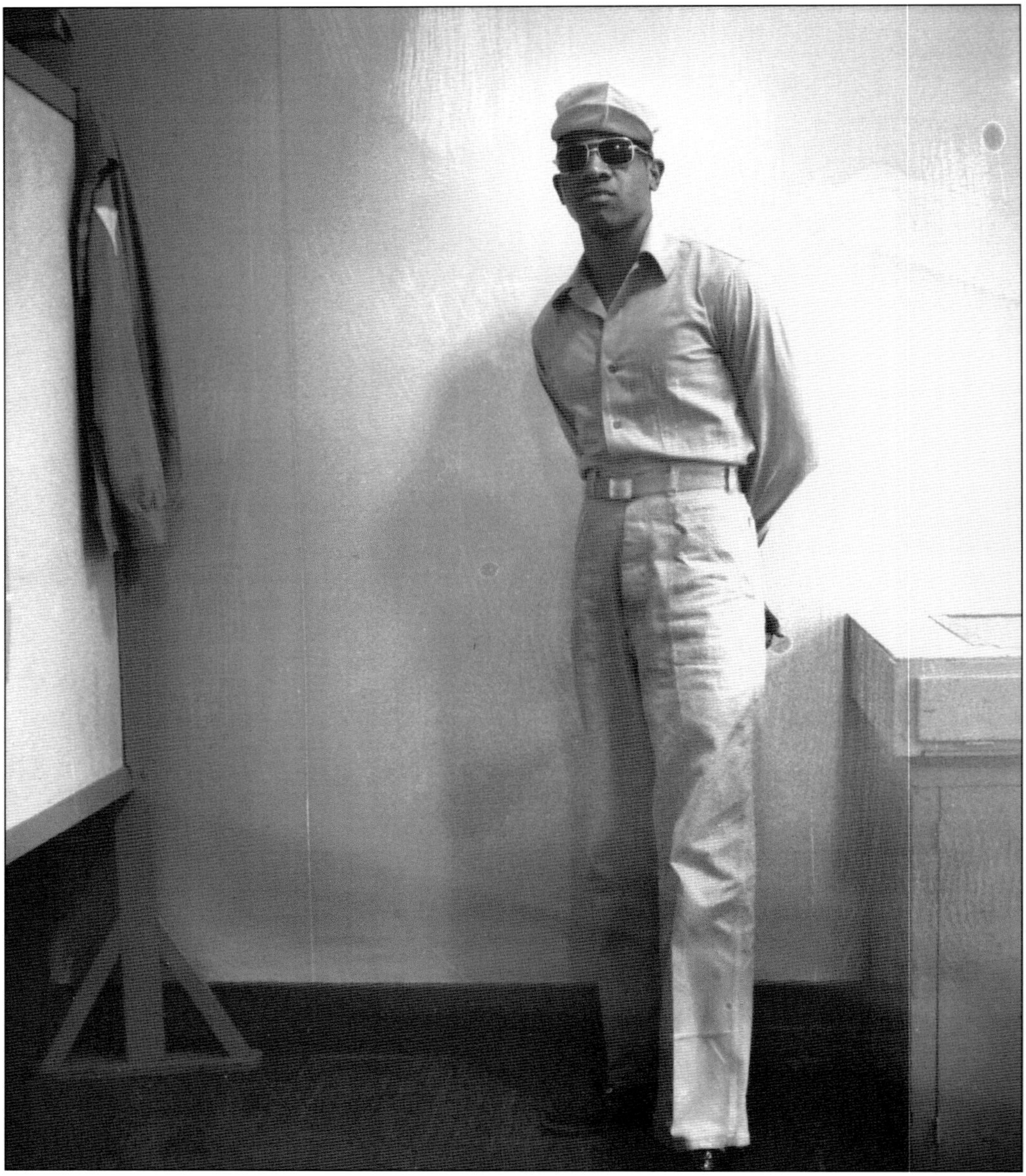

Prison uniforms allowed little leeway for individuality. This inmate, however, managed to impart his own style to an otherwise drab uniform. He is also representative of an increasingly urban inmate population that began to grow after World War II.

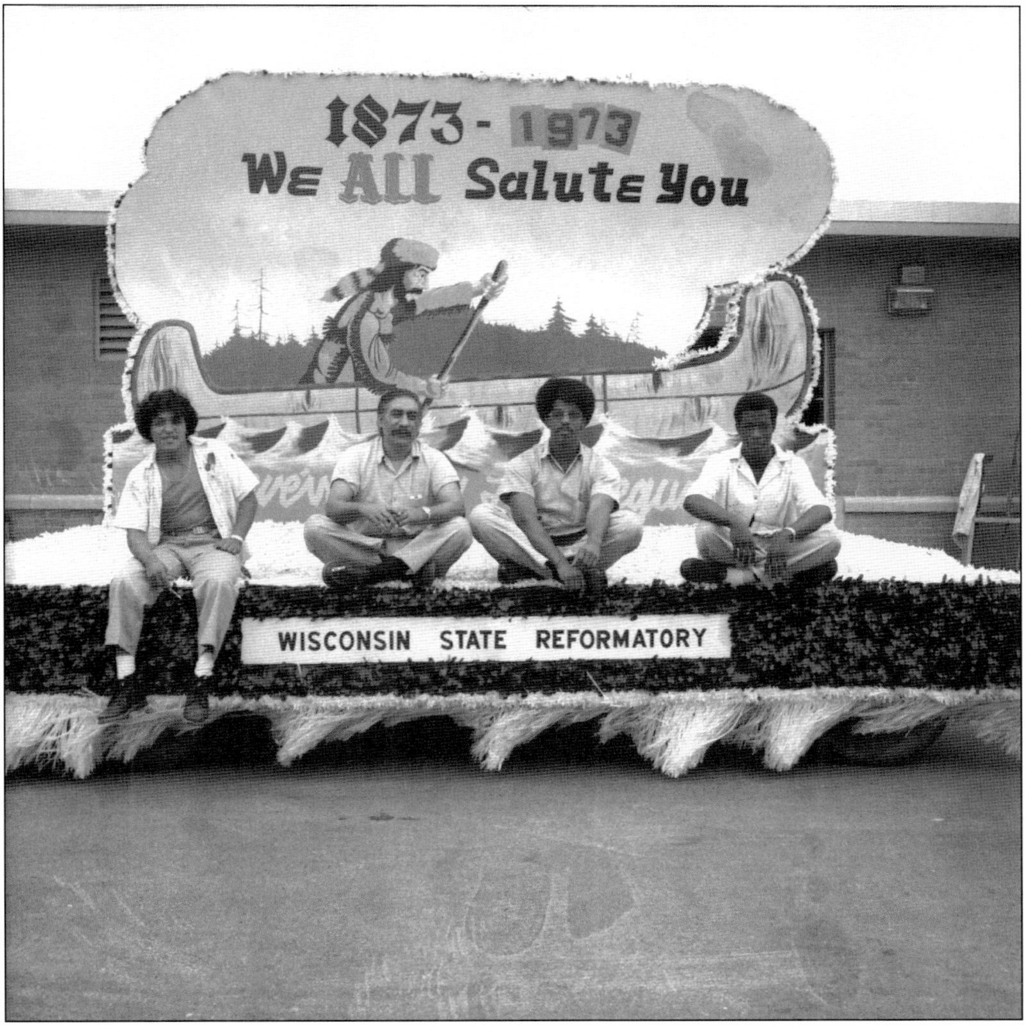

In 1973, reformatory inmates helped the village of Allouez celebrate its centennial by building a parade float. Community interaction was a hallmark of the reformatory's culture through the early 1970s. Its transformation into a maximum security prison for adult offenders, however, has reduced such interaction

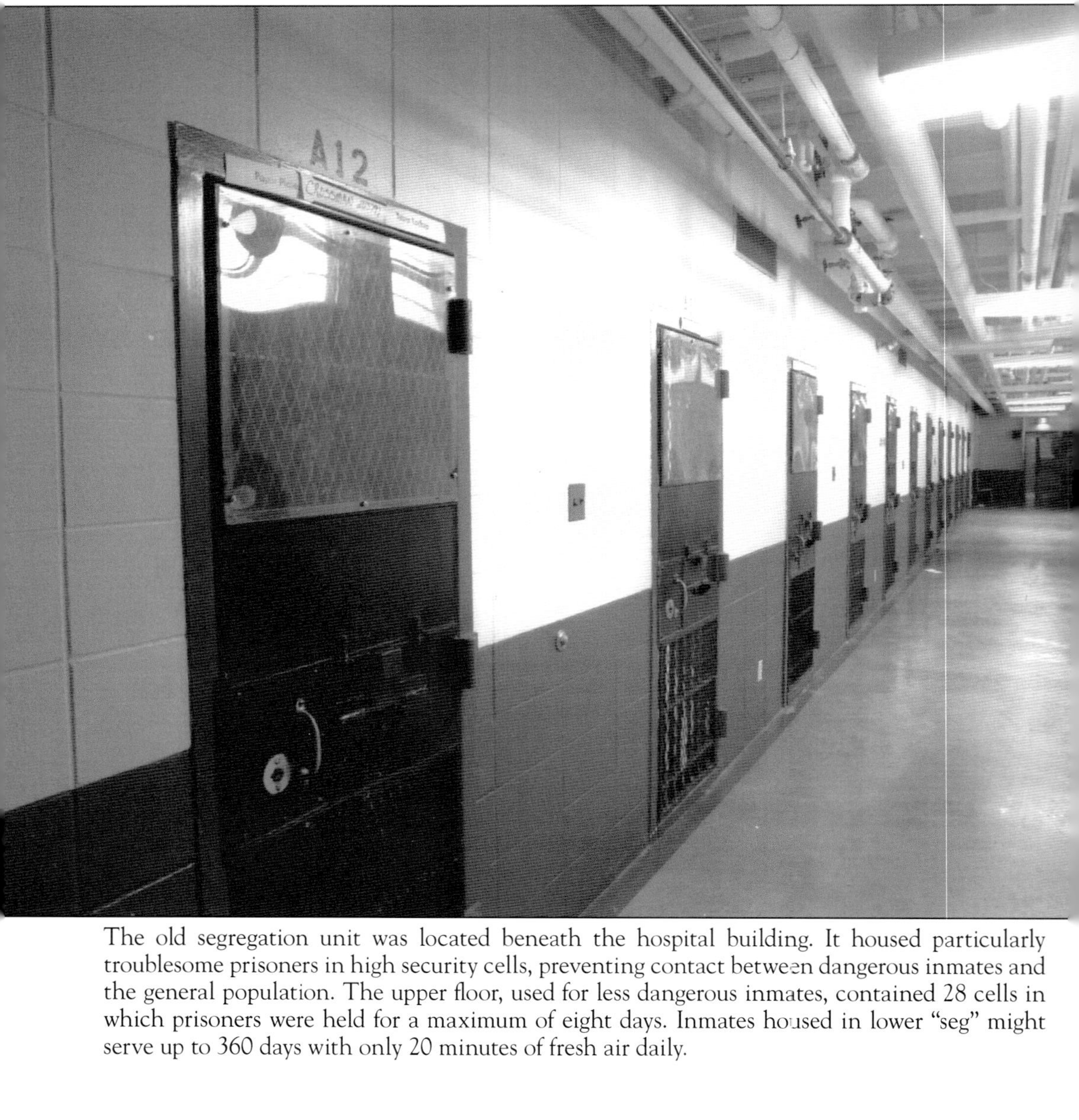

The old segregation unit was located beneath the hospital building. It housed particularly troublesome prisoners in high security cells, preventing contact between dangerous inmates and the general population. The upper floor, used for less dangerous inmates, contained 28 cells in which prisoners were held for a maximum of eight days. Inmates housed in lower "seg" might serve up to 360 days with only 20 minutes of fresh air daily.

Eight

REFORMATORY RIOT

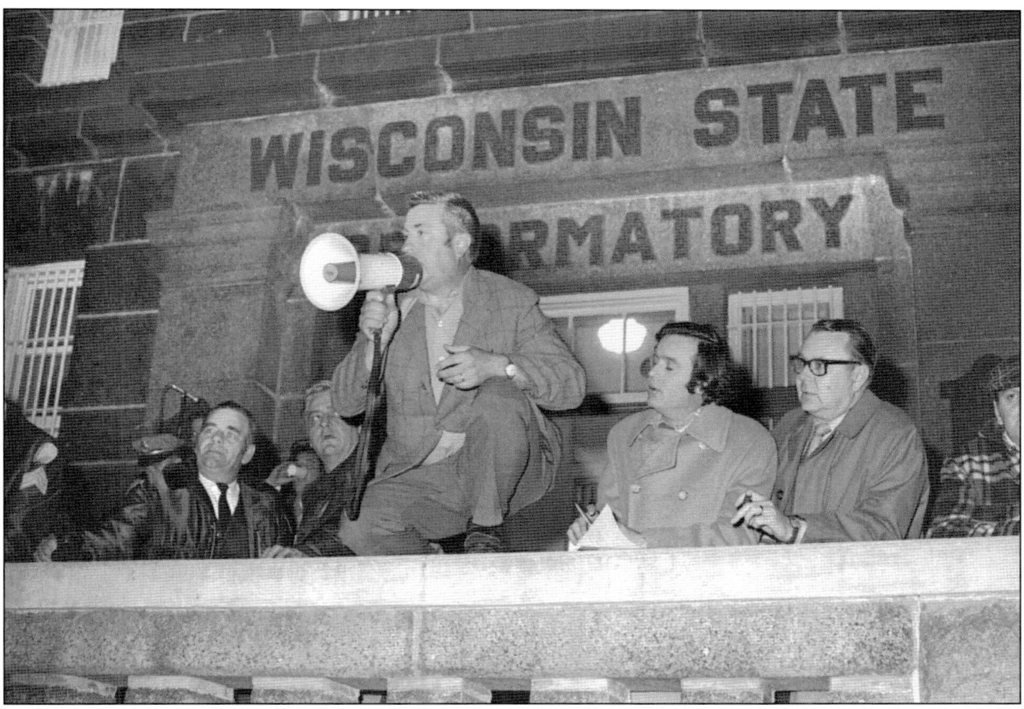

Norb Froelich, Brown County sheriff, barks orders through a bullhorn on the night of the November 12, 1971, riot. A dining hall disturbance led to significant damage to the dormitory and classrooms; guards as well as inmates were injured.

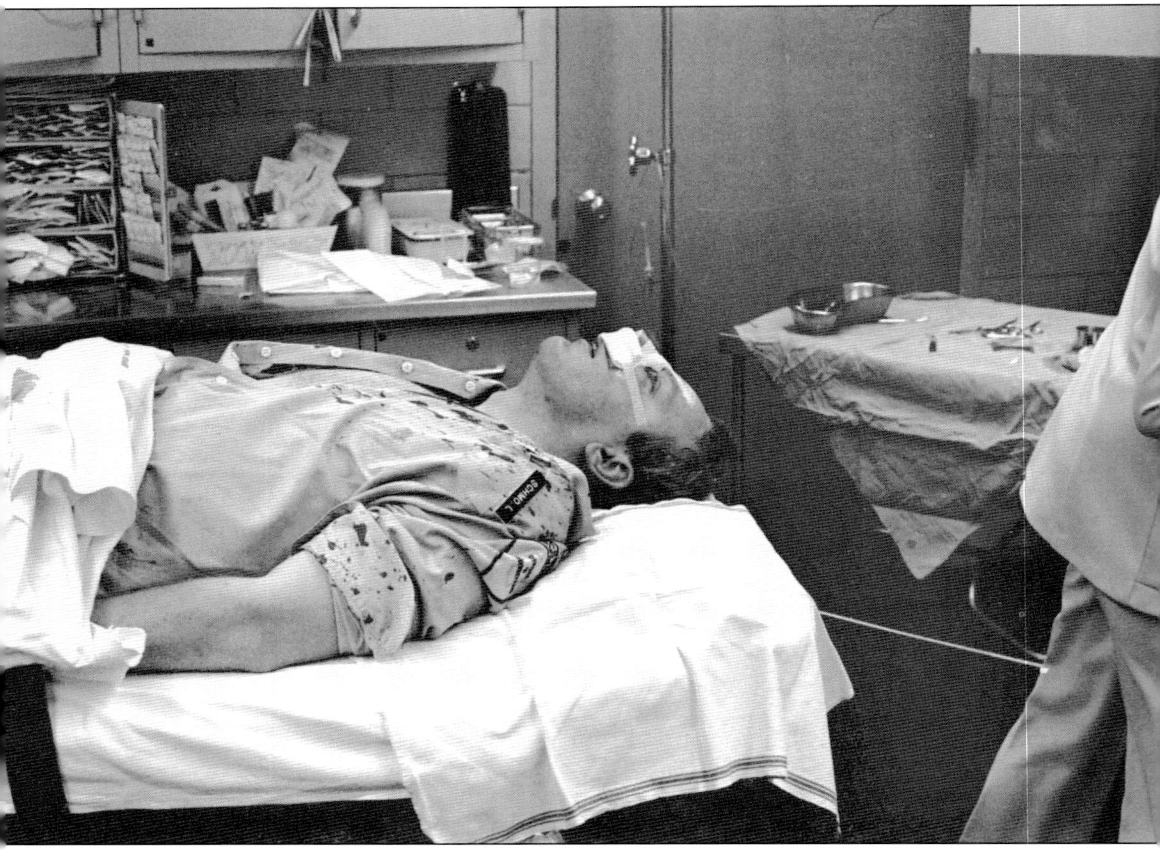

Reformatory corrections officer Herbert Schmoll lies bloodied and battered at Green Bay's Bellin Hospital in the aftermath of the prison's largest inmate riot. Schmoll suffered a broken nose and lacerations.

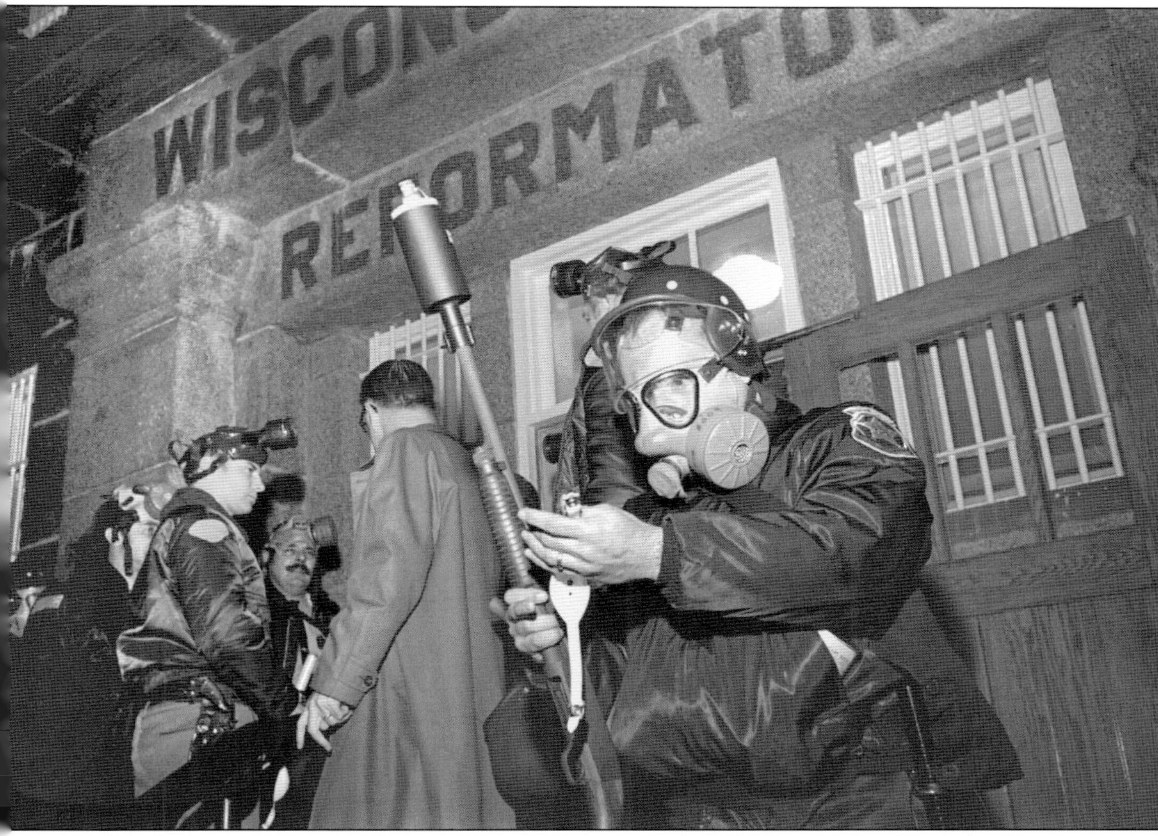

Armed with a riot shotgun and teargas, a Brown County sheriff's deputy stands on the front steps of the reformatory on the night of the biggest riot in reformatory history. Over 350 law enforcement officers were called into action that evening.

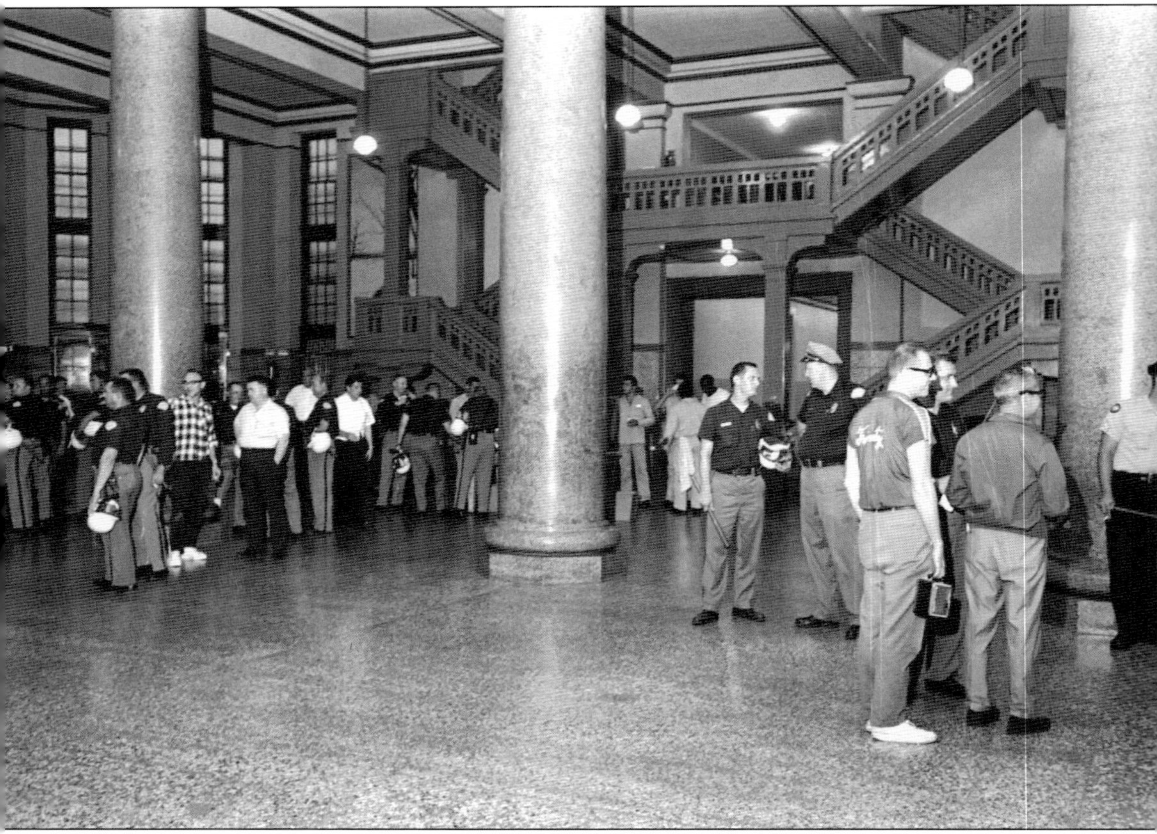

Reformatory corrections personnel and Brown County law enforcement officers gather in the prison's rotunda on November 13, 1971, the day after the riot.

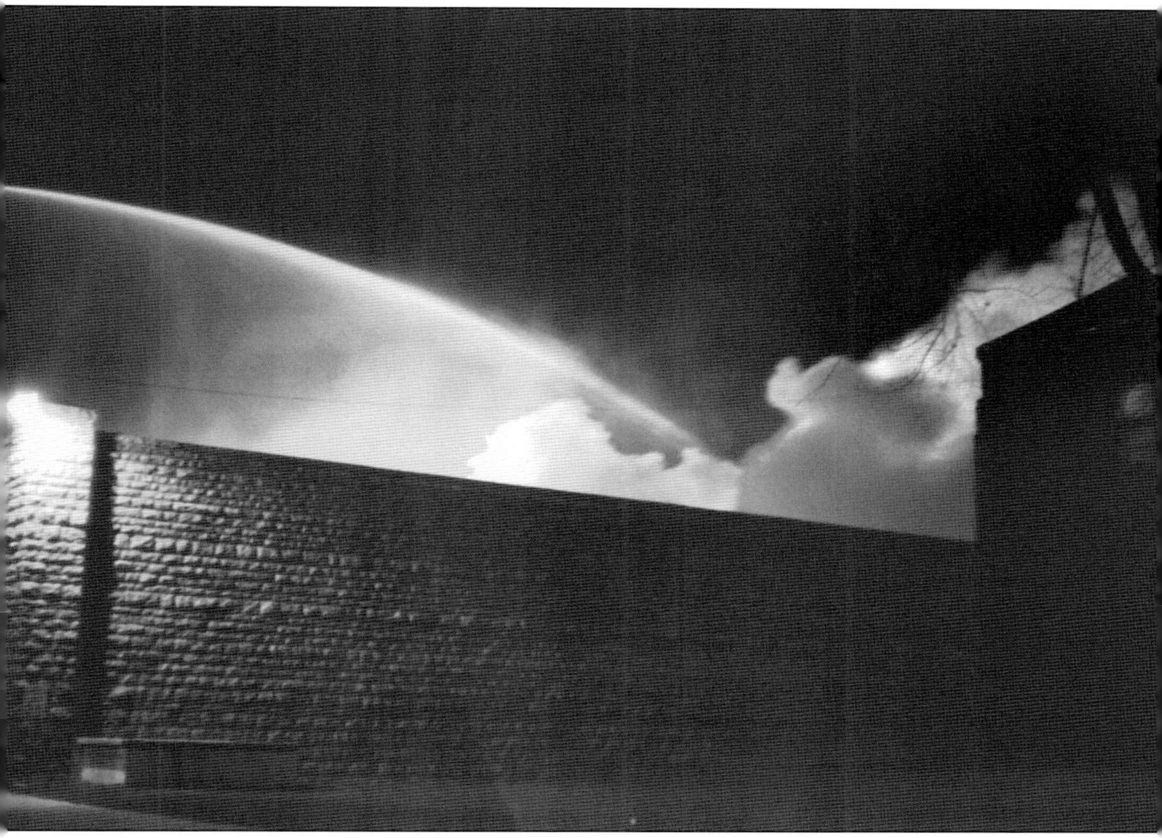

Under the glowing night sky, a fire unit pours gallons of water into the burning dormitory from over the north wall on the night of November 12, 1971. Damage caused by the inmates was estimated at $250,000.

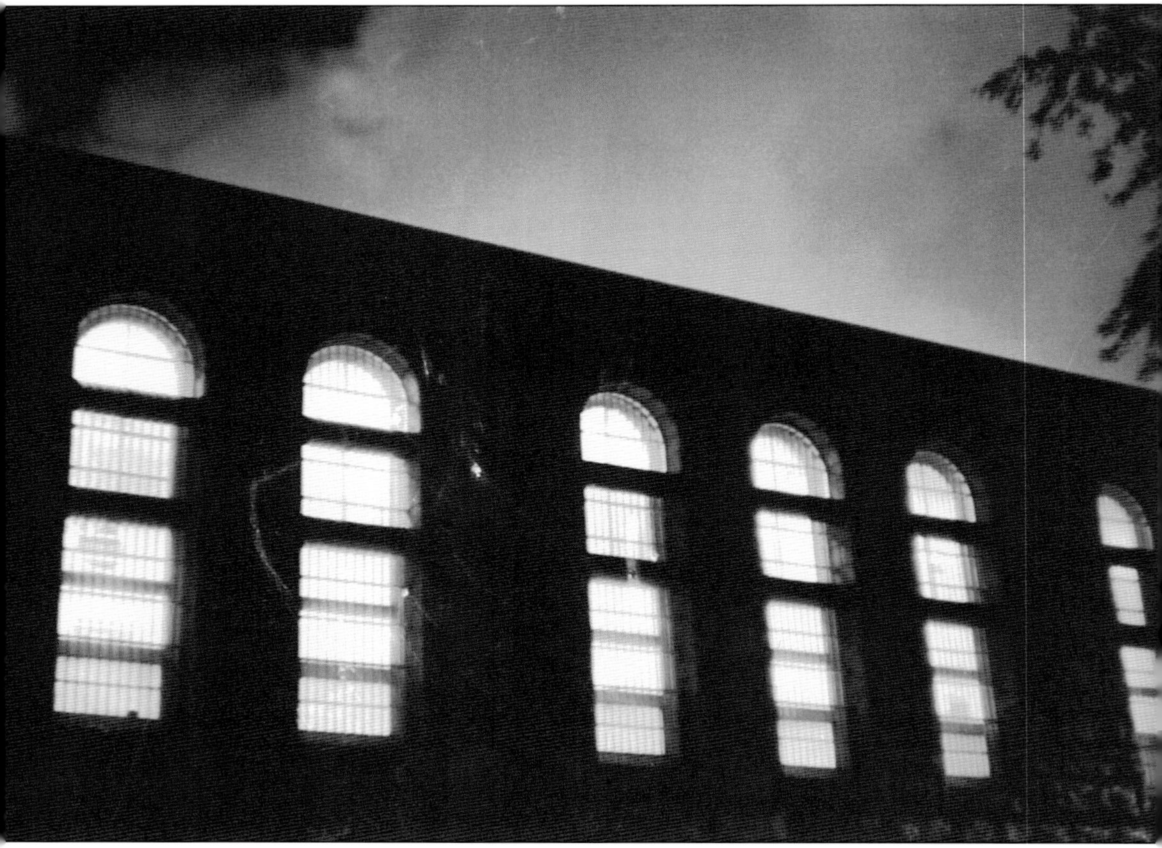

Lights of the North Cell Hall burn brightly against the smoke-filled sky as firefighters continue to fight the blaze that destroyed much of the old dormitory building. After disciplinary hearings, inmates Herman Krause and Willie Moore were both placed in "indefinite lower segregation" for their roles in the disturbance. Both individuals claimed that they were denied their procedural rights. They later filed a class action suit on behalf of all the inmates at Green Bay, who were "denied the right to due process."

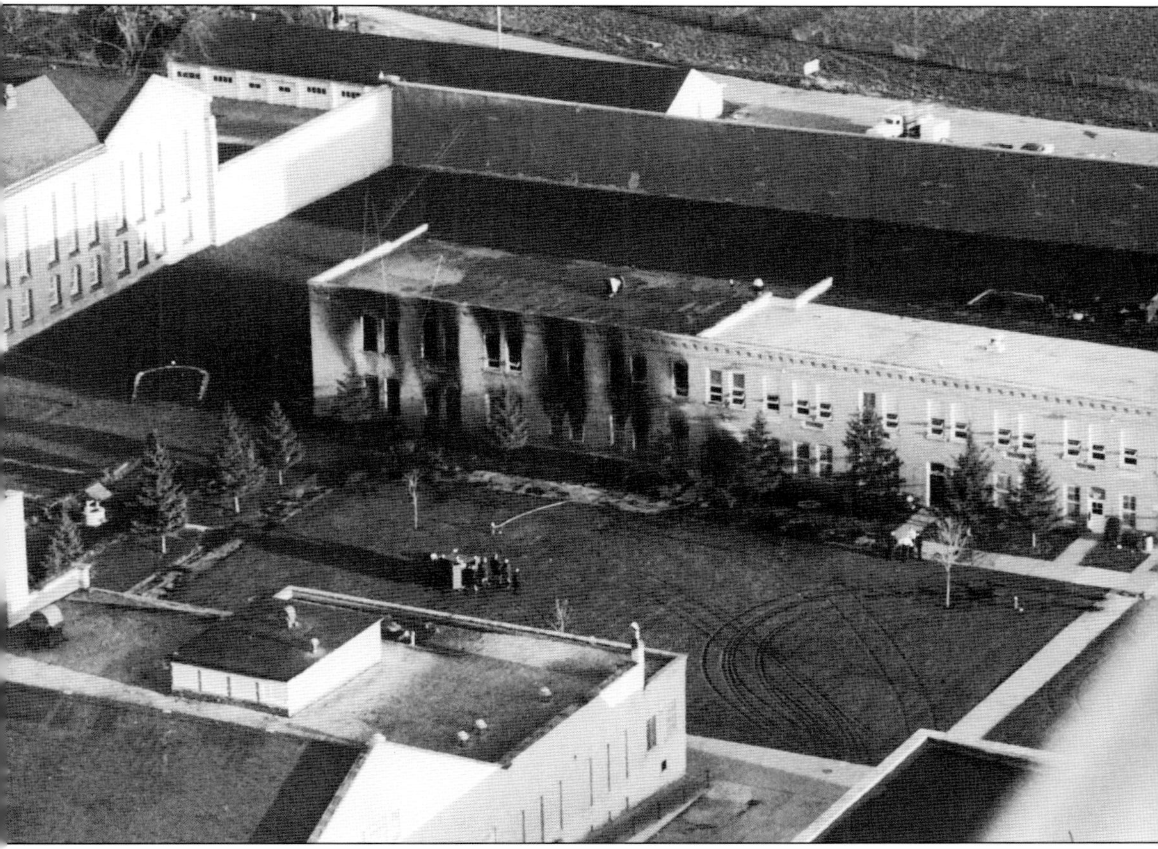

The charred windows of the old dormitory building are visible in this aerial photograph taken by legendary Green Bay photographer Henry LeFebvre in the aftermath of the riot. About 100 feet of the building was destroyed during the disturbance. The gutted section was subsequently demolished.

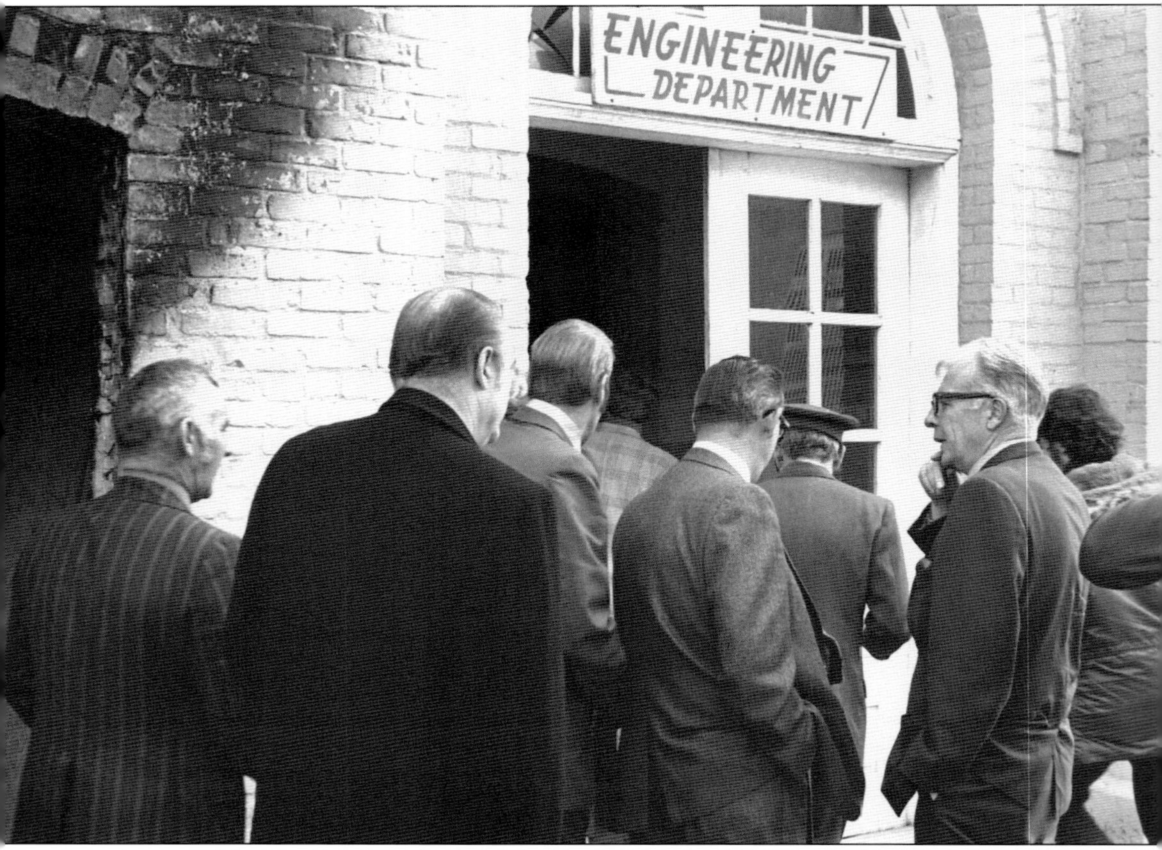

State and local officials gather outside the dormitory and shop buildings a month after the riot. In the aftermath of the riot, the institution developed much needed improvements to its security procedures.

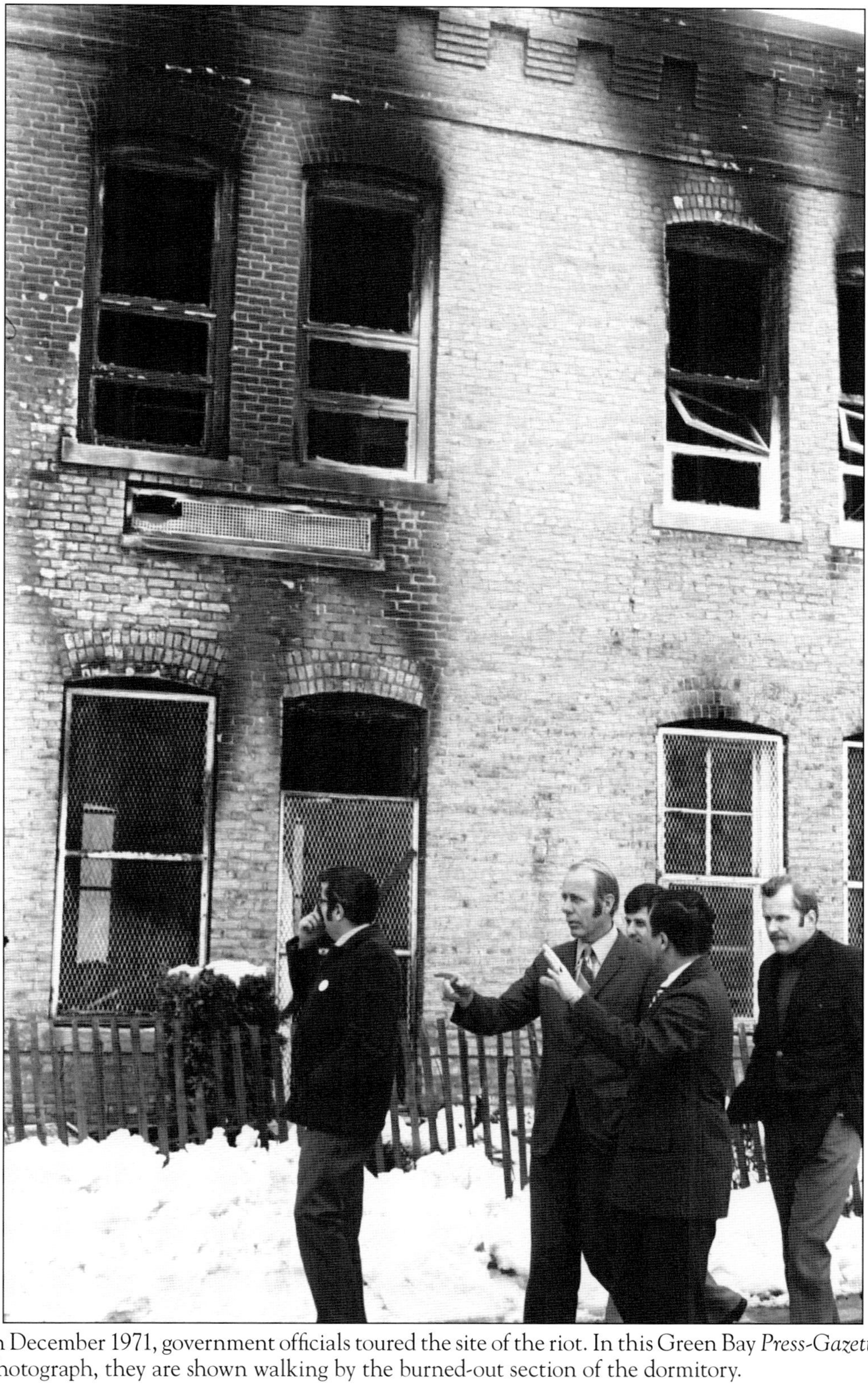

In December 1971, government officials toured the site of the riot. In this Green Bay *Press-Gazette* photograph, they are shown walking by the burned-out section of the dormitory.

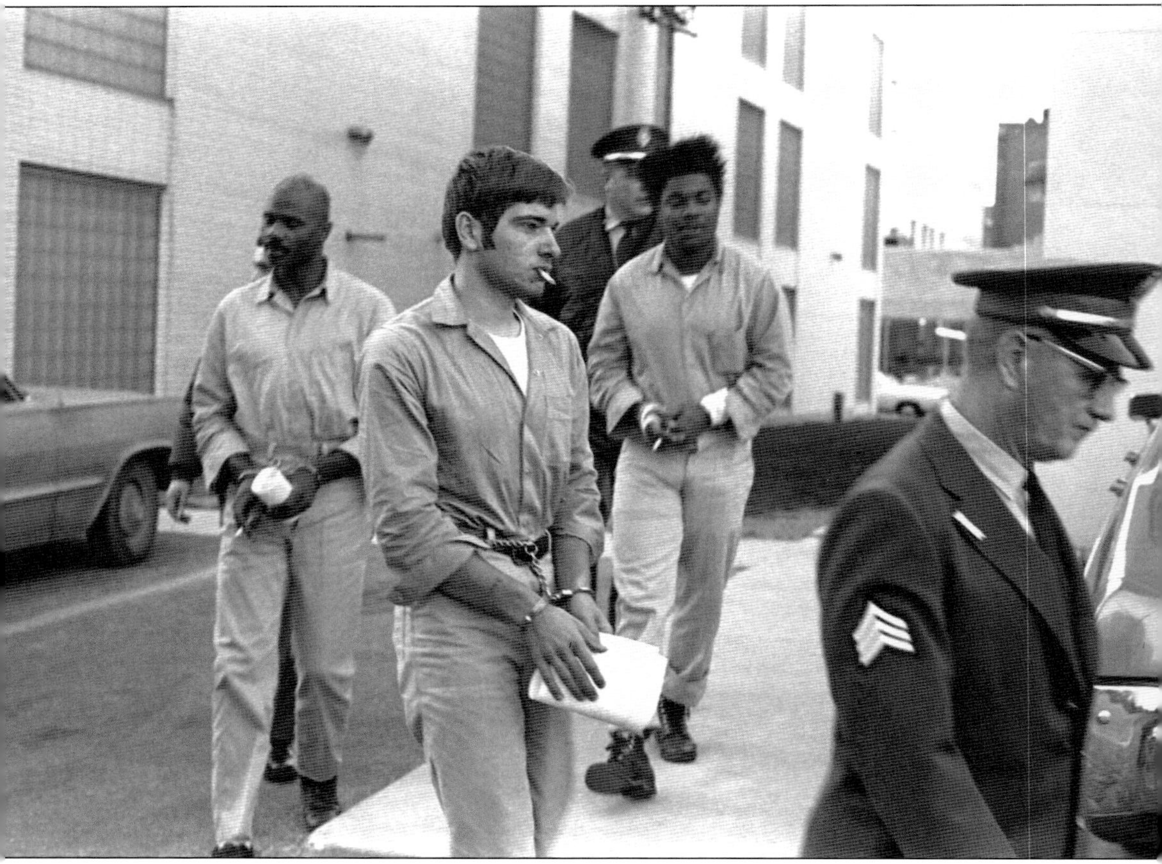

Participants in the institution's worst riot are led to their arraignment in Green Bay on November 16, 1971. The riot started in the cafeteria during the evening meal when about 235 of the institution's 635 inmates began throwing chairs, trays, and garbage cans. By the time it was over, 13 guards and three inmates were injured.

BIBLIOGRAPHY

Allen, Harry E. and Clifford Simonsen. *Corrections in America, 5th Ed.* New York: McMillan, 1989.

Bowron, Charles W. "*Wisconsin State Reformatory*" in *The Blue Book of the State of Wisconsin*, compiled by J. D. Beck. Madison, WI: Democrat Printing Company, State Printer, 1907.

Brockway, Z. R. "*The Reformatory System*" in *The Reformatory System in the United States, Reports Prepared for The International Prison Commission*, compiled by S. J. Barrows. Washington: Government Printing Office, 1900.

Dilulio, John J. Jr. *Crime and Punishment in Wisconsin*. Milwaukee, WI: Wisconsin Policy Research Institute, 1990.

Kroncke, James F. and John McLimans. *The Wisconsin State Reformatory*. Green Bay, WI: Training Office, Wisconsin State Reformatory, 1969.

Sanborn, Frank B. "*The Elmira Reformatory*" in *The Reformatory System in the United States, Reports Prepared for The International Prison Commission*, compiled by S. J. Barrows. Washington: Government Printing Office, 1900.